MILA

Dear Mama-Bella,

Happy Mother's Day!
& much love

Sabrina

Andrée & Bertrand

10 May/92

MILA

Sally Armstrong

Macmillan Canada
Toronto

Canadian Cataloguing in Publication Data

Armstrong, Sally, date.
    Mila

ISBN 0-7715-9156-X

1. Mulroney, Mila.   2. Mulroney, Brian, 1939-
3. Prime ministers - Canada - Spouses - Biography. *
I. Title.

FC631.M8A75 1992   971.064'7'092   C92-093329-7
F1034.3.M8A75 1992

The publishers would like to thank the Photo Section of the Prime Minister's Office for providing many of the photos used in this book and for the colour photographs of Mila (and Nicolas) Mulroney that appear on the jacket.

Macmillan Canada
A Division of Canada Publishing Corporation
Toronto, Canada

1 2 3 4 5   FP   96 95 94 93 92

Printed in Canada

For Ross, Heather, Peter, and Anna

Acknowledgements

First of all, to Mila Mulroney, many thanks for allowing me to stand so close to you and your family, for answering hundreds of questions, and for enduring the tape recorder at dinner, on the road, and whenever there was ten minutes away from the madding crowd. Thank you, as well, for being so candid with me and bravely sharing your thoughts and private life.

To the rest of the Mulroneys, Caroline, Ben, Mark, Nicolas, and Mr. Prime Minister, thank you for your time and help and trust. And Bogdanka Pivnicki, your stories about life in Yugoslavia, and your tireless efforts in supplying me with information and in finding teachers and school friends are much appreciated.

To Bonnie Brownlee, who must have started to feel as though we were a tag team, thank you. From you I learned not only the mysterious ways of protocol and party politics, but also how to stay upright in a van when a motorcade is careening through the streets, and how to move out of a crowded room and into an elevator in five seconds flat.

My gratitude goes to Gilbert Lavoie, a journalist who understands the business of story-telling better than anyone else. Thank you for your support and for introducing me to the Ottawa press gallery and those-in-the-know on the Hill.

Many others were helpful in vital ways, including Kim Cross and Lonnie Robillard, who bailed me out in Zimbabwe, when I exploded not only my transformer but theirs as well. Without your technical expertise and good-natured understanding, I'd still be on chapter three. And Michael McSweeney, thanks for cheerfully telling me the colourful behind-the-scenes stories I needed. Bill McCarthy and Dagmar Galt, thank you for searching through seven years' worth of photos to find the ones we wanted for this book. Peter Bregg, thanks for your photographic advice. And Heather McDonald, Ann Palmer, JoAnne Godard, Hélène Chalifoux, and Robby McRobb, I appreciate your help.

As well, I want to thank Greg MacNeil, the publisher of *Homemaker's Magazine* and editors Mary McIver, Cheryl Embrett, and Shiraz Bagli, who were so generous with their support and help and advice through this project. And Judy Brandow, the editor of *Canadian Living*, who sent me to Stellarton in 1983 to do a story on Mila Mulroney, a woman I knew nothing about. And Bob Dees at Macmillan for walking me through the early stages of this book, even though it was five o'clock in the morning in Vancouver when he placed the calls.

My enormous respect and gratitude goes to Philippa Campsie, the editor-in-chief of Macmillan who was assigned to this project. This is a woman who has a very nice way of saying, "You can't get there from here." She is a brilliant editor who lavished on this book her talent, her enthusiasm, and her energy.

And last but never least, to the people who graze in my kitchen, the ones who made Thanksgiving dinner wonderful even though I was in Africa doing research, and the ones who thought Christmas with a computer in the kitchen and a manuscript on the table was an okay idea. The people I'm crazy about, who endured "the book." Thank you all.

Sally Armstrong
Toronto, January 1992

Prologue

Montreal, December 19, 1991. A gentle snow is falling on Marlowe Avenue when the dark blue car rolls up to the front door of the semi-detached red brick house with the white front porch. Mila Mulroney steps out of the back seat, climbs over the snow bank, and walks up the stairs to the front door of the house where she was raised. She lets herself in and catches her father's eye. "Milica," he roars. "You're home."

Usually Mila arrives with Brian and the children. When her father sees that she is alone, his first question is, "So where's everybody?" Mila explains that Brian is in Ottawa presiding over a first ministers' conference, the first one since the failed Meech Lake Accord, and he simply can't get away. Nicolas is being inducted into his Beaver pack. Caroline is in England. Ben has a school project to finish up before the Christmas holidays. But, Mila assures her father, "As soon as the Beaver investiture is over, someone will drive Mark and Nico here. Soon, Tata, they'll be here soon."

Today is Slava, the Pivnicki family's patron saint day. And no matter what else is going on, Dimitrije and Bogdanka Pivnicki expect their children to be home for Slava.

Almost everyone in the house is speaking Serbo-Croatian. Mila's sister Ivana has come from Toronto. Her brother John, who lives nearby in Montreal, is here with his wife Manuela Soares and their baby. Plenty of Yugoslav friends are here, too. The Pivnickis don't have any other relatives in Canada, but Boba says half of Yugoslavia has slept on her couch and they're just like family.

Dr. Pivnicki looks over the crowd with pride. Ever since he arrived in Canada thirty-one years ago, he has worked hard to establish the Yugoslav community in Montreal. And he and Bogdanka (Boba) have raised their three children as Canadians with a rich Yugoslavian heritage.

In this house Mila isn't the wife of the prime minister of Canada. She is Milica, the Pivnickis' first-born child. A voice from the kitchen calls her: "Come. Stir." Mila settles in at the stove, sniffs the cabbage rolls in the huge pot, and pushes them around with a wooden spoon. "How do you do this, Mama? They smell so good." There's enough food in this kitchen to feed a small village.

Boba has been preparing for Slava all week. There's German potato salad and Russian salad. There's pita (cheese and spinach pie) and urmasice (a Bosnian dessert) and kifle (almond and walnut cookies). "Somebody check the roast beef in the oven," orders Boba.

Mila is comfortable in her old place in the kitchen, the place she stood so often as a teenager, helping her mother prepare meals, washing the dishes, listening to the family stories. She has hosted six parties this week for more than 200 people at 24 Sussex Drive. There are still a dozen Christmas events she must go to with Brian. The two of them have been travelling for six out of the last fifteen weeks. It's nice to be home.

In the house on Marlowe there is no press to report on Mila's comings and goings. Here she can joke with her brother and sister, pick a perogie out of a pot with her fingers, talk to old family friends and neighbours who knew her before the paparazzi did, steep herself in her heritage, knowing she will pass that heritage on to her children.

When Mark and Nicolas arrive, she talks to them about the traditions. Near the front door is an icon of St. Nicolas. There is a candle burning beneath it. And there is the traditional bread of Slava, called kolac, which Boba bakes every year for the feast, and zito, a paste made from almonds and wheat flour. The priest came earlier to bless the kolac, the zito, and the house.

When people start arriving at six o'clock, they taste the kolac and the zito before joining the others in the living room. It is supposed to bring good luck. Some guests even take a piece home with them.

''*Sretan Slava*,'' (Happy Feast Day), Mila says as she greets guest after guest. One of them, a ninety-one-year-old man, tells the story of Slava to the uninitiated. It's important to Mila that her children understand their roots and know the history. The story goes like this.

More than 900 years ago, pagan Slavs migrated from the north of Asia to the south, where they came into contact with Christians. Although the Slavs were reluctant to give up the gods of thunder and rain and sunshine they had always worshipped, under the influence of the Christians, they eventually abandoned their old religion. However, their form of Christianity retained some old traditions, and their god of the home became identified with a Christian saint, usually said to be St. Nicolas, but sometimes called St. Mark, St. John, or St. Matthew.

For the Pivnickis, it is St. Nicolas and Slava is celebrated on December 19. (Although Catholics consider December 6 to be St. Nicolas's day, the Orthodox Church retains the Julian calendar, so its saints' days are different.) It's rather close to Christmas, which can be awkward if you're the wife of the prime minister of Canada and have dozens of official obligations as well as a family Christmas to prepare. But miss Slava? Never.

Mila Mulroney believes strongly in family, in traditions, in the ties that bind people together. Her neighbours say she was like that as a child. Always present when the Pivnickis entertained. Always curious about other people and what they did when they weren't discussing history, politics, or religion in her parents' living room. They knew the tall pretty teenager would do something interesting with her life. She was an intelligent youngster who could engage anyone in conversation. They thought she might become an architect, maybe a designer. She was always talking about how she'd preserve and restore the old buildings in Montreal if she had her way.

Tonight they don't want to talk about her life in the nation's fishbowl, or the whirlwind trips she's taken to Gabon, Zimbabwe, Paris, Rome, San Francisco, and western Canada in the last few months, or even the GST. They want to reminisce. So does Mila.

This house holds a lot of memories for her. There are photographs of a little girl with long thick braids and of Mila with John and Ivana. This is the house they lived in when she started high school and university, when she had her first date with Brian. She remembers walking down these stairs on her wedding day, and running to the front porch during the party for her first wedding anniversary because there was a commotion in the street. Brian had bought a moped for her so she could get to classes and he was driving it up the street. She was just twenty years old then.

Times have changed for the people in this house too. Dr. Pivnicki is seventy-three years old. He has an inoperable brain tumour, but he still goes to work at the Allan Memorial Institute of Psychiatry three days a week to see patients. The family can hardly speak of his illness. In fact one of the only people at Slava who isn't speaking Serbo-Croatian is Dr. William Feindel, leader of the surgical team that operated on Dr. Pivnicki last April. He's introduced as "the man who saved Mita's life."

Mita is a strong and brilliant man, very much the patriarch. Boba drives him to work each day since he can no longer drive a car. Then she goes to the church to cook, to help with the rummage sale, to work on fundraising projects. Boba, at sixty, is a stylish, energetic woman. She's the storyteller in the family, the soft touch, the healer. Mila is a combination of the two, practical yet sensitive like her mother, self-possessed and strong-willed like her father. She has grown up into a savvy, ambitious adult with a sixth sense for knowing what to do.

When she left this house in 1973, little did she know that she'd become a household word in Canada. She'd already had an interesting life as a child in Yugoslavia, as an immigrant in Montreal, as an uptown girl at Westmount High School. No one told her the best was yet to come.

Chapter One

We're aristocrats with a democratic style.
Dimitrije Pivnicki

It was a path she'd taken many times before. The young woman with the dark wavy hair and the beautifully cut clothes walked through the park with her four-year-old daughter in tow. Down the broad avenue lined with majestic chestnut trees, through the park, over the bridge where the Miljacka River runs through the centre of Sarajevo. This late summer day was much like any other, except that whenever she met friends along the avenue they'd look furtively around and whisper to her, "If he's smart, he'll never come back." She nodded in agreement and clutched her little girl by the hand.

After several such encounters, she took her daughter home to their two-room apartment, a luxurious accommodation in this Yugoslavian city in 1957, considering the communist rule and the strict orders they had to live under. More and more often when they went out for their walk, the same words of advice would be passed

1

along to Bogdanka Pivnicki: "If he's smart, he'll never come back."

It had been only a few weeks since Dimitrije Pivnicki had left Sarajevo for Canada, where he was to study medicine at Montreal's Royal Victoria Hospital. It wasn't safe to tell anyone that he would never come back. Not even best friends in the privacy of a living room could be trusted with such information. This was a communist country after all. The borders were closed, no one was allowed to leave. If you managed to find a reason to be temporarily absent, a reason such as study- ing medicine in a foreign country, you would guard the opportunity with great care. You certainly wouldn't explain to an outgoing, inquisitive little four-year-old that Tata was leaving for good and that soon, she and Mama would be leaving too.

With Dimitrije away, Bogdanka, who was pregnant with their second child, took another job. By day, she worked as a registered nurse in an eye clinic. When that shift was over at 3:30, she went to a laboratory to work as a technician. Their daughter Milica, who was nick- named Mila, was left with a housekeeper all day.

After several months, Bogdanka, who was known as Boba, noticed that something was wrong with Mila. She was having nightmares, she began to limp. A visit to a doctor friend proved that there was nothing physically wrong with the little girl. The doctor told Boba, "Your daughter is grieving for her father."

Mila had heard the comments in the street, and she thought her beloved father had left them forever. But soon, parcels began to arrive from Montreal. There were letters Boba could read to Mila in which her Tata sent her his love. And there was a doll and from time to time other small surprises for her. Even though Boba couldn't tell her little daughter what the plan was, she reassured her that they would see Tata again very soon.

Dimitrije (Mita) Pivnicki was born on November 12, 1918, in Novi Becej, into a family of doctors and lawyers. They were privileged, educated people who lost everything when the communists took over in Yugoslavia in 1944.

His father, a quiet, brilliant man, had been called to the bar in 1899 and had a very successful law practice in Novi Becej. His mother, who was strong-willed and outgoing, wanted Dimitrije to be a lawyer, and it was expected that he would take over the practice and follow in his father's footsteps, maybe even going on to become involved in politics.

Dimitrije graduated from law school just as war broke out in Yugoslavia in 1941. Because of the German occupation, his parents didn't want him to stay in the country. With the help of influential friends, they managed to get him into Hungary, where he took up the study of medicine.

When the war finally ended, everything had changed. Dimitrije's father had died. The law offices had been abandoned. The communists were in power, and the land his family owned had been nationalized. Their country home had been confiscated. The house in the city was divided into several apartments, and his widowed mother was living in two rooms in the former servants' quarters.

"I realized I couldn't go back to the old ways. It's almost impossible to imagine how helpless you can become in a country where such radical change has occurred. Friends had disappeared. Those who remained couldn't help you to get back on your feet," he says. After spending the next eighteen months in the medical corps of the army, Dimitrije returned to school, this time to the medical faculty at the University of Belgrade. He graduated in 1949. Although he was trained as a psychiatrist, the communist party sent him to the small town of Mostar to work in the internal medicine department of the general hospital. Two years later, he was moved to Sarajevo, in Bosnia, where he began to study and practise neuropsychiatry. That's where he met Bogdanka Ilic.

Bogdanka had been born in 1931 on a farm near a small village called Batkusa. "My mother and father had to work all day in the fields and at dusk they did chores in the barns," says Boba. "I never saw them. My mother died [of unknown causes] when I was eight years old. I hardly remember her at all.

Before she died, Boba's mother spoke to Draga Ilic, a doctor who was Boba's great-aunt, and asked her to take care of the little girl and to educate her. In those days, girls from the farm were not sent to school. Boba had met Draga before at the Ilic family's feast day, held each year on May 6. She adored her great-aunt and longed to stay with her, to go to school, to learn the ways of that sophisticated household in Belgrade.

After her mother died, Boba thought that her great-aunt had forgotten about her mother's wishes. No one came to take her away. Six months later, there was a memorial service for her mother in Belgrade. Boba became ill after the service and had to stay with Draga when her father and four brothers and sisters returned to Batkusa. "I think I worked my way into their hearts," says Boba today. She never returned to the farm.

As a teenager, she witnessed the brutality of war and learned the lessons of survival and loyalty. Her next-door neighbour, Dragan Vuckovic, had taken in a young woman their own age and hidden her from the Nazis throughout the war. The young woman's family had been slaughtered. Dragan and Bogdanka lived in fear that their friend would be discovered. (In fact, she survived and married Dragan; today they live in New York City.) When the communists arrived, Boba experienced a new kind of occupation, this time by the Russians. Although they had to share their house with soldiers, Boba and her adoptive parents were spared some of the worst aspects of communist rule, probably because her parents were both doctors and thus in a position of privilege in a communist regime.

After the war, she moved with the family to Sarajevo, where she trained to become a nurse. Soon after graduating from college, she met Dimitrije Pivnicki, an outspoken scholar thirteen years her senior. They were married on September 6, 1952, and together moved into the residence for doctors that was attached to the hospital.

The residence was an old convent, once occupied by nuns who had been ousted by the communists. The red brick building had dark, narrow hallways that connected about thirty rooms. There was one toilet for everyone to share and no bathing facilities. The Pivnickis took their weekly baths at the public bath house on Saturdays at 6:30 in the morning. They lived, as all the doctors in Sarajevo did, in a two and a half by six metre room. They had two single beds, a washbasin on a three-sided corner cupboard, a hotplate on a counter in the opposite corner, and a desk.

The cramped space never stopped them from entertaining their friends, however. Boba, who loved to cook, often had people over for supper, serving their meals while they perched on the desk, or sat on the beds or the floor with their plates balanced on their knees. Their guests were for the most part other doctors and their families who lived in the cloister. In a certain way, Mita was recreating his father's salon with the intelligentsia of the day—Serbs, Macedonians, Moslems, Croats—who enjoyed discussing history, politics, religion, the future.

When Boba realized she was pregnant, she and Mita worried that they didn't have enough space for a child. However, Mara Kafka, a friend who lived in an adjoining room, said she would move in with another friend and give her space to the Pivnickis. By the time Mila arrived, they occupied the two rooms—one was used as a kitchen with a bed for Mita's mother, Majka Tassa, and the other housed Mita, Boba, and all their worldly goods, including the basket that would be the baby's crib.

On July 12, 1953, the day before Mila was born, the Pivnickis were getting ready for one of their dinner parties. Boba had to go to the market, as she did every day, since they didn't have a refrigerator. On this day she left the house at 5 a.m. to make sure she'd be there as soon as the stalls opened so she could get enough food to serve her guests. At about 6 a.m., when she was still half an hour from home, her water broke. Because she didn't have any labour pains, she didn't understand what was wrong and rushed to her mother's house.

Draga smiled and said, "You're in labour." Boba returned home with her grocery bags, and Draga set out to fetch Mita, who was at the public baths.

The party went on as planned, while Boba checked into the hospital next door. After dinner their guests played a game called Preference, which is similar to bridge in that one person of the foursome is the dummy. That player would go and sit with Boba at the hospital on the other side of the convent walls.

At noon the next day, a sunny July 13, Milica made her appearance. Her arrival was heralded with joy. Her father had been the only child of parents who had longed for a child for seventeen years. When he was born, it was like a miracle for them. Seven years later, his mother gave birth to a daughter, Milica. Mita adored her, and he was devastated when she died of meningitis at the age of two. Even while he and Boba were dating, he used to say that some day he'd have a daughter and he would call her Milica. The nickname would be Mila, a Serbo-Croatian word that means "dear."

For the first ten months of her life, Mila slept in the basket beside her parents' bed and was watched over by her adoring grandmother during the day when the Pivnickis went to work. In May of the following year, the Pivnickis were told that an apartment would be available for them in September. The family decided that it would be better for Mila to spend the summer with Majka Tassa at her home in Novi Becej, instead of waiting in the cramped apartment. Even now, thirty-seven years later, Boba begins to cry when she recounts the story. "My little daughter was gone until the end of September. I knew it was better for her. But I missed my Mila."

At last the apartment was ready—two bedrooms as well as a living room. Because both sets of grandparents had had large furnished homes before the communist takeover, they owned more furniture than they needed for the quarters they were now forced to share with others, so they sent some pieces to the young couple to help furnish their new place. At last, the Pivnickis thought, they would put down roots.

Mila had an unusual relationship with her father for those days. Yugoslavian fathers in 1953 did not push baby prams down the avenues nor dote on their daughters, as Mita Pivnicki did. In fact, Boba remembers, having a daughter was usually considered nothing to brag about in that place; sons were the prizes parents sought.

Like Mita, Boba Pivnicki wasn't one to bow to conventions. Her adopted mother had been one of the first woman doctors in Yugoslavia and the first woman director of a prison. Her grandmother was a suffragette. For Boba, having a daughter was plenty to brag about.

Mila was left at home while her parents went out to work. There were no nursery schools in Yugoslavia, so she spent most of her days with Anka, a woman who had worked as a maid for Boba's mother. Although Mita's mother, Majka Tassa, who had an enormous influence on Mila, came to stay in the winter months, most of the time Mila had to rely on herself. She had to find other children to play with and, for the most part, had to invent her own games.

It is not unusual in Yugoslavia for people to drop in for visits. Boba says she remembers often coming home from work to find that friends had dropped in and Mila was entertaining them. Boba doesn't remember telling her what to do, but she'd find her pouring imaginary tea for a visitor and making sure the apartment looked nice and the visitor was comfortable. Although she wasn't involved in lessons or sports, Boba says little Mila managed to organize the neighbourhood kids and take charge of the people around her.

She also began, at the age of two, to show an interest in fashion and good grooming that would stay with her throughout her life—an interest that she came by honestly. Bogdanka says that during World War II bombing raids over Yugoslavia, her family would rush to take cover in the bomb shelters, but "I would never go until my braids were done."

Boba could knit beautifully, so although there was little in the shops to buy, she always made sure her daughter was well dressed. She remembers that Mila loved to look nice even as a little girl and never left the apartment without a tiny purse she had received as a gift. She even made the front page of the newspaper when she was three years old.

She had been to Dubrovnik to visit her grandparents for the May Day holiday. The first of May is Labour Day, an important holiday in communist countries; it is also the day the beaches are officially opened. Mila appeared on the front page of the newspaper, her hair in braids, wearing a bathing suit and carrying the ever-present purse. The caption read, "The beaches have opened. This young bather is prepared. Is her purse to collect shells or to carry her sandwich?"

On her return from one of those trips to Dubrovnik, the five-year-old Mila demonstrated an independence that would become typical of her style. Mita had already left for Montreal and Mila had come down with pneumonia. Boba decided that Dubrovnik, where her parents now lived in a small villa, was the best place for her to recover. Boba, who was working and struggling to take care of John, the son who had been born on November 15, 1957, five months after Mita left, simply couldn't give her convalescing daughter the attention she needed.

Mila's grandparents, whom she called Baka and Deda, loved having their little granddaughter with them, and their villa seemed an ideal place for a youngster. They had a garden with fig trees and an extra lot where they kept chickens and hens. (Not only was it unheard-of in those times to have an extra lot, but raising chickens in the city just wasn't done.)

Mila spent almost a month with Baka and Deda. When it was time to return to her mother in Sarajevo, Baka wrote ahead and told Boba what time Mila would be arriving. Unfortunately, the mail service was chaotic in Yugoslavia at the time and somehow the letter went astray. Boba didn't have a phone, and neither did Mila's grandparents. "It was the end of autumn, she was supposed to be coming home, but I hadn't received word," Boba remembers. "It was very hard on me to have her away so long. I missed her terribly. She was a very active, loving child.

"One day, I was coming home from work. I was tired and feeling very low. I saw a little girl in front of me and thought, 'Oh, that's Mila.' Then I thought I must be imagining it, because I wanted it to be her so much. Suddenly the little girl dropped the hand of the man she'd been walking with and started to run toward a group of children. The kids began to yell, 'Mila, Mila.' It was her. I didn't know that she was arriving.

''When she got off the plane and realized I wasn't there, she'd asked a man in the airport if he would bring her home. She was only five years old. I could hardly believe it. I didn't know what to say. I offered the man a cup of coffee, he accepted, drank the coffee, and left. I never saw him again in my life.''

The conditions of her early life have shaped Mila's personality, her style, and her spontaneity. Her mother, Boba, sits in the living room of her semi-detached home on Marlowe Avenue in Montreal today and shakes her head when she describes the formidable energy level her eldest daughter has, her attention to detail, her commitment to her children, her husband, her friends, her causes, and even casual acquaintances. She says, ''I always knew exactly what I wanted from an early age. So did Mila. Did I teach it to her or is it in our genes? I don't know.''

After about eighteen months, Boba received word from her husband that it was time to come to Canada. Not only did she have to manage the trip, the passports, and the exit visas, but she had to handle the deception involved in leaving with Mila, who was now five and a half, and John, who was just a year old. No one was permitted to move out of the country, but it was possible with luck and with connections to get special permission to leave on a holiday.

It had been difficult enough to get Mita away. He'd been working in the library of the hospital in Sarajevo when he read in a medical journal that the Royal Victoria Hospital in Montreal was looking for an enthusiastic doctor who would be interested in joining a research team. He wrote to them immediately. Three weeks later, they responded with a job offer, a bursary, and a visiting visa from the Canadian government. He wondered how on earth he'd get exit papers.

Boba is the street-smart one in the marriage and she knew what to do. "I knew I would have to pull strings and that I'd have to prove that he would come back and finish his work here. My mother had a friend in the government, so I decided to go and visit her. She was very sharp with me, saying my husband was anti-communist and was politically undesirable. I argued with her. 'My husband is a scholar,' I said. 'The university here is too small for him.' I was very convincing and finally she gave me a name, a top person in the government, to write to. Eight or nine months later, a door opened and he got out."

Boba wondered how she'd pull off a similar exit for herself and the children. "One day I was walking in the park with Mila. She was pushing John in the stroller. We ran into a man called Dr. Kovacevic, the doctor who had helped Mita to move from Mostar seven years earlier so that he could continue with his psychiatric work. He asked me how my husband was getting along in Canada. I told him he needed an extension to finish his work and that I wanted to go and visit him. He told me exactly who to see in the government. We'd never been close to this man. We hardly knew him and yet, twice, he played an important role in our lives."

Yugoslavians didn't hold their own passports in those days. If you were granted leave, you would be issued a passport. When Boba finally got permission to leave, they offered her a passport but said there weren't any for the children. She refused to accept it. Back she went to the government offices asking people to help her, hoping for the luck she feels she's always had. At last, they issued exit papers for her and her children that were good for one year. Mita had obtained tourist visas for them in Montreal. Nobody knew Boba was leaving for good, except a few intimate friends who helped her. She remembers being afraid to discuss anything about her departure. You never knew who would inform on you.

When Boba left she carried, as she puts it, nine items with her and they included her two children. Her friend, Mara Kafka, who had given her the extra room in the convent when Mila was born, took her to the train.

The six-hour trip to Zagreb was uneventful. In Yugoslavia, as in many European countries, when families travelled, they carried food with them; sandwiches and cheese that was invariably shared with their fellow travellers. Boba found lots of people to help her with her two small children, and they passed the time eating sandwiches and talking to other people on the train.

A friend met her in Zagreb with fresh milk for the children and helped her to change trains for the two-hour trip to the sea port of Rijeka, where they boarded the ship. The ship Mita had sailed on was called the *Croatia*. Boba's ship was called the *Serbia*. It was a cargo ship bound for New York, with stops at Dubrovnik, Messina in Sicily, and Algiers.

13

In Dubrovnik, Boba received permission to stay overnight with her adopted parents. During that visit, her father warned her not to take a single piece of jewellery or any money or valuables with her. When it was time to leave, her parents took her back to the ship. It was November, a miserable cold and rainy day. Draga started to cry. She wondered if she would ever see the Pivnickis again.

As a final reminder of what her departure was all about, the minute Boba got back on board, two policemen approached and demanded that she hand over her valuables. She told them she didn't have any, but she was searched anyway. So was Mila. They even examined John's diaper to make sure nothing of monetary value had been hidden away.

A dock strike in Algiers tied them up for several days, so Boba took the children off the boat and went sightseeing and shopping. Then they set out for the north Atlantic and the danger of its high waves, rough seas, and stormy weather. The children were seasick; so was Boba.

One day when the seas calmed down a little, Boba rested in a lounge chair on one deck while Mila went exploring on another. A few minutes later Mile, the ship's engineer, came striding down to Boba's deck with Mila in tow. Boba remembers, ''He was so furious with me I thought he was going to slap me. Mila had been climbing around the ship trying to reach the barnacles that were stuck to the underside of the life boats to add them to her shell collection. Mile was afraid she was getting too close to the ship's railing. I guess I trusted everyone on the ship. We were friends in misery.

Every one of us had left Yugoslavia for one reason or another.''

The twenty-nine-day voyage across the sea to Canada would be a reminder to Boba about the cost of freedom, the importance of family ties, the strong stock they came from. ''We're survivors,'' she says today, ''because we came from a part of the world where trouble is present.''

Mila's earliest memory is of her father leaving for Canada. ''My father was a softie. My mother was the disciplinarian. I felt the loss, I was very much an only child. I had to stay with a maid all day, since my mother was at work. At the end of each day the maid would present my mother with a litany of things I'd done wrong during the day. It wasn't a happy experience.''

She also remembers the departure that day in Rijeka. It all seemed like a big adventure until she discovered sea sickness. She remembers spending most of the voyage in the infirmary eating oranges and French-fried potatoes.

When the ship docked in New York on December 1, 1958, it happened to be one of those unusually warm days that had everyone in shirtsleeves. Mila remembers it being enormously exciting; she recalls clinging to her father's knees as he hugged her little brother, John, the baby he'd never set eyes on.

They took the train to Montreal (Dr. Pivnicki didn't have a car) and arrived in Windsor Station the next day during the biggest blizzard of the year. Mila stared out of the taxi window as they made their way through the snow to the two-bedroom furnished apartment over a tavern on Pine Avenue, in an old neighbourhood of walk-ups and duplexes that were homes to the students and professors of McGill University.

Inside the apartment was a trunk brimming with winter clothing: hats, scarves, and snowsuits that Dr. Pivnicki had collected for his family. For Mila, it was like having an early Christmas. She surveyed her new surroundings from the fire escape and watched the comings and goings in the tavern below. She soon decided who to trust on the street.

For Boba, it was the beginning of a painful adjustment. The entire apartment vibrated every time the air circulation system in the tavern went on. Even worse was the construction of an overpass opposite their apartment that began a few months after they moved in. The noise and accompanying mess severely tested Boba's peace of mind. She was dreadfully homesick. She didn't speak either French or English and didn't know a soul in Montreal. The climate was another shock. Getting the children dressed up in snowsuits, scarves, and hats every time she had to go out was a chore she was unaccustomed to.

Her solace became her children, and she raised them the only way she knew how—with lots of family togetherness, very strict rules and, as soon as she made some friends, visits to other Yugoslavian families. ''It was a very hard time for me. I was often depressed and unhappy. We were landed immigrants, but for the first while, when I was so lonesome, we didn't apply for a citizenship visa. I used to get a babysitter for half a day and go to the antique shops. I would buy something old, a cup, a saucer, anything that reminded me of

Yugoslavia, and bring it home hoping it would make me feel better.''

Shortly after their arrival, Mila was enrolled in the St. Urbain Street Nursery School. Her parents were anxious for her to learn to speak English. But most of the other children at the school were also Eastern European, and Mila learned to speak Czech instead of English, so her father decided to spend every bit of money they had saved to register her at Miss Edgar's and Miss Cramp's School (ECS), a private girls' school where he felt she would not only learn to speak English but would quickly adapt to Canadian ways. Located on a hill at the edge of exclusive Westmount, the school educated the daughters of Montreal's elite.

When Mila looks back on those days she says, ''No one at school knew how I felt, but there was definitely a sense of being different. You master the language at school but then you go home to an entirely different environment. One of the mothers at ECS said to my mother, 'It's very sad what you're doing, making Mila go to this school. You don't even live in the area.' ''

Although Maisie MacSporran, who was headmistress at ECS when Mila was there, remembers her as a lively little girl, Mila left the school after grade three because her parents were told she didn't fit in. Concerned by this judgement, Dr. Pivnicki took Mila to the Allan Memorial Institute, where she took the most comprehensive IQ test available in Montreal. Her test results were very high. Her father took the scores to the school, handed them to a woman in the office, and said, ''There you are. And now I'll take my child home.''

She was then enrolled in public school in the working-class district of Côte des Neiges. In the meantime, Dr. Pivnicki had hired Binty Mustard, a teacher recommended to him by neighbours, to teach Mila to speak English. "I remember her as a dark, bright, happy little girl," says Binty. "She wasn't prepossessingly pretty. She wasn't at all frightened. She seemed very self-assured for a little girl of her size but not brashly so. I also remember that she was always attractively dressed. Although she was a vital and interested little girl, she'd have preferred to play with my daughter Julia's dolls than to study the lessons we had for the day. However, she learned very fast, she never needed a great deal explained to her, so she was only with me for about three or four months; after that she didn't need me any more."

Her daughter Julia, who is a year older than Mila, has a slightly different memory of Mila coming to their house. "She'd be skipping along the sidewalk, braids flying behind her, and always very neatly dressed with a lot of attention to detail. She had big black bows in her hair, which made her look very Eastern European. She always wore a pure white blouse and a black tunic. I remember she liked playing with my doll's house. We'd rearrange the furniture over and over again. We didn't have a mutual language but I babbled on in English and she never seemed to be bothered by that."

Mila remembers her efforts to fit in at the various schools she attended. "It's not as though I wasn't dressed properly. My mother bought me nice clothes, but the selection was slim. I had my one nice blouse, my one nice skirt, and my school tunic, which she bought big so I would grow into it. In those days my style was my Yugoslavian immigrant roots—braids and clothes big enough to grow into. I remember wearing the same winter coat four years in a row when I went to Rosedale School. The coat was royal blue. Every year, my mother changed the buttons, brass buttons one year, royal blue buttons the next year. It was a good quality coat and wasn't frayed or anything, but I knew it was the same coat and my friends all knew it was the same coat. That sort of thing makes you feel different. Clothes became a badge of belonging for me. That they're the right size and right for the season is important. I'm not alone in this; most immigrants want to fit in, they don't want to be different.''

She wasn't very stimulated by any of the schools she attended. Instead, her source of stimulation tended to be her parents' friends. Professional people from all over the world gathered in the Pivnickis' living room to debate the issues of the day. Dr. Joseph Divic, another psychiatrist who arrived in Montreal from Yugoslavia in 1961, says the Pivnicki home, which by now was a walk-up apartment on Ridgewood Avenue, was like the literary salons of continental Europe. ''Professors, philosophers, doctors, and lawyers gathered there for conversations at the highest intellectual level.''

From the time she was a small child in Yugoslavia, Mila had always been a part of these adult gatherings, usually because there was nowhere else for her to go in the tiny apartment in Sarajevo. In Canada, the Pivnickis kept their Eastern European style, entertaining good friends with spicy food and stimulating conversation, and the children were never excluded.

Mila was clearly the apple of her father's eye. Dr. Divic says her father had a powerful effect on her. As soon as he met them he saw the closeness between father and daughter and felt she had all the characteristics of a much-loved first-born child. "First-borns think everything is possible and that everything should be granted to them. They're very close to their parents and have direct access to authority. All of this is typical of Milica."

Dr. Divic remembers a conversation he had with Milica (he never calls her Mila) the day after he arrived in Canada. She was eight years old. "Her mother was teaching her how to address me. 'Call him Uncle Yotsa,' she suggested. Yotsa is a nickname for Joseph or John, which is my first name as well as the name of Milica's little brother. Well, Milica thought that was impossible. To her it was inconceivable that someone could be an uncle and have the same name as her little brother. She refused to call me Uncle Yotsa, and until she got married, she called me Uncle Divic."

The Pivnickis' circle of friends also included Carla and Herbert Muller, psychiatrists from Germany, another psychiatrist, George Peterfy, and his wife, Marion, from Hungary, and a lawyer, Eugene Jurisic, and his wife, Olivera, from Yugoslavia. Dragan Vuckovic, Boba's former neighbour, who now lives in New York City, describes Mita Pivnicki as "an unusual man, highly educated, always surrounded by books, even as a young man. He's a man who likes to read, talk, and discuss things. He prefers to associate with people like that."

Mita and Boba were also active in the Serbian Orthodox Church in Montreal, where the family worshipped on Sundays. That connection brought another circle of intellectuals to their home. Mita felt he was re-establishing in Canada the traditions he preferred from the old country. "We're aristocrats with a democratic style," he says.

Even though the conversations in the Pivnickis' living room would serve Mila well in the years to come, at that time they didn't appear to have much of an effect on her school work. Her best subjects were languages, and she had a passion for literature. She loved the Grimms' fairy tales and the novels of Charles Dickens and Pearl Buck. She read *The Good Earth* a dozen times. But even in her reading she sometimes felt that she didn't fit in. "The teacher would say, 'Read this and decide what the theme is.' I'd read it and decide on the theme but I never got it right. I really think it's because my roots were different. I saw things differently, so in the teacher's eyes that made me wrong."

Mila, her brother John, and her sister, Ivana (born in 1961), were each treated a little differently, according to their place in the family. As the eldest, Mila learned to take responsibility for the younger members.

John's earliest memory of his big sister is of her taking care of him. "When I think of her in those days, I think of her hand. She was always holding my hand, always pulling me places. She would check my ski boots, make sure I didn't fall. She was the big sister and she was always in charge of us. I remember an accident on the street when we were little. A girl had fallen off her bike and cut her face. Mila took charge. 'Get this, call that.' She was always the one to take care of everyone."

Ivana, eight years her junior, agrees. "Mila had the responsibility of being the eldest. She was the first-born, the one who remembered Yugoslavia. She knew the grandparents. That was important to the family. Actually, I think Mila liked having the power and the authority to be in charge of us. I'm much more spoiled than she is. Johnny is more quiet. Mila is different, she's very strong. But we always look out for each other." Boba established that kind of thinking in each of the children because, as she says, "If you're happy in the home, you can survive outside the home."

Chapter Two

Can you imagine? He was thirty-three years old. I had a curfew of eleven o'clock.

Mila Pivnicki

By the time Ivana was born, on October 14, 1961, times for the Pivnickis had changed. Mita had finished his studies and no longer had to support his family on the $100-a-month pay cheque he'd had as a resident doctor at the Royal Victoria Hospital. Boba says that's when she decided to put down roots in Canada. Until then, they'd lived in furnished apartments, first over the tavern, then over a tea room farther down Pine Avenue. Now they were living in an apartment on Ridgewood Avenue, with a playground for the children and parkland behind the building.

Boba still missed her family, but the aching was beginning to wane after three years. "I began to buy furniture. I started to feel at home." Although she wouldn't see her native Yugoslavia again until Mila was thirteen years old, she says, "It felt like I'd had half of Yugoslavia to my house in Montreal. There was always someone from there sleeping on my couch."

Mila and her best friend, another Yugoslavian, Johnny Despic, were the leaders of a neighbourhood gang on Ridgewood. They found all the adventure and intrigue they wanted in what Johnny remembers as a deep, dark forest behind the apartment building. In fact, he says today, it was only as big as the space it took to put up another apartment building, which is what the "forest" later became.

"Mila was outspoken, frank, opinionated," he says. "We had a very special friendship that lasted even after her family moved away. We skated together in the winter months and saw each other at parties in the summer. We used to speak to each other in Serbo-Croatian when we didn't want the other kids to know what we were saying. When we were about fourteen, we liked each other an awful lot, but nothing ever came of it."

Johnny Despic also recalls Dr. Pivnicki, whom he describes as a very severe man but more sophisticated and better educated than the average Canadian. "I remember when I was only six years old, going into the house on Saturday afternoons and finding him sitting on the living room couch reading Plato."

The Pivnickis had begun to prosper in their new country and in 1963, the family moved to a house in Notre-Dame-de-Grace (NDG), a middle-class district in Montreal. It was on a pretty tree-lined street close to Westmount and it felt like home. Mila started attending Rosedale Public School. Then a car accident forcibly reminded the family of the frailties of what had started to become a comfortable lifestyle.

In May 1963, they were out in the family car for a drive when an ambulance taking an eighty-one-year-old man home from the hospital ran a red light and crashed into them. The patient in the ambulance died. Dr. Pivnicki suffered a severe concussion. Mrs. Pivnicki's face was lacerated when the rearview mirror shattered; she needed more than a hundred stitches to close her wounds. A friend of the family who was sitting in the front seat with Dr. and Mrs. Pivnicki broke both legs. Two-year-old Ivana was on the floor in the back seat and was unharmed. John, who was five, needed a few stitches to close a gash on his forehead. And Mila, who was nine, flew into the front seat from the back seat and broke her nose.

Mila remembers seeing bodies being stretched out in the park at the corner of Girouard and Côte St. Antoine, where the ambulance finally came to a halt. So many people required immediate attention that her injury was relegated to minor status. A week later, the doctor's office called to say her X-rays revealed a broken nose and that she should return to the hospital to have it rebroken and properly set. She thought it sounded like a horrible procedure. Her mother was still in the hospital recovering. Her father was trying to juggle the children, his work, and visiting hours at the hospital. Mila made a fuss and eventually convinced him that her nose didn't need further attention.

Although the accident had badly shaken the Pivnickis, it didn't seem to put them off car travel.

"We went somewhere every weekend," recalls Boba. "We loved the Eastern Townships in Quebec and we often drove to Vermont for the day."

The car was also used for summer holidays. "We used to drive to Virginia Beach on vacations," says John.

"Whether we liked it or not, we were together." They stayed in efficiency units because, as Boba says, "We needed to economize, but we also preferred to eat our own food." Myrtle Beach in South Carolina, Lake George in New York, and Florida were also holiday spots they frequented.

They travelled by car every year until after Mila and John had left home. Only then did Boba and Mita switch to air travel. Years later, when Brian Mulroney was president of the Iron Ore Company of Canada and had a private jet at his disposal, he once suggested that the Pivnickis fly to Florida with him and Mila. He was surprised to hear Mila say they would rather drive. "She was paying a compliment to her parents when she said that," says Boba.

Mila recalls those holidays. "We were all stuffed into the car, we stayed in one hotel room, my mother cooked. We learned a lot about each other."

By now the younger children, John and Ivana, were students at a private junior school called The Priory, another Westmount establishment for educating the privileged offspring of the area. The Pivnickis joined the Mount Royal Tennis Club and signed Mila up for Saturday morning tennis lessons. In the locker room one day, she ran into Julia Mustard, the little girl she'd made friends with when she was still struggling to learn English. "It was like meeting up with an old friend," says Julia. "We were a bit shy with each other at first, but then we started hanging around together. We both lived in NDG, just outside of Westmount, and we both wound up at Westmount High School.

"I had a feeling her mother was very stern, even though I never knew what she was saying because it was always said in Serbian. I remember Mila being called away from my house because she had to help at a tea her mother was having. I always had the sense that she had a stricter upbringing than I did or our friends did. Looking back, I realize it was an Eastern European influence on child-rearing. I never felt her parents tried to take away her energy, but they were very strict. I wished they weren't so strict, because it meant we couldn't do some things together."

For instance, Mila had to iron every Wednesday, clean the house every Friday, and do the dishes every time her mother cooked. She also attended ballet classes at Iona School for six years, performing in annual recitals even though she didn't like it and felt she was too tall. She went because her parents said that's what she was to do.

"We used to sit in her basement giggling and talking about boys," Julia says, "especially the ones we had crushes on. Her little brother was always there, playing with Meccano on the floor. We tried smoking cigarettes, and I remember we did a lot of drawing. Mila had an interest in art and would often say she wanted to be an artist when she grew up. My family were artists, but her house was different. Her father had an intensity about him. I often thought that the artist was a side of Mila most people didn't see."

It was at about this time that Mila figured out she could work around the strict rules in the house if she played her cards right. As it turned out, her strategy was also her entry into the arts. "The only way I was allowed out at night was to go to a concert or the ballet. So as soon as I was old enough to get to the theatre on my own, I went—of course!''

Mila acknowledges that her parents were probably too strict. ''In Europe you abide by certain rules, in Canada it's not the same. They adapted a bit, but I was certainly raised in a different way from a lot of kids my age.'' Her brother says Mila managed her share of teenage antics such as smoking in the basement without getting caught, ''because she was savvy, quick on her feet, good in a crisis, and she seemed to know instinctively where to draw the line. When Ivana had parties, the entire house shook; when Mila had parties, things never got out of hand.''

When Mila was fourteen, the family moved to Marlowe Avenue, the home Mita and Boba still live in today. There Mila met Monique Brossard, who lived next door and became a close friend. Today Monique says, ''We hardly see each other any more, but I know I can count on her for anything and she knows she can count on me.''

Their friendship formed at first because Mila wanted to learn to speak French and Monique wanted to learn English. But, Monique explains, there was more to it than that. ''Mila was very interested in other cultures. One time, she asked if she could come with my family to midnight mass on Christmas Eve, and she wanted to attend Reveillon with us afterwards. She always invited me to Slava, the feast day her family celebrates on December 19. She was very proud of her Yugoslavian roots.

''It also struck me, especially during family events such as Slava, that Mila would entertain like her mother.

I had to help with the dishes in my house, but in her house the kids were treated like adults, they helped with everything.''

The two girls spent all their free time together, helping each other with homework, spending weekends at the Brossard cottage in Ste-Adèle, north of Montreal, and hanging around the park in their neighbourhood. Monique recalls a story that typified the young Mila. ''A tiny bird flew into the living room window. It hit the glass and fell to the ground. We rushed outside and picked it up. It was badly hurt but still alive. Mila said, 'Let's take it to the SPCA—they'll take care of it.' Well we went there and were told to wait in the waiting room. We waited and waited for what seemed like a very long time. At last, we asked the person at the desk what was going on. She said, 'Oh, we had to sacrifice that bird.' Mila started to cry. It was an ordinary little bird but it upset her a lot.''

When they began dating boys, the two would agree that whoever arrived home last would throw a pebble at the other's bedroom window as a signal to sneak down the stairs and out into the backyard to compare notes about their dates. ''I think we were more anxious about telling each other the details of the evening than anything else,'' says Monique.

Monique remembers Mila showing her a copy of an academic paper that her father had written about the game of chess and how it is analogous to the moves we make in life. He wrote it at a time when he was worrying about what the future would hold for Mila. She wasn't doing as well in school as he had hoped, and he was concerned about the choices she would make in her future. Mila was very proud of the paper and wanted to share "Tata's" comments with Monique. The paper began:

> Chess is the nicest game, a game of kings as it was called. There is great stress on the beauty of the positional sets and arrangements. There is an invisible dynamism behind each set enhancing or limiting further development. The game has to be played with elegance and according to rules which are reflections of those we find in life....
>
> A player starts at the point where he is in an abstract way equal with all other players in the world. When the figures are set on the chess board, before the first step is taken, we are equal and may remain equal up to the third or fourth move. All our babies are identical, they cry, eat, evacuate, they sleep and cry again. It continues that way up to three or four years of age and then suddenly differences become evident.

Mita's observations touched his daughter. She would remember his words when she had children of her own.

By the time she was in her mid-teens, the Mount Royal Tennis Club had become the centre of Mila's social life. There were tennis clinics and tournaments and swimming lessons by day and club house dance parties by night. When they weren't at the club, the younger members congregated in nearby Murray Park to plan parties and sorties into downtown Montreal.

Coleman Bonny, one of the tennis gang, remembers Mila was a good player, very athletic, but never driven to excel in the tournaments they all entered. She was tall and lean, appeared older than her age, and was clearly concerned with how she looked, he recalls. "Some of the girls ran around in cut-off jeans, others in long white Bermuda shorts. Mila was one of the latter. She never looked scruffy, was always tanned and well finished—more so than the other girls. The only time I ever saw her looking dishevelled was after dances when she'd be soaking wet from doing the twist or the limbo all night. I bet she washed her hair every day. She didn't suddenly turn into this person as an adult. I bet Jacqueline Kennedy Onassis was the same as a child."

Coleman used to pick Mila up on his motorcycle, something he was never sure pleased the Pivnickis. "Her upbringing was as strict as everyone says, but she lived in a really stable home. Her parents had a tight grip on her, but she had a lot of respect for them. We'd come racing home on the motorcycle—her long dark hair flying—to make it in time for her curfew. She was wild but not crazy. I don't remember her having close girlfriends, she hung out more with the guys than the girls. It was always Mila who had the ideas for what the gang should do. She was the leader, never the follower."

Throughout those years, the presence of Mila's younger siblings was obvious to everyone who knew her. Taking care of John and Ivana was expected of her. "Whether we liked it or not, we were always together," says John. "When Mila started to be interested in boys, it couldn't have been so great to have a little brother and a little sister around all the time, but even if she didn't like it, she had to keep an eye on us."

These were the 1960s, and rock concerts at the Forum and protest marches on the street were plentiful in

31

Montreal. Mila attended the concerts and sat up in the ''greys'' (the cheap seats near the ceiling of the Forum) with her friends, where so much marijuana smoke drifted to the rafters that she wondered if you could get high just sitting there.

Although rock concerts were frequent outings, there was only one demonstration that Mila really wanted to take part in. It was a march on the Russian Embassy to protest the censorship of Solzhenitsyn, Sakharov, and other intellectuals. Her mother was against the idea. After a long-drawn-out argument, Mila capitulated and stayed at home while her friends attended the protest. To this day she says that she only gets into a fight when she's sure she's 100 percent right. ''Obeying my parents wasn't usually a problem. I knew, for instance, in the case of the protest march, that my mother was concerned about my safety. On other occasions, I understood where she stood about me missing a curfew. It didn't seem complicated to me. I usually felt that there was little point in arguing back.''

Everyone who knows the Pivnickis recounts stories of the arguments around the dinner table. ''Our family revolved around the dinner table,'' says John. ''Our father was really busy, he'd had to do all of his schooling over again, but we ate dinner together almost every night. My father was loud, there was always a lot of yelling and screaming going on at the table—it often had to do with report cards. Mila was a good student, but Father had an idea that she should be a brilliant student.'' Her mother says she did very well in subjects she liked, but in the others, ''Well, it was a source of arguments.'' John says that, regardless of the arguments or the noise level during the meal, "everything would be fine after dinner. We weren't allowed to hold a grudge."

Mila says they are a very vocal family, and she thinks it's because their father is a psychiatrist and he used to tell them that people who held their feelings in had problems. He encouraged the Pivnicki kids to laugh, cry, and yell together. "It's hard to hold a grudge when that's what you're used to doing," says Ivana. Mrs. Pivnicki thinks it's a family trait. "I can't wake up in the morning without my morning cup of coffee and my morning argument," she jokes. However, the children knew that when their mother said she had "a cramp"— which meant she had a gut feeling that something was wrong—there was little point in arguing back.

Mila's life was very much managed by her parents. But as much as she felt she was being raised in a way that was different to her friends, Mila loved the Eastern European style of her home and felt nourished by it. "The house was always filled with music," she recalls. "My father would be sitting at his desk reading or conducting the music. My mother would be in the kitchen making something delicious. There would be a smell of rich Turkish coffee brewing. I remember the sun streaming into Tata's den on Marlowe, the cat curled up on the ottoman, Tata at his desk, the coffee, the music. I liked my life."

When the kids were old enough, they were registered in the Snow Larks Ski School. Although on most winter weekends they lined up for the ski bus at the nearby Côte-St-Luc shopping centre for transportation to Avila (the ski hill in the Laurentians where they took all-day lessons), occasionally Mita and Boba would drive them to the hills and watch their youngsters ski.

John recalls that Mila was a very strong skier. She remembers that John had better equipment than she had. John agrees that the younger kids in immigrant families usually have better things than the older ones. He feels it's because the parents are settled and more able to deliver the dream they had for their children.

A story Mila tells seems to offer proof not only of her position as the oldest child in an immigrant family but also of the sense of humour that she has about those days. "My mother had this friend from Latvia who knitted me a hat. This was not a hat Canadian children wore. This certainly was not a hat that skiers wore. But it was the hat I wore skiing. I called it my Heidi hat. When we went skiing, I had to take care of my brother, check his ski boots, make sure he didn't get hurt, things like that. Well, my brother, being younger, had clip-on ski boots. I still had the lace-up boots. So I used to think of myself in my Heidi hat and my wooden shoes. I looked like someone from out of the ark."

Although Coleman Bonny was the boyfriend she went babysitting with, played tennis with, and watched television with, her first big crush was on a boy called David Cahn, who took her to her first formal dance. It was the German Ball in Montreal, one of the social season's debutante balls. Although Mila wasn't a debutante, she and David attended the ball with David's parents. David's mother, Elaine, says Mila was a good conversationalist, she had a certain confidence and, in her opinion, she was easily the prettiest girl in the room.

David also had the dubious distinction of being the beneficiary of Mila's early attempts at cuisine. John remembers "a spaghetti dinner that went wrong, but David ate the whole thing." When he sees his old high school girlfriend on television now, David says he isn't the least bit surprised. "I knew she'd do something important with her life."

The strictness and family expectations didn't stop when Mila went to Sir George Williams College (now Concordia University). Her high school marks hadn't been good enough to get her accepted at a university so she'd spent a year at prep school. Westbury College was a small private school with an enrolment of about one hundred students. Kenneth Ward, her math teacher there, says, "She was a very bright student, but she needed a bit of structure and attention. In our small classes, she had that and started to blossom."

The hippy era had just begun and Ward saw the "Down with the rich and down with the establishment" slogan of the time as a blight on young people. He remembers Mila as being polite, not rebellious in the way that was so trendy at the time. "She was popular, but very conventional."

Mila studied arts in her first year at university, "but by second year, the writing stopped me. I did some aptitude tests and was told to switch into maths. I chose civil engineering because I had an interest in renovating old houses in Montreal and wanted to be an architect. I felt there were wonderful old houses that were in danger of being destroyed by modernism. I wanted to save the exteriors and renovate the interiors.

"There weren't many women in engineering in those days—three in my class if I remember—but schooling isn't my fondest memory. It seemed to be my weak link."

While she didn't establish lasting ties with other students, she was involved in a number of projects at high school and university. She played Mrs. Blackwell in *The Life and Death of Sneaky Fitch* when she was in grade ten at Westmount High School. She also joined the high school year book committee and, at Concordia, took part in the annual fashion show.

Mrs. Pivnicki remembers that a hairdresser from the show had a photo of Mila dressed in hot pants and high boots that covered her knees. "He showed that picture to me in the hairdressing salon one day and I said, 'Give that to me, you have no business having a photo like that of my Mila.' " The young man meekly handed over the photo.

Mila also volunteered in the campaign office of Michael Meighen, the Conservative who was trying to buck the Montreal Liberal tide and win a Conservative seat in Westmount. A friend of hers told her there were lots of young people working at the headquarters and they were having fun. After listening to the other candidates speak, Mila decided that she'd offer her help to the Conservatives, even though her own family voted Liberal. Although she didn't meet Brian there, she discovered later that he was the guy with the deep voice who used to call to speak to Michael; at the time Michael was vice-chairman of the Conservative Party of Quebec.

Michael Meighen says, "She was a real asset to the campaign, even though she knew nothing about politics. She answered the phone and was the first person to greet people at the door. She was very good because she projected an aura of warmth and friendliness. She was believable, always exactly as she appeared, and no one ever got the feeling she had a second agenda.''

It was hardly a surprise to anyone that when Brian Mulroney came into Mila's life, he was in for a scrutiny that would test his mettle as well as his patience.

They met at the Mount Royal Tennis Club on July 14, 1972, the day after Mila's nineteenth birthday. She was sitting by the pool, enjoying two weeks off from her summer job as a hostess at the Yugoslavian Pavilion (which was still open on the Man and His World site five years after Expo 67 closed). It had been a particularly adventurous summer for Mila: her first job, her own money. She loved the freedom it gave her. And working in the Yugoslavian Pavilion allowed her to explore the history and customs of her native land.

A serious relationship was the furthest thing from her mind. She was enjoying university and feeling confident about her academic ability for the first time in her life. She had plans for the future. And they didn't include the thirty-three-year-old man in the red bathing suit who kept asking about her. Her friends said that he wanted to meet her. She didn't pay much attention. She saw it as a smooth line and dismissed it.

Soon Brian came over to where she was sitting. Just as they were introduced, there was a sudden summer downpour. He told her he'd meet her inside. There he started making plans for the evening. Mila told him she had to babysit her brother and sister. Brian said that was all right, he'd come along to her house. When he left her that

night, he announced that he'd pick her up the following
Friday night. The next day a dozen red roses with the
longest stems she'd ever seen arrived at the house.

At first Brian's attentions only made Mila's life ''interesting,'' but after a few weeks of dating each other
every night, she began to change her mind about him.
''There are certain traits that I really like in people. I like
a sense of humour, open-mindedness. I like people who
are hard working, have goals and ambitions. I like to
learn from my friends, grow with them. Most of the
people I'm close to have some of these qualities. Brian
has them all. He's not pretentious, not negative, he
always has a nice thing to say about people. He's very
flexible, he made me laugh more than anyone ever had
before. As I got to know him, I realized he was very
capable—he became one of the youngest junior partners at Ogilvy, Renault when we were dating. He was
respected and reliable.''

Brian talked about marriage from their very first date.
He asked if any of her friends were married. He talked
about his friends who were married. He asked her if she
looked forward to getting married. He often sent her
flowers, and whenever a vendor passed their table in a
restaurant, he asked Mila to choose the flower she
wanted. It was always a rose and always a different
colour. One night, they were having dinner at an Irish
pub on St. Catherine Street, and the flower vendor
asked Brian if he'd like to buy a rose for his daughter.
They never went back there again.

Mila wasn't sure where the relationship was going,
but she realized it was moving fast. ''Can you imagine?
He was thirty-three years old. I had a curfew of eleven

o'clock. My mother used to wait at the door each night with the light on.''

Mrs. Pivnicki didn't make it easy for Brian Mulroney. ''He used to come to the house every morning to drive her to school. We didn't like that. He invited her to go to Russia with him to see the Canada Cup hockey series. I said, 'No, over my dead body. If she goes to Russia, she'll go on my ticket. And what does she know about hockey anyway?' Every time he sent her flowers, she hid them in her room because she knew I didn't approve. I would say, 'Why are you receiving gifts if you're not giving something? Gifts are extremes.' I thought he was too old for her, I really did. But Mila kept saying, 'He's the man for me. We'll have a very good family.' I still didn't like it.

''One night I woke up because I smelled smoke. I have a phobia about fires. I rushed out of my bed and heard Mila's voice. I called out, 'Mila, what is it?' She answered, 'It's Brian.' He was on his way home from the airport. It was midnight. He'd stopped in to see Mila and he was having a cigarette in my front hall. I said, 'Out—now!' It was my rule.

''One day, Brian came to me and asked, 'What is it you don't like about me? I have a good profession. I come from a good family. I have a good job.' I said, 'It's your age. She's very young. I want her to finish school.' He raised his voice and said, 'Bobo'—he called me Bobo in those days—'I never met anyone like Mila. Whether you like it or not, I'll be around her for forty years.' He won me over. My husband liked him from the very beginning, but he grew on me more slowly. He was a handsome man, the envy of all my friends. He proved me wrong. He's a good family man.''

When Brian went away on a two-week holiday in November, Mila realized she had fallen in love with him. He called after six days and said he was coming home and wanted to talk to her. They went to the Alpenhaus and over beef fondue and wine, Brian said, "Maybe tomorrow we should go and pick out a ring." Mila replied, "I have a dentist appointment." He wanted to talk about when and where they would get married. Mila felt there could be no discussion until he'd asked her father for permission to marry her. "I thought the person proposing should go through the formalities of speaking to my parents before buying a ring. It was a standard approach to marriage then. I think if you take those steps there's a larger commitment."

They went home to talk to the Pivnickis. Brian sat in the living room with Dr. Pivnicki. The doctor, using an old chess analogy, said, "Well Brian, you're holding the white pawn. That means you go first. So why don't you tell me what's going on?"

The Pivnickis gave their blessing in the end. After all, as Mila points out, her parents had been married when her father was thirty-four and her mother was twenty-one, so they could hardly claim that a wide difference in ages was a barrier. Brian became part of the Pivnicki family, and they came to enjoy his antics and his demonstrative love for Mila as much as she did.

Soon Brian's friends began to notice the strong-willed independence of his bride-to-be. Madeleine Roy (who is married to Bernard Roy, one of Brian's best friends) remembers the night she met Mila, at a party before any of them were married. "Brian hushed her for something she said. A few minutes later, in the kitchen, Mila said to me, 'If he thinks he's going to tell me what to say, he'd better think it over again.' "

By now, Brian had let Mila in on his plans for the future. "We were sitting having dinner when he told me he intended to be the prime minister of Canada one day. I was up for it. Ignorance gives you a lot of confidence!"

One of his closest friends at the time, Lowell Murray, says, "Brian was extremely protective of Mila. I think he felt a real sense of responsibility for her and to her parents. Her parents certainly had some misgivings. Brian was a practising lawyer who was well known in Montreal and had quite a long bachelorhood. The world he took Mila into was a world of people his own age and interests. Since they were all older than she was, he went to some pains to make sure she felt at ease. Compared to the way he treated other women he'd brought into our group, he was particularly attentive to Mila and watchful that she was at ease and that the others were being nice to her.

"His close friends knew he was serious about this relationship because of the way he treated her and because he wanted to have her around him all the time, not just at social gatherings. I remember having lunch with him and cautioning him not to lose his heart to someone so young. I told him that some of us were worried since he'd been a bachelor for such a long time, but he was absolutely determined to marry Mila."

They were engaged on December 19, 1972, the feast of Slava. Brian told his mother, Irene, the news on a plane flying between Quebec City and Montreal. Irene remembers the trip well. "I had been in Shannon visiting relatives, and Brian called to say he'd meet me and fly back with me. He's a generous and thoughtful son, so I didn't think too much of his offer. Then he gave me the news that he'd met the girl he was going to marry. He brought her over to my apartment soon after that and we clicked right away. I felt I could be easy with her and that she'd be part of the family. Did I ever feel relieved! Brian had no shortage of girlfriends. The one he'd bring home to be Mrs. Mulroney was what bothered me.''

And so the relationship was blessed from both sides of the family—time enough, thought Boba, to leave the young couple alone. This momentous occasion became an infamous family story known to insiders as the Cat Story. Ivana tells it best. ''My parents whisked my brother and me off to the Fairview Mall so the young couple could—at last—be alone together. We no sooner left them alone in the house for this intimate moment together than the phone rings. It's a neighbour who says, 'I hate to disturb you,but your cat has just been hit by a car.' Brian checks it out and sure enough, there is a dead cat on the road. He has to go out onto the street with a shovel and pick up the cat and put it into a box in the backyard. Mila is hysterical and crying. When we return, I'm sent immediately to my room because at the age of eleven, I'm too young to hear bad things like this. I tear upstairs and, being the snoop that I am, I intend to listen to the conversation from the stair top. I raced into my room to get something and there was our cat lying on my bed. I scooped up the cat, ran down the stairs, and said, 'Is this why Mila is crying?' Brian had been consoling Mila for three hours, and to this day he's convinced that some poor cat was sacrificed for Mila's chastity.''

Chapter Three

*I used to show her house to my friends. One time she
and Brian were in the bedroom when I was showing
my friends around and Mila said, 'Mother, this has to
stop.'*

Bogdanka Pivnicki

The bride was beautiful, the groom handsome. The
wedding party consisted of a collection of hot-shot
lawyers from Montreal—Michel Cogger, Bernard Roy,
Yves Fortier, Lowell Murray—a bevy of Yugoslavian
bridesmaids, and a French-Canadian maid of honour,
Monique Brossard. The guests included six nationali-
ties and enough Yugoslavs to make the reception rich
with stories and customs from the old country and the
bride's childhood.

Milica Pivnicki and Martin Brian Mulroney were married in the Church of the Ascension in Westmount on a
sunny May 26, 1973. Monique Brossard, who'd been
Mila's best friend for the five years since they moved in
next door on Marlowe Avenue, remembers, "Everything
was perfect. Every single detail was taken care of. It was
as though this wedding had been planned for years."

Certainly the preparations were elaborate. Dozens of
parties were given to honour the couple, as well as a

series of bridal showers that included the wives of senior partners at Ogilvy, Renault, the law firm where Brian worked. (Unheard-of, harrumphed some of the wives, that such attention should be lavished on a newcomer and at that, one so young.) Gifts arrived daily at the Pivnicki house. Hours were spent on fittings for the beautiful hand-sewn gowns the bridesmaids wore and Mila's elegant long-sleeved, high-necked bridal gown with lace appliqué and a cathedral-length train.

On her wedding day, Mila wore a single strand of cultured pearls and loops of ribbon caught up in a bow in her hair, and she carried a bouquet of daisies. The wedding was a traditional Catholic ceremony with about two hundred guests. Mila, says her mother, was more serene than she's ever seen her, or any bride for that matter.

The reception was held at the McGill Faculty Club, a staid old downtown club with overstuffed leather chairs, gloomy oil paintings of former deans, and dozens of little reading lamps. The Pivnicki kids had frequented the club with their father, and Mila had always insisted that when she was married, her reception would be there. Boba had wanted a reception that embraced their Yugoslavian roots: a feasting table and dancing into the small hours of the morning. But Mila and Brian felt that their friends would prefer a cocktail party, and anyway, they had to catch a five o'clock flight to Paris to begin their honeymoon.

When Brian Mulroney rose to make his speech, he told the gathering that he had a very special thank you for the person who was responsible for his bride being there that day. Dr. Pivnicki sat a little straighter in his chair. The future prime minister continued, "Obviously this day couldn't have taken place without some decisions by a very strong Yugoslav patriot. I can safely say that without him, I wouldn't be marrying Mila today." Dr. Pivnicki smiled at the people at his table. "This is a man who bears full responsibility for the Pivnicki voyage across the sea to Canada." Dr. Pivnicki nodded in agreement. And then Brian Mulroney did what no one had managed to do in twenty-nine years. When he said to the gathered guests, "I refer of course to Marshal Tito, the man who forced Mita Pivnicki to bring his family and my lovely bride to Canada," the room full of Yugoslavs erupted with laughter. Until then, no one would have dared to praise the name of the hated dictator to Yugoslavs.

Their three-and-a-half-week honeymoon in Europe got off to a memorable start when they discovered that the Hotel Le Commodore in Paris had no record of their reservations. When they finally checked in, they found that the elevator doors were lethal weapons—they swung open into the corridor, nearly knocking the honeymooners out cold. Honeymoons, Mila soon decided, are very revealing. "You spend all this time together for three weeks. We were two very different people. Our upbringing was different. Our religions were different. We had a lot to learn about each other." They also had a lot to teach each other. "He learned to like the classics through me. I learned more about politics from him. I found that being around him brought out the best in me."

After taking in all the tourist sights in Paris, they flew to Vienna, then rented a car and drove to Yugoslavia, where Mila introduced Brian to her grandparents in Dubrovnik. Unfortunately, Baka and Deda were frail and ill, and the meeting was difficult for Brian because he didn't understand a single word of the conversation. "It must have been a tremendous culture shock for him to go to Yugoslavia," says Mila. "My grandmother was so senile. The poor woman—she wouldn't have her teeth in and her gums were all swollen. I had a lot of trouble with this. I would be terribly upset every time we left the house. I knew Brian was a gentle man. But I didn't know how patient, understanding, tolerant, and good-natured he would be in a situation like this."

They flew to Belgrade, where more than fifty relatives, all clutching bouquets, came to the airport to meet their flight. Their hotel room looked like a florist's shop. Every time someone came to the door, Brian would say, "Do you have a wife? Here are some flowers for her. You don't have a wife? Well, give these to your girlfriend."

On the way home to Canada, they stopped in England to attend the wedding of a friend of Brian's. When they got back to Montreal, they settled into the apartment Brian had been living in on Clarke Avenue in Westmount. Brian went back to his law practice at Ogilvy, Renault, where he'd established a reputation as a first-rate labour and corporate lawyer.

They'd been in the apartment two months when they found a semi-detached house in Westmount at the corner of Devon and Upper Belmont and decided to become home-owners. "The apartment was his. The closet was his. I had one in the hall," says Mila. "Not only that, everything in the apartment was green—the walls, the carpet, the sofa, and even the bedspread. I put our wedding gifts around and bought an aquarium so there'd be something alive in all that green, and I added plants. But we needed a place that was both of ours.''

The new house had white walls and old wall sconces and room enough for Brian to do his work and Mila to do her studying. And when children came along, there would be room for them too, but the house was small enough that they could take care of it themselves. They lived there for three years.

Their marriage didn't begin as the partnership it is today. Mila says that her early married life was a matter of two strong personalities getting to know each other. For instance, she says, ''I like sleeping in a cold room with the windows open and lots of covers on. Brian doesn't. The first year I was married I thought I'd changed my name to Jesus. Every morning when Brian got out of bed he'd yell, 'Jesus, it's cold in here!' I took him to see Nureyev—he fell sound asleep. I like classical music, he didn't. I wasn't a sports fan, he was.''

Brian says, ''I didn't realize it at the time, but as the relationship developed, I began to see certain things in a different perspective. After some period of time, it dawned on me that I was finding out that her assessment of people and policies was invariably accurate. I wondered if it was instinct. She had her own antennae and radar that were extremely effective, and I began to realize that her judgement was extremely good and reliable. It took a little while. We were married for a few years before we really became partners, then she became very much a part of everything that I do.''

His friend Lowell Murray agrees. "At first, I thought Mila was a bit in awe of him and the people he was introducing her to. But then it became clear as time went on that he was deferring to her, that he had a lot of respect for her."

As their partnership began to establish itself, it became the driving force behind what most people saw as the family firm. Brian had ambitious political plans. Mila was prepared to help him achieve his goals. They saw themselves as a pair of beautiful people "off to see the world," like the Huckleberry friends in the song "Moon River."

"Those were wonderful days, a golden time in Montreal," Brian remembers. "Mila is full of life, an exciting person to live with. She's always interested in everything, from travelling to the symphony. I even managed to persuade her that there was value in going to a hockey game, but that took a little while. We had a wide circle of friends. We were young and had lots of energy. We worked hard and enjoyed life, so it was a very good time for us. We loved to go to movies, order out, and walk around Stanley Street and Crescent Street. There were no clouds on the horizon." This was when they began to build up the art collection that Brian had started as a bachelor. They bought the paintings by Stanley Cosgrove, Lawren Harris, and Molly Bobak that hang in the halls and rooms of 24 Sussex today.

Mila viewed her future the way most nineteen-year-olds would consider a backpacking tour of Europe. The road ahead would be filled with unknowns and excitement and occasionally peril, but she was up for the ride. Brian travelled a lot, and even when he was home, he left early and worked late, so Mila led her own life and began what she would later remember as a training program for the job she would ultimately hold as the wife of the prime minister of Canada.

One of the first things she did as a newlywed was hire a cleaning woman two days a week. She felt she'd done enough cleaning and ironing at her parents' house to last a lifetime. If she did any more, it would be her choice.

Mila is intensely loyal to the people she loves, and her first priority was Brian—his job, his friends, his interests. Even in the very early days of their marriage, Mila would put together dinner for ten at the drop of a hat if Brian had clients to entertain. Sometimes she'd come home from her lectures at university at four or five o'clock, and Brian would call and tell her that he was bringing home eight people for dinner. She'd get back in the car, drive downtown to the Atwater Market, and by the time the guests arrived at 7:30, she'd greet them as though she'd been waiting all day for them. Then, as often as not, when her guests had left and she'd tidied up the kitchen, she would get her books out to finish her assignments.

"I sometimes felt like I was living a double life. I'd get to school a bit late for class in the morning and the professor would say, 'I saved this seat in the front for you, Mrs. Mulroney'—always with a heavy emphasis on the 'Mrs. Mulroney.' I'd study in the library after classes and get as much done as I could. I cut classes a few times when Brian wanted me to go on trips with him. It was hard to juggle everything. My mother used to help me, and Joe Kovecvic, a Yugoslav friend and handyman, used to help me. It was hard, but really those were good days. I loved entertaining and meeting all those interesting people.''

An almost uncanny ability to remember names served her well. Her brother credits that talent to an early and continued exposure to numerous visitors with long, complicated eastern European names. Mila also mastered a brilliant technique for pairing people with events. For instance, throughout her adult life, she's been able to greet a person she's met perhaps once before not only with the right name but with a remark such as, ''The last time I saw you, your husband had just had surgery. How is he?'' It's a skill that takes people by surprise and often wins them over quickly. Her friends call it the ''Mila connection.'' Whether the guests at her dinner parties were clients of Brian's or young Tory colleagues, they were invariably knocked out by this nineteen-year-old engineering student's seemingly effortless charm.

Soon after they were married, Mila became pregnant, but she miscarried in September after a long, uncomfortable flight to Saint John, New Brunswick. ''Brian was negotiating a settlement in a labour dispute at the port in Saint John. There were four men, all smoking, and me crammed into this little plane. I knew something was wrong, but I didn't want to say anything until we arrived in Saint John. The next morning, I lost the baby.''

Mila returned to classes immediately, but she was already beginning to see a different way of life unfolding in front of her. Brian needed her and wanted her to travel with him. She wanted to get pregnant again soon. Although her classes were important to her, she began to think about her choices for the future. She was reminded of her father's academic paper likening the game of chess to life.

> Unless a chess player sees at least three, four, five or more moves ahead he will be a loser... It is less important that he remember the moves of the beginning. It is much more important that he see where he is driving and in what direction he is going. If you glance at a chess board at the time of the twentieth move, you can't reconstruct what had led to that set of figures. If you are a good player who knows the game and can "project" your own moves into the future, your reactions as well as the reactions of your partner, you can predict the ending of the game.

Mila was shrewd enough to know that her life and her ambitions were also being mapped out while she entertained Brian's friends, attended classes, and ran her household.

This was the newlywed who turned up at Shirley Corn's door at the end of the summer of 1973, at a time when most of the neighbours on Upper Belmont Avenue were beginning to fold away the lawn chairs and turn in for winter. Shirley, who has two children of her own and is seventeen years older than Mila, remembers answering the doorbell that day and finding this "smiley" woman saying, "Hi. I just moved in next door. Your house looks lovely. Can I come in and see what you've done with it?"

For Shirley this sounded like potential disaster. "One of the reasons you move to a neighbourhood like this is you don't want suburbia. I listened to this woman and thought, 'Oh God, here it is—suburbia.' But then I got to know her. She's lots of fun and is forever talking me into doing things that I never imagined I could do. I'd been a nurse before I retired to raise my children, but now I had an urge to go back to work and a chance to do something totally untraditional—selling bags [the kind you carry your merchandise home in] to stores. Mila is a risk-taker. I was scared to take the job, but Mila gave me the nerve to do it. When I first met her, I used to think, 'God, she must have bad breath or something.' I mean, how can anyone be so nice all the time and be so up about things like curtains and decorating?

"She knew every discount place in the city, and when we went shopping at those places, I would only see junk," says Shirley. "But Mila would zero in on something terrific that was all squished up on the rack and insist that I try it on. She had me put together in twenty minutes flat."

To her friends in Montreal, she's the best bargain shopper in town. She introduced them to Brana's, the wholesaler in the east end (now out of business), and to Madison Textiles on Amherst Street, the fabric store where she taught everyone else about mixing and matching patterns in 1975, before anyone else was doing it. She told them where to get shoes dyed and how to put clips on shoes so it would seem as though you had dozens of pairs. Ivana says she always used to think that Mila would wind up in the design business. "She has such an eye for shapes and colours and style."

Shirley says, "This is a woman with a very high energy level. She's a pusher, an achiever who lives as though today will never happen again."

Not long after her miscarriage, Mila became pregnant again. The baby was due in late May. Her exams would be over by then, and a three-month summer vacation seemed plenty of time to adjust to motherhood before school began again in September. Shirley Corn says Mila's spirits and energy level remained amazingly high throughout her pregnancy. "She was one of those women who could barf, wash, dress, and go. God, I was envious."

Three and a half weeks beyond the baby's due date, her labour pains finally started. She knew that this signalled not only the arrival of a baby but also the arrival of her mother and who knows how many other relatives at her house, so she started cleaning cupboards. She cleaned all day and called Brian at five o'clock to tell him her news. They were having Michel and Erica Cogger for dinner and decided to go ahead with the plan.

At two o'clock on the morning of June 11, 1974, Mila woke Brian up and in the midst of a driving rain storm, they dashed to the hospital. The delivery wasn't easy—it was a breech birth, and Mila had toxaemia.

In those days, fathers were not allowed in the delivery room—they had to sit in the waiting room until the doctor came out to announce the birth. At 8 a.m. Mila's father arrived at the hospital to go to work, and Brian asked him to check on Mila. Dr. Pivnicki returned to say he was the father of a five-pound, eleven-ounce baby girl who had been born more than an hour earlier. The doctor who delivered the baby had finished his work and gone home without telling Brian the news. Brian was furious, but his mood quickly turned to elation as the news of his daughter's birth sank in. "There was a celebration all over Montreal that day," he says.

Their lives didn't change a great deal with Caroline's arrival. Mila tackled motherhood with a relaxed attitude that is unusual in new mothers. She would bundle her baby in receiving blankets, thinking that the tight wrapping would make Caroline feel secure. When her mother came to babysit, she would peel off the blankets and say, "Let this child breathe and feel some freedom." Most first-time mothers are threatened by interference and worry that their baby will suffer from inconsistent treatment. Not Mila. When her mother took care of Caroline, which was often, she did it her way. When Mila was in charge, she followed her own instincts. Caroline thrived on this system.

As her mother had been, Caroline was an integral part of her parents' lives. "I used to think that if people were coming over, the baby should be upstairs," says Brian. "But Mila said, 'No, our children have to be with us, have to be used to being around people.' Caroline wasn't three weeks old when she was with us in a little push-chair at a restaurant in Montreal. She was the start of it—we took the kids everywhere with us. A lot of people remark today about the extent to which the kids are a part of our lives. They come into our dinner parties whether we're entertaining the Queen of England or a king from someplace or the president of the United States."

Mila was fortunate throughout those years to have a close-knit supportive family. As is the custom in the Pivnicki home, Boba was often there to help Mila. She would bring prepared meals over and tuck them into her daughter's fridge so that Mila wouldn't have to cook. Boba was known as a great cook, but she says, "Mila taught me something. Everyone has different tastes. My husband is European. He likes to taste different foods. Brian is a man who likes basic food. Mila didn't know how to tell me that her husband didn't want to eat what I cook. One day I saw a dish I'd left in her fridge the week before and asked Mila why it hadn't been eaten. 'Mom, Brian likes plain food, spaghetti, things like that.'"

In time, Mila persuaded him to try the Yugoslavian dishes she'd been raised on, and he began to like them. But the independence she'd gained in the process of breaking away from her mother's style of cooking was an experience she intended to repeat.

One day soon after she was married, she telephoned her mother and told her that she had bought a dog. Boba asked her why and Mila replied briskly, "I'm a married woman. I'll do what I like." Boba says the dog was untrainable but lovable. "It had one ear up and one ear down. It came from the SPCA. It wouldn't respond to a name. We tried everything, but the dog wouldn't listen. And guess who looked after him? I did. They were going to Brazil: 'Mama, will you keep the dog?' They were going to Paris: 'Mama, will you take the dog?'

"One day they came back from a trip and brought me a beautiful gift in a Gucci bag. I screamed, 'Gucci!'

when I saw the bag. And the dog jumped up. So that became the dog's name—Gucci.

"When Brian and Mila moved to Ottawa ten years later, they left Gucci with me. Nobody wanted a mess on the Persian carpets at Kingsmere where they were going to live."

Even with a baby and a puppy in the house and her commitments as a student, with the help of her cleaning woman, Mila kept her house immaculate. Her sister-in-law, Olive Elliott, says she's always been like that. "The house gleamed just as much as it does now. There were polished tables and fresh flowers and a feeling of relaxation and welcome in the house. It always astonished me that a woman so young could handle everything so well. For instance, when my husband and I moved back to Canada from Iran where he'd been working, I wanted to go and see my sister in New York, so Mila invited my husband and two of our children to stay with them for three weeks—just like that. Can you imagine? She's always organized and on top of everything."

Mila's sister, Ivana, called her a clean freak when she was growing up, because Mila not only kept her own place tidy but she was always pushing Ivana to clean up after herself. Another characteristic that Shirley Corn remembers and her husband, Harvey, swears he'll never forget is Mila's fetish for changing furniture around. "Even after she moved to Ottawa, she'd come back to Montreal to visit and she'd come in the house and start yelling, 'Shirley, you've had the living room like this for six months. Aren't you tired of it?' Then poor Harvey would come home with his arms full of briefcases and try to sneak past the room so that Mila wouldn't see him. It never worked. She'd grab him and say, 'Come on, Harvey, be a doll, help me to move this cabinet.' A little while later she'd be looking at it and saying, 'I hate it—let's move it back.' The day she and Brian moved, Harvey cheered, thinking his moving days were over!''

One of Shirley's favourite stories about Mila typifies her willingness to jump in and learn something new. Only this time, her jump had unexpected repercussions. ''Harvey's mother died. We were sitting shiva here. Mila says, 'Explain it to me. I understand it's like a wake and after the person is buried, people come to the house, but what do you do?' I said, 'Well, the immediate family always has dinner together because you receive people in the afternoon and then go back into the living room again to receive guests from seven o'clock to ten.' Mila said, 'I know what I can do to help you, I'm going to make one of your meals. What do you want me to make?' After going back and forth for a while with me saying, 'Don't bother,' and her saying, 'I insist,' I said, 'Well, your turkeys are delicious, I'll have a turkey for about twelve people.' She asked when she should have it ready, and I said I'd prefer that she have it here at six o'clock.

''That evening, just before six o'clock, Brian comes walking up our path with a huge turkey on a platter. When he sees the mezuzah on our door, a sign that Jewish people live in this house, he suddenly realizes, 'Oh my God, there's bacon on this turkey.' So he strips off the bacon and feeds it to his dog Gucci. Anyway, when Harvey answers the door Brian takes a deep breath and says to him, 'Look, I don't need this on my conscience, so I am going to tell you, Harvey, there was bacon on this turkey. You do what you want with it.'

"Harvey comes into the kitchen and says, 'Shirley, I have some terrible news for you.' My family's kosher, you see. I said, 'What?' He said, 'There was bacon on the turkey.' I look at my watch, all these people are going to be arriving at seven o'clock to sit shiva. Then I look at all the people in my living room waiting for the next course and I said, 'Harvey, I'll think about my sin tomorrow, take the turkey to the table and start carving.'

"When we start to eat, I can't look at anyone and I want this meal to be over fast. Harvey starts to cut the meat. He gives some to my Auntie Fanny, who is the senior mourner, she's my Yiddish auntie who immigrated here from Russia. Although she's not living any more, she was elderly then and always kept kosher. When Auntie Fanny takes a bite, she says, 'Oi, this toikey is so good! Shoiley, you have any idea what she puts on it?' At this point my face is in my plate, I can't look at my husband, and I say, 'It's paprika, Auntie Fanny.' And she says, 'What do you take me for, a dumbbell? I know from paprika. This isn't paprika, it has that taste, that delicious taste. Those Yugoslavs, Shoiley, they have very good recipes.' She will not leave it alone and she's eating that turkey. Then, God forbid, she says, 'Harvey, do me a favour, give me another piece of that toikey—it's delicious.' And I'm saying to her, Auntie Fanny, I don't think you should eat any more of that turkey. And she shoots back, 'Why? Now you're stingy with the meat?'

''At the end of the evening—and remember it was a sad occasion—Auntie Fanny says, 'Shoiley, do me a favour, ask Myla'—she never called her Mila—'for the recipe.' I said, 'I promise you, Auntie Fanny, I will.' I thought, 'What will I do? I'll think of things like rosemary or some kind of ingredient that Jewish people her age don't usually use.' I told her all the things on my list. She said, 'I know from rosemary and from all the things you're telling me. This was not that, Shoiley, there was something else on that toikey that was delicious.' Anyway, we finally let it drop.

''A couple of years later when Brian was running for the leadership of the Conservative party, Auntie Fanny was very active in the Golden Age Association in Montreal, and Mila and I were sitting around trying to think of ways we could help Brian. Well, we thought talking to the Golden Age group might be a really good idea, especially in the Jewish community. They were mostly Liberals and here was a chance to meet someone from their own community who had met Conservatives and could talk about them as friends and people who understand the concerns of the Jewish community. So who was better to be our spokesperson at the Golden Age Association than Auntie Fanny?

''I call her and say, 'Auntie Fanny, I need a special favour.' Well, she didn't have children and was always very good to me so she said, 'Shoiley, anything.' I went to her house and we had tea and I said, 'Auntie Fanny, I really would like you to help my friends.' And I went into the whole thing about how Brian is sympathetic to Israel and to Jewish causes and after all, he's married to an immigrant, he understands what it was like to come

here. She listened, then she turns to me and says,
'Shoiley, I'm not an educated lady but I'll tell you one
thing, a person who doesn't give her recipes is not the
kind of person you should be friendly with and it's not
the kind of person you should vote for.' She would not
talk to the Golden Age Association. For her, the worst
possible sin you could commit was not to share a
recipe.''

Shirley and Mila were part of a tightly knit group of
Montreal women called the Ballet Group. It had its
beginnings in 1974 when ''the girls''—Mila, Shirley,
Cathy Campeau, Madeleine Roy, Shirley Ann Mass,
Anelie Bubalo, and later, Andrée Beaulieu—decided
that the only way to get organized about attending
symphony performances was to order tickets in ad-
vance and plan a night out. Mila agreed to get the group
organized. She ordered the tickets and made a dinner
reservation for afterwards.

As it turned out, Mila was the only one who really
enjoyed the performances and that was only because
she was brought up with classical music and therefore
knew the repertoire. The others were falling asleep. So
they decided that a little action with the music would be
helpful and agreed that ballet tickets were probably a
better idea. Although they used to pick each other up
and usually travelled as a group in Cathy's station
wagon, invariably one or two had prior commitments
and had to get there solo and, as often as not, late.
Disturbing the other patrons by climbing over them to
find your seat wasn't permitted, so the late arrival had
to stand out in the hall. So they decided to get a box.

''The best part was going out for dinner afterwards,'' says Madeleine. ''We'd solve all the world's problems and apparently we entertained the people sitting at the tables around us at the same time. The restaurants on Mountain Street would wait for us. They wouldn't close on the nights the ballet group went downtown because we were so funny.''

The group was Mila's inside circle. They entertained each other at dinner parties, helped each other with the charitable work all of them were very involved with, and relied on each other for advice and support when they needed it. Mila started the group and was the instigator for most of the things they did.

''Don't get the idea that Mila was boring or a saint,'' says Madeleine. ''When we're together, we smoke and drink and tell funny stories. But there isn't one of us who doesn't go home and straighten a few pillows after being with her.''

Like most of her friends, the women in the ballet group were much older than Mila. Cathy Campeau, for instance, whose husband at that time was a partner in the same law firm Brian worked in, was eleven years her senior but became one of her closest friends because the two had so much in common. A do-it-yourself decorating philosophy is one way of describing their mutual interests. Tearing houses apart is another way. Their we-can-do-anything style bonded the two women together.

One day, Cathy was helping the contractor she'd hired to renovate her basement. There was an accident, and about eight sheets of gyproc came crashing down on top of her. In fact, the contractor was also caught when he rushed to her rescue and knocked more layers

on top of himself. "We were like a gyproc sandwich,"
Cathy says.

"Mila happened to telephone at the time and the
maid who worked in our house was panicking and
telling her I was being squashed by this giant pile of
gyproc. Mila was on her way to some event, she was
dressed to the nines, but she dropped everything and
came rushing over to my house. I refused to go to the
hospital in an ambulance, so Mila fashioned a stretcher
out of some of the construction board and helped the
contractor slide me into the back of my station wagon.
He drove while Mila supervised me. We got to the
hospital and found out I had a fractured pelvis."

In 1974 Brian was named as one of three commissioners
to the Cliche Commission, which was established to
examine racketeering in the construction industry in
Quebec. "This royal commission was going to interrupt
a six-billion-dollar-a-year business," says Brian.
"There'd been a lot of violence, murder, and destruction. These were not choirboys we were dealing with.
The Sûreté du Québec intercepted a communication
that the commissioners were being threatened, so they
insisted we have police drivers and around-the-clock
protection for our families at our homes.

"One day we received word that one of the witnesses
was going to do something. I called home to check on
Mila and the baby and couldn't get an answer, and I
thought something had happened. We jumped in the
car and roared all the way home. As it turned out, Mila
was washing the baby and couldn't hear the phone, but
I realized that something might have happened.

"We were uncovering a web of violence and corruption that had held the construction industry in Quebec hostage for many years. A lot of people knew about it, but it was the shock of the destruction of the Baie James project that got the inquiry going. This was an inter-union battle. They drove bulldozers into the power plants. They burned the place down, destroyed the biggest construction project in the history of Quebec. Everyone had to be evacuated by helicopter and plane because they'd even burned down the bunkhouses. They had guns up there. They were running the place like something out of the Wild West. The battle was for union control of the project, so you can imagine what that meant in terms of influence and kickbacks. We exposed some pretty tough characters. We were under serious threat."

Mila made it all sound like an adventure, telling her neighbour, "Hey, Shirley, we're going to have all these men around, isn't that fabulous?" But the situation must have been difficult. Caroline was playing with security guards at the front door of the house. Brian was being driven to work by policemen. Neighbours called Mila to ask why there were strangers sitting in cars parked across from her house. This was not part of the beautiful people script. But Mila insisted that she wasn't afraid. "I was studying so hard at the time— perhaps ignorance was my excuse. I didn't go to the hearings. We did have threatening phone calls, but we had bodyguards, so I figured we were taken care of. I didn't worry. I think worrying about something like that is a waste of energy and time. When your time is up, it's up. I'm not going to lose sleep over something that isn't in my control."

Throughout this period, Mila managed to run her household, attend classes at Concordia, entertain their friends, and prepare meals for the security guards. John, who was also an engineering student (he was in chemical engineering at McGill University), wasn't able to see much of his sister, but Ivana was just starting high school and loved visiting her big sister's home. She would often stay overnight, not just to help her sister but because she wanted to be part of what was becoming a fairly glamorous lifestyle. She felt free to bring her friends over to Mila's house. So did Boba. "I used to show her house to my friends. One time, she and Brian were in the bedroom when I was showing my friends around and Mila said, 'Mother, this has to stop.'"

At the same time, Mila was developing her own style. The long, straight 1960s-style hair, parted in the middle, was cut shorter with the saucy bangs that would become her trademark along with her long, carefully manicured nails and the clothes with the bold colours and remarkable design.

An election was called in 1974, and her friend Michael Meighen decided to run again for public office. She'd worked for him in 1972, before she met Brian, and now he needed her help again. The campaign headquarters were anything but glamorous, with makeshift telephone equipment and wires tangled up on the concrete floor. Whenever the door on St. Catherine Street opened, a blast of cold air rushed in.

One of Mila's fellow campaigners, Molly Fripp, was then the headmistress at Miss Edgar's and Miss Cramp's School in Montreal, the school Mila had

attended briefly as a child. Molly remembers the dedi-
cated, no-nonsense, fluently bilingual campaign
worker as being an asset who was worth her weight in
gold. What really impressed the people around Mila
was not only her willingness to work—if it wasn't her
turn and they called because they were short of people,
she'd come along anyway, bringing the baby and a
playpen with her—but also her patient, courteous man-
ner with everyone she met, whether they were the party
bigwigs or those who had arrived to stuff envelopes.

"She greeted people with such warmth, they couldn't
help but feel appreciated. And it didn't seem to matter
whether she was making sandwiches while standing on
a cold concrete floor or answering the phone," Molly
remembers. Others agree that Mila is one of those lucky
people who can stand in a doorway yet seem to be in the
centre of the room.

If 1974 and 1975 were eventful years in Mila's life up
to that point, in retrospect, they were simply a warm-up
for what was to come in 1976. Brian's law career was
soaring. Mila was still attending classes at university
and taking care of fourteen-month-old Caroline. In the
summer of 1975 she discovered that she was pregnant
again. It promised to be an exciting year ahead.

Mila never completed her university degree. When
Brian decided to run for the leadership of the Conservative party, she dropped out of school, because it was the
only thing she felt she could return to at a later date. "I
couldn't figure out how I would study full time, travel
with my husband, and take care of two children.

"Now I wish I had completed my degree. I can't go
back because there is a ten-year limit to finishing an

engineering degree, but if I were to do those years again, it's the only thing I would change. I would have taken that year. Brian would have travelled without me. I think that in this country there is an unfortunate belief that people who don't have a university degree are somehow not as successful or as appreciated as those who do. It's almost like the volunteer who doesn't receive a pay cheque—as though it's not a job. I put it on a par with that. I think it would have been easier for me as a political wife if I had finished my degree. Now that I have the confidence to do other things, I may go back and do an arts degree.''

Soon after she dropped out of school, she ran into the woman who had been her needlepoint teacher as a child. ''I was rushing around Steinberg's with two babies in my cart trying to get my groceries when I saw her. She came up to me with this la-de-dah accent and said, 'Mila dahling, you were *such* an ugly child. It's amazing how you've turned out.' It was the business of looking different, being different. I was very much a Yugoslav child.'' No matter how well she fitted into her life in Canada, married to a prominent lawyer, praised as a gifted volunteer and hostess and an energetic mother, she would be reminded again and again that she had started as an outsider.

Chapter Four

It was one of the hardest things I ever did. I didn't even
get a chance to bond with my baby. But it was
important to Brian that we go to Florida right then.
He needed me. It was a question of priorities.

Mila Mulroney

Montreal in the mid-1970s was an exciting place to
be. The Montreal Expos were a young team, the
Canadiens were at the top of the league, the Soviets had
come to town to play hockey, and the excitement about
the upcoming 1976 Olympics caught the imagination of
Montrealers. Theatre was flourishing, and the city was
making a name for itself as a fashion centre.

Brian and Mila Mulroney were enjoying life to the
full. The crowd they spent their time with were the
young power brokers in Montreal—Michel and Erica
Cogger, Jean and Michelle Bazin, Lowell Murray, Michael Meighen, Peter and Mary White, Bernard and
Madeleine Roy. Except for Lowell Murray (whom Brian
had met as an undergraduate at St. Francis Xavier University in Antigonish, Nova Scotia), they were all graduates from the law school at Laval University in Quebec
City (their tag name was the Laval Mafia). They'd been
talking politics ever since they met. Was Stanfield really

a good leader? Who would replace him? Could the Conservative party win another election?

Mila had been a Conservative campaign worker, and although she stayed outside the fray, she understood the conversations taking place in her living room. With the exception of Bernard Roy, each one had talked at one time or another of becoming leader of the party. It was accepted that eventually one of "the boys" would take a shot at the top. Mila always felt that Brian was the one member of the group who could raise the money and the sponsors needed to mount a leadership campaign. But at this stage, it was a topic of conversation rather than a concrete plan.

On a hot July weekend in 1975, Brian and Mila drove two hours to the Eastern Townships to spend the weekend with Michel and Erica Cogger. Michel was anxious to talk to Brian alone and invited Brian to take a walk with him. Brian remembers that walk in the woods very well. Robert Stanfield had just resigned. Brian told Michel that he'd called Stanfield and tried to convince him to stay on. "I thought it was terrible that Bob was resigning as leader of the Conservative party," says Brian, "but at that time none of us knew how ill Bob's wife, Mary, was." They talked about the various possible successors to Bob Stanfield while Mila and Erica stayed back at the house watching their little girls splash in the garden pool.

It had always been the contention of the Laval Mafia that the Conservatives had to have a leader who could win in Quebec if they were going to win a national election. They realized it was numerically impossible to form a government without Quebec and other French-speaking areas of Canada. Michel said, ''I know a candidate who can lead the Conservative party to victory, because he can win in Quebec as well as the rest of the country.'' Brian asked whom he was referring to. Michel said, ''You.''

Although Brian had been as involved as the others in the discussions in his living room and was ambitious, this was the first time anyone had actually proposed backing him as a leadership candidate. Brian remembers telling Cogger, ''You're out of your mind.'' Cogger insisted the idea had merit. But Brian had more on his plate that particular summer than political ambitions. He'd been approached by the Iron Ore Company of Canada. There were attractive opportunities for the young lawyer in the big multinational firm. While his friend Cogger told him that there would be dozens of Iron Ore offers down the road and only one crack at the leadership of the party every ten years, Brian was not prepared to change his course, at least not right away. They walked back to the cottage, and that was the end of the conversation.

On the way home from the Coggers', Brian and Mila discussed Michel's proposal. Neither felt sure that an entry into a leadership race was the right move for them at the time. But although they'd been married for only two years, Mila knew that politics had a powerful attraction for her husband. She guessed silently that the Iron Ore Company might have to look for another candidate.

Brian had been a backroom boy in politics ever since he was sixteen years old. At St. Francis Xavier University, he'd shown himself as a cocky young freshman who refused to observe what senior students called the "Lord of the Rings" rule on campus, that is, the rule that freshmen were not allowed to speak to upperclassmen. Mulroney spoke to whomever he wanted. He became a heavy hitter in the student model parliament and was good on his feet as a debater and public speaker. At Laval law school he continued politicking, often claiming that Prime Minister Diefenbaker would call to chat with him. Nobody believed him, so one day he invited the Chief to come to Quebec City and address the class. Everyone was astonished when Diefenbaker turned up.

After graduation in 1964, Brian and his Laval gang gravitated to Montreal and lucrative jobs in law firms. Their lifestyle involved working hard and playing hard. Bernard Roy smiles when he recounts the days when they used the Carrefour bar in Montreal's Place Ville-Marie like a head office. He says they would gather there to talk business and politics over martinis and to meet other people, mostly women, who worked in the Place Ville-Marie complex. At first they spent their weekends driving to Quebec City to visit girlfriends, usually in Bernard's old Triumph. Later, at rented cottages in the Laurentians, they learned to ski and perfected the art of partying.

"I have very fond memories of those days," says Bernard. "I've heard all the stories about Brian's behaviour at that time, but I do not have a recollection of him behaving in an embarrassingly impaired way." Another friend, Lowell Murray, feels the stories about Brian burning the candle at both ends are grossly exaggerated. "When Brian was a bachelor, he worked until seven o'clock at night. His mother used to clean his apartment for him. She'd cook a roast of beef and leave it on the counter. As likely as not, he'd take a slice of that for supper and go to bed or watch television or be on the phone to people. You couldn't be successful in the world he was in—the world of labour and corporate law—if you were out every night."

Brian's political manoeuvring continued, and by 1967 he was the Conservative party's link to Daniel Johnson's ruling Union Nationale party. In 1972 he was co-chair of the Conservatives' Quebec campaign.

The next year, in January 1973, he was asked to be a partner at Ogilvy, Renault, and just a year later began work on the Cliche Commission, where he developed a name for himself as a tough negotiator, a street fighter who wouldn't give in to any amount of pressure, no matter how dangerous. In fact, he was seen as a hero in Montreal at that time, a man who had thumbed his nose at the corrupt and terrifying world of organized crime.

Because of his role as a commissioner, he'd received dozens of requests to speak at functions. Until the Cliche Commission had completed its examination and report, however, he could not accept the invitations. Eventually, in fall 1975, he agreed to travel across the country to fulfil the speaking engagements. It was just eight weeks after the weekend he and Mila had spent with the Coggers in the country. Michel decided the time was ripe to present his argument again.

He convinced Brian to use the speaking tour to test the waters for a shot at the leadership of the Conservative party. After all, Cogger insisted, Brian had nothing to lose; he was making the trip anyway. Although Brian felt the bid was premature, he agreed that as long as he was going and as long as his pal Cogger went with him, he would test the waters. Mila stayed behind with Caroline. (In those days there was never a question of her campaigning with Brian. She says her role was expected to be strictly one of support. She assumed he would be all right with his friends Cogger, Murray, Meighen, Bazin, and Roy.)

By the time they returned from the speaking tour, a lot of people, including the media and Conservative party people, were starting to talk about Mulroney as a candidate. Weeks later he was drafted as a candidate for the leadership race by a group of supporters at the Bristol Place Hotel in Toronto. That night he went home to Montreal and said to Mila, ''This may sound a little weird. As a prospect, running for the leadership doesn't make any sense.'' One of his concerns was that he was the only candidate who was not a member of Parliament. ''I was thirty-six years old. I had never run for public office. I had never even been elected churchwarden in my life. But after Mila and I talked about it together, we decided to go for it.''

Mila approved of her husband's gutsy approach. She too was a risk-taker and understood his feelings. Moreover, she had already established her priorities. Brian came first. Although she was pregnant at the time with their second child and felt she was in no position to take part in the leadership race, she was prepared for the challenge. More than anything, she believed that her husband was the man for the job.

She felt it was an opportunity not to be missed. "I don't think anyone has the right to say no to opportunities like that. If Brian was prepared to risk it all, to try something new, then who was I to stop him? The last thing I want is to be the person who has to wonder about the missed opportunities, the missed chances. I couldn't have lived with myself.

"I'd worked for Michael Meighen as a volunteer when he ran for election, so I knew a little bit about what was involved. But I also knew this would be different. When you're a volunteer, you can detach yourself from the candidate. You don't have any of the responsibility. You just work and root for the candidate. I worked long hours, the graveyard shift (as most young volunteers did when I worked for Michael Meighen). But as far as Brian was concerned, he didn't even know exactly what this would entail. This country is very big. Until you actually start travelling it, you don't know the depth of energy you need. But I was up for it. I decided I'd have to learn along with Brian this time."

At about the same time, Mila decided to take steps to rectify a problem of her own. She had rhinoplasty. She says it wasn't because she disliked her appearance. "I had lots of friends and always felt attractive when I was a teenager." Rather, she needed surgery because of badly deformed nasal passages that were the result of the broken nose she'd received in the car crash when she was nine.

When Caroline was a baby, Mila found that she was having difficulty sleeping. She couldn't breathe through her nose. She went to see a doctor at the Royal Victoria Hospital and asked him what could be done. He said that bone chips left over from the fracture were causing her breathing problems and that they were easily removed. Then he asked her, "What's a pretty girl like you doing with an ugly nose like this?" He suggested that she see a plastic surgeon to have her nose straightened while she was having the bone chips removed.

"I probably wouldn't have done it just to straighten my nose, but as long as they had to operate to do something else, I decided to go ahead with it." She recovered quickly and returned to her role as chatelaine of the house that was now becoming command central for the Laval Mafia, Conservative party people in Quebec, and potential supporters and volunteers.

On November 13, Brian made it official. He was entering the race to become leader of the Conservative party. On December 16 he went home to Baie-Comeau to tell his home town what he was up to. Mila flew up to Baie-Comeau in a small chartered plane with several reporters. She remembers that it was terribly cold, that she was wearing a red Pelerina "swing" raincoat, and that everyone kept pushing her into chairs to sit down because she was pregnant. But mostly she remembers that her husband gave the speech of his life.

Brian likened Baie-Comeau to all the small towns and cities across the country. One of the reporters there was Bill Fox, a Southam News correspondent who would in 1984 become Brian's first press secretary. He says, "I'll never forget that day when Brian looked out at all those people and said, 'It's a great country when the son of an

electrician can aspire to the highest office in the land.'
He was obviously very proud of being the son of an
electrician and he put a lot of emphasis on the 'aspire'
part. I remember being struck by how personable his
wife, Mila, was and how new she was to the game of
politics.''

By December, Mila realized that she was going to have
to postpone the rest of her education. She dropped out of
university just one semester short of an engineering
degree. She and Brian joined Michel and Erica Cogger at
the Nassau home of business friend Peter Thomson for a
Christmas holiday, leaving Caroline with the Pivnickis.
They left on Christmas night. ''Brian needed me,'' says
Mila. ''We had a lot to discuss. We didn't have a tree,
there was no celebration in Nassau. It wasn't like Christmas. I've almost wiped it out of my memory. We had
Christmas with Caroline when we came back on January
6. I don't think you scar children like that. Caroline was
only eighteen months old. She didn't know anything
about dates.'' In less than eight weeks, the vote to declare
a new leader for the Conservative party would be taken
at the Château Laurier Hotel in Ottawa.

There were twelve candidates in the race. At first,
Brian Mulroney was ranked dead last, but support for
his candidacy grew, and as it grew, so did his hopes and
expectations. He says, ''As you acquire supporters, you
start to look at the other candidates, and there's a
natural inclination to feel as time goes on that maybe
you can do this. Maybe the others are less well quali-
fied. By Christmas, we were looking at the race this way.
In January we were, in the minds of many people, in
first or second place. At the convention on February 22,

we were number two on the first ballot [after Claude Wagner]. That meant there had to be ten or eleven behind me.''

It was at that convention that Marjory LeBreton, a Tory party insider who is currently deputy chief of staff in the Prime Minister's Office, first noticed Mila Mulroney. ''Their section in the Civic Centre was to my right. She was sitting there with Brian. I was up in the stands watching her and I thought, 'She is a person upon whom this man leans.' I remembered her because she was so pregnant and the room was so hot and smoky. When the vote was announced, she'd move in, shield him, keep control of the situation. Coming into the convention, I would have bet my mortgage that Brian Mulroney would win.''

Nevertheless, early on in the convention Brian and Mila knew that a win was impossible. After a speech delivered by Diefenbaker imploring the party to elect a leader who already had a seat in the House of Commons, they knew their shot at the top was lost. So, although for television viewers the results were not in, the Mulroneys knew the outcome before Brian was eliminated on the third ballot. Together, Brian and Mila had reached for the brass ring, and for the first time in their married lives they had missed.

Brian was bitterly disappointed by the results of the leadership race and by what he saw as the duplicity of some of the people he'd counted on who had changed their vote at the end. Losing a leadership race is in many ways tougher than losing a general election because it is the party, the club, the family who defeat you. Leadership races are like a civil war, splitting apart friendships and families. The divisions continue long after the ceasefire.

His friends understood how he felt. One of them said, ''Imagine being Brian Mulroney, the hot-shot lawyer in Montreal, the respected Cliche commissioner, the handsome, debonair deal-maker, losing to a guy known as Joe Who. It was a very difficult time.'' Moreover, his friends confide, they used to talk about it with him all the time, analysing it over and over again. Brian replayed the loss in his mind and it continued to bother him. He was also bothered by the number of people whom he felt had let him down. Some friends of twenty years had turned up in someone else's camp.

Those who have fought a leadership race, or supported someone who did, understand the letdown and the aftermath. When Jean Chrétien lost the Liberal leadership race to John Turner and Brian Mulroney defeated Turner at the polls, Chrétien turned up at a cocktail party being given by Jean Pierre Cabouat, France's ambassador to Canada, boasting about the outcome had he been the leader. ''I would have kicked the shit out of Mulroney had I won the leadership,'' said Chrétien. Then he went on to take John Turner's attributes apart one by one. Those who listened understood that these were the words of a defeated candidate.

The aftermath was tough on everyone, on Brian, on Mila, and on their friends and colleagues. But Mila felt it was hardest on Brian, and he was her priority. She understood the sense of betrayal he felt. She also knew how heartbreaking it was to have been the candidate who came in late, started at the bottom of the heap, rose up dramatically to a point at which winning seemed possible, but lost in the end. It takes a long time to heal such wounds.

Less than three weeks after the convention, on March 9, 1976, Benedict was born. Brian was still so popular in Montreal that he couldn't walk down the street without six or seven people stopping to shake hands with him. He couldn't sit through a meal at a restaurant without well-wishers approaching the table. So when they arrived at St. Mary's Hospital with Mila in labour, the nurses all gushed, "Hi, Mr. Mulroney. We've been waiting for you." Mila watched the fuss being made over her husband and thought, "Hey, *I'm* the pregnant one. *I'm* the one with the suitcase. This is a maternity ward, isn't it? What about me?"

Ben was a breech birth. The labour was long and painful, but when he finally arrived, he was gorgeous, says Mila. "He even had a perfect part in his hair and a wonderful little square face with big blue eyes. He was an easy baby. He seemed to know that this was a time of reflection for us. When it was time to eat, we'd say, 'Wake up, Ben,' and he would. When it was time to sleep, we'd say, 'Go to sleep, Ben,' and he'd go to sleep."

When Ben was one week old, Mila left him with her parents so she could accompany Brian to Florida to put their post-leadership-race lives back together. Though they took Caroline with them, Mila says, "I couldn't be getting up all night with a new baby. It was one of the hardest things I ever did. I didn't even get a chance to bond with my baby. But it was important to Brian that we go to Florida right then. He needed me. It was a question of priorities. I made the decision to go, thinking it was the right decision. It was okay with me. The baby was important. But Brian's well-being was more important. The baby would be okay with my mother.''

They spent ten days in Florida discussing what had happened and making plans for the future. "We had a chance to decompress, to talk out all the things we wanted to talk out. We put all the puzzle pieces on the table.'' The pieces included career, job, house, family. Career and job are two different things for Brian, says Mila. "He'd always loved politics and always had his finger in it. As vice-president of the Conservative party and as a lawyer he was able to bring the two together. Now he felt they were separated. He went through a period of time when he said he would never be involved in politics again. But I knew that was a wound speaking.''

As for house and family, they wanted a bigger house. Although their house had three bedrooms and a den, they felt it was time to invest in something larger. Mila also wanted Brian to spend more time with his family. As a labour lawyer he might have to work eighteen days in a row, often in another city. As a backroom politician, he could easily spend every night of the week talking shop over dinner and martinis. Mila wanted to discuss the kind of attention a family needs. She wanted more control over their lives and their time together.

While they thrashed out their future, they walked on the beach, sat on the balcony, went out for dinner. And they called home five times a day to check on Ben and found time to spend with Caroline, whom they had barely seen during the three weeks leading up to the leadership race. "Down there we verbalized what we wanted and what we didn't want. We decided that for the time being, we didn't want such an intense life. We needed more time with the kids, being together as a family. We wanted time to travel and we wanted a job that we could control rather than a job that controlled us.''

After ten days in Florida, they had a different perspective. They had talked about what they meant to each other and where their relationship stood. They knew who their friends were. It seemed that some people who were very close and supportive during the leadership bid suddenly vanished when Brian was defeated. Although the healing process was not complete, Mila says, ''When I think about it, that was one of the healthiest times in our lives.''

When they returned to Montreal, Brian decided to leave law practice and go into business. He'd had several good offers and eventually accepted the one from the Iron Ore Company of Canada. He started as vice-president, and a year later became president and chief operating officer. The job included perks such as membership at the swanky Mount Royal Club, the use of a private fishing camp in Labrador, two company planes at his disposal for business and personal use, and four box seats behind the Canadiens bench at the Forum. (That particular aspect of the job didn't really thrill Mila, since on a scale of one to ten, her interest in and knowledge of hockey barely registers.) The job at Iron Ore rocketed the Mulroneys into a new level of affluence that included a house at the top of the hill on Westmount's Belvedere Road.

Before starting the job, Brian worked out a lucrative contract that guaranteed lifelong financial security but stipulated that he stay away from politics for five years.

He also took time to move out of his law office at Ogilvy, Renault and resettle in the business world. And he spent a lot of time reflecting. Although he'd said he would never re-enter the political arena, Mila knew that his love of politics would probably mean that he would one day try again. Moreover, Brian was still meeting with his friends and rehashing the details of the leadership race.

Mila says 1976 was sad "because we'd fallen short of something we'd tried hard to reach. But Brian had left a strong impression out there. He conducted himself well, raised his profile, spoke well, had good ideas, got enough notoriety to help him down the road. It was an enlightening, eye-opening experience that helped us in '83."

But even the excitement of a new job didn't erase the memory of the leadership bid. Mila stood by steadfastly. When her friends came to the house asking about Brian, she'd insist that they speak to him themselves. The two of them went to the movies or sat in the backyard and read books. She watched over him carefully, because she knew that in time his wounds would heal, and in her opinion this was a man worth waiting for.

Mila remembers this as a period when their relationship strengthened. "We became friends and recognized that the important things people talk about in a marriage can come true. The trust between us became strong and it continued to build. We worked out the glitches and became each other's best friend. I saw it as a foundation-building time."

Mila found her new life easier. She had fewer commitments. She started doing things for herself—taking an
exercise class every day, working as a volunteer in the
Children's Hospital, reading to children on the cancer
ward. She volunteered at the Montreal Museum of Fine
Arts and started a play group with other moms in her
neighbourhood for the under-five-year-old kids who
weren't in school.

She also enjoyed redecorating her new home. Her
sister-in-law Olive Elliott was with Mila the first time
she saw the house on Belvedere Road. Mila looked at
the walls and the floors and said to Olive, ''Nobody
loved this house.'' Then she and her friends went to
work stripping off layers and layers of old wallpaper and
peeling glued carpets off the floors.

The house had a very old kitchen that needed to be
replaced. There was no closet in the front hall (instead
there were coat hooks in the bathroom). The project
was perfect for a woman who prided herself on her
decorating ideas and who loved renovating old houses.
She painted the mouldings yellow. The living room,
which was thirty-five feet by eighteen feet, was done in
old pine panelling with bookcases and two seating
areas. She painted Caroline's room hot pink. She decorated the bathrooms to fit around the old-fashioned
tubs with their ornate feet. The master bedroom had a
fireplace, a window seat, and a dressing room. Mila
turned the house into a showplace.

She was already known as a woman who adores
bright colours and appreciates fine fabrics and bold
designs. Olive says, ''She has an eye for detail that goes
beyond decorating and picking beautiful clothes. She

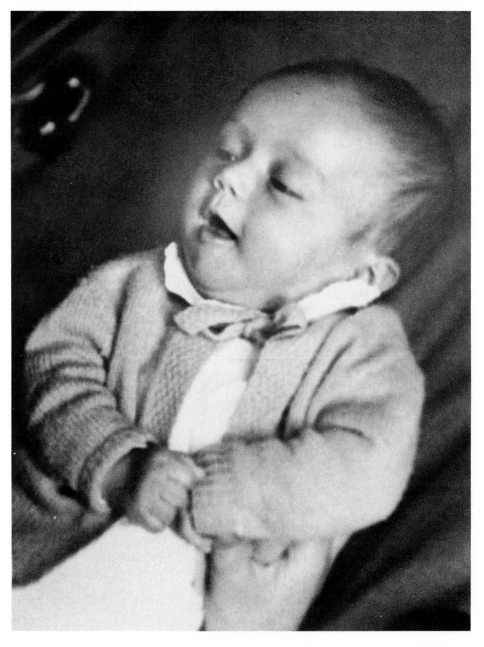

For the first ten months of her life, Mila slept in a basket beside her parents' bed, in a cramped two-room apartment in Sarajevo.

"Yugoslavian fathers did not dote on their daughters, as Mita Pivnicki did." The Pivnicki family is on the right: Mila's mother, Boba, and Mila, holding her father's hand.

The family finally was permitted to move to a larger apartment. Mila and Boba survey their new surroundings from the balcony.

"If he's smart, he'll never come back," friends would whisper to Boba Pivnicki (left), as she walked with her daughter in the park. Mita went to Canada when Mila was four. Boba was pregnant at the time, and managed alone for eighteen months before following Mita to Canada with her children.

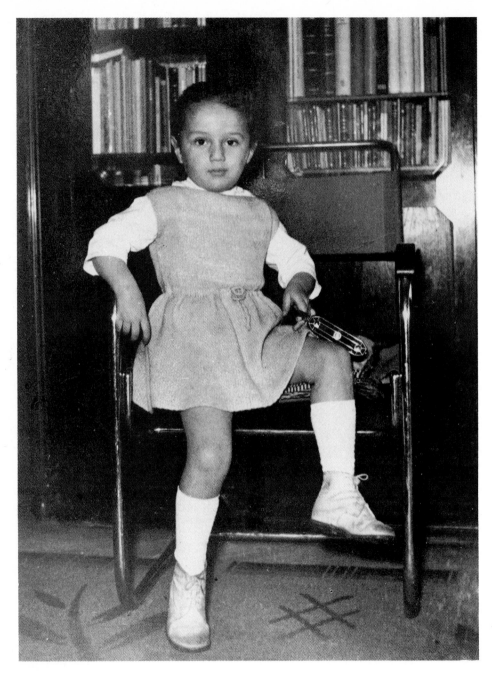

Mila had been given a tiny purse that she carried everywhere with her. Although the shops in Yugoslavia were often empty, she was always neatly dressed, because her mother knitted most of her clothes.

"In those days, my style was my immigrant roots – braids and clothes big enough to grow into."

Reunited with her father in Montreal. A close family friend described Mila as "the apple of his eye."

When Mila was taken to visit the Parliament Buildings in Ottawa as a child, she could not have dreamt that she would one day have an office of her own there.

Her brother John's earliest memories are of his big sister taking care of him. ''She was always holding my hand, always pulling me places.''

The Pivnicki family, several weeks after the car accident that took place in 1963. Boba's arm is still in a sling; Mita is holding Ivana, the youngest child.

The following caption appears beside Mila's high school yearbook photo:
"We were all born originals, let us not die copies."
Happiness is: A full stomach.
Ambition: Sculptor.
Pet Aversion: Pressure.
Prototype, "The Person."
Weakness: Just so stories.

Mila (far left) with friends at the Man and His World site in summer 1972, the summer she met Brian Mulroney. Mila is in the costume she wore as a hostess at the Yugoslavian pavilion. It was her first job and she loved the freedom it gave her.

Mila and Caroline, playing in a friend's swimming pool. "Mila tackled motherhood with a relaxed attitude that is unusual in new mothers."

Brian and Mila show off their new baby in front of the Pivnicki's house in Montreal. Mila was still attending university at this time.

Mila with Caroline, around the time that Brian was serving on the Cliche Commission. Caroline used to play with the security guards who protected the family. Threatening telephone calls were a routine experience.

Mila with Caroline and Benedict. Brian had lost his leadership bid in February 1976, and Benedict was born less than three weeks later. That summer, Brian started work for the Iron Ore Company of Canada.

After winning the leadership of the Conservative Party, Brian campaigned for by-election in the Central Nova riding in Nova Scotia. The family spent the summer at Pictou Lodge. Mark, the youngest, had been born in 1979.

Installed at 24 Sussex Drive. Mila is pregnant with Nicolas, who was born exactly a year after Brian's victory at the polls.

sees things most people don't see. We went to a play in New York one time and afterwards, over dinner, we discussed several aspects of the play. I was astonished at the minute details she remembered.''

From their beautiful home on top of the hill, the Mulroneys led the good life. Every few months they'd spend four or five days in New York, where they had a company apartment across from Central Park. They visited Europe several times a year, staying at the Ritz in Paris. They had a terrific trip on the Orient Express with three other couples. And often, when Brian travelled to head office in Cleveland, Mila went along with him.

Since the time zone in Florida is the same as Montreal and the company plane was prepared to leave whenever they wanted, they travelled to Florida three or four times a year, staying at the St. Andrews Club near Boynton Beach, between Palm Beach and Miami.

On one of those trips, Mila remembers going through the usual checklist of equipment they travelled with: strollers, playpen, babies' bottles and diapers, and so on. When they arrived in Florida Brian did the checklist in reverse, watching each piece of vital equipment as it came off the plane. When he was satisfied that everything for the babies was accounted for, he dismissed the plane, assuming that he had all the family's luggage. ''The plane took off and flew back to Montreal with Brian's suitcase on board. He didn't have a stitch of clothes to wear, except for what he was standing in.''

During this period, Julia Mustard ran into her childhood friend again. Julia felt very far removed from her old pal. ''Our lifestyles were different. I was single and had a career in fine arts and wanted to travel. She was so traditional, so establishment. She'd gone the way I'd hoped she wouldn't go, but was always afraid she might go. I felt our schoolgirl relationship had ended and that disappointed me.

''When we were in school, I was very anti-establishment and spoke against the school system. She was always much more of a participant in the school activities. But still we were friends. When I saw her on television during the leadership campaign, it seemed odd to watch her. There's a sense of knowing someone in the spotlight and not being quite sure if she's the person you know. She's a very talented, smart woman. But she seems to be in the shadow of her husband. I know she's capable of anything, so it's hard for me to watch her sitting on the sidelines.''

Mila became pregnant again in 1977 but miscarried. On April 29, 1979, their third child, Mark, was born. She didn't enjoy her pregnancy this time. ''To give you some idea about how big I was, I weighed in at 191 pounds when I checked into the hospital to have Mark. I was so hungry during that pregnancy, I kept a chair in front of the fridge. I was like a tub of lard. No, there was no tub, just lard.

''A friend of mine, Anelie Bubalo, was also pregnant. We both had babies the same age and she'd decided that one was enough. I convinced her that it wouldn't be fair to her baby to have only one, so she decided to have another one and we were pregnant at the same time again. She had a heart murmur and had to stay in the Montreal Heart Institute for the last few months of her pregnancy. I went to visit her one day. I was hu-mungous. Here she was lying on a hospital bed in a beautiful silk nightgown, on embroidered sheets (she brought her own since she was to be there for such a long time), sipping water from a teaspoon. She looked like she'd put on about four ounces. I was wearing a tent dress with a frill around it and mukluks and eating everything in sight.''

When Mila went into labour with Mark, she was in the grocery store with Ben and Caroline in the shopping cart. She left the store, dropped the kids at home with the mother's helper, and asked Joe, the handyman who worked for them, to drive her to the hospital. Once there, she called Brian. But Mark wasn't ready for life on the outside and postponed his arrival. ''When I went home after two days I felt so bloated, fat, and uncomfortable, I could hardly stand myself. I was waiting at the door for Brian to get the car and a nurse said to me, 'Oh just a minute, I'll get your baby.' Well that did it. I started crying and couldn't stop.''

A week later, labour began again. This time, Mila didn't bother to rush to the hospital. Instead she called Brian and said there were two chairs in the window of a department store on Sherbrooke Street that fit the description of the ones he wanted for his office and suggested he go with her to see them. They drove the two children to the Pivnickis, went to look at the chairs, decided to buy them, selected fabric to have them upholstered, and then drove to St. Mary's Hospital.

Mark arrived early in the evening. Although he weighed more than nine pounds, he was put into an incubator because more than twenty-six hours had elapsed between the time Mila's water broke and the time the baby was delivered. She remembers how odd it was to see her fat, healthy baby with his curly hair and dimples stuffed into an incubator. Brian was allowed into the delivery room this time. It was an experience he says he'll never forget.

In a biography called *Mulroney, The Making of the Prime Minister*, Ian MacDonald, a good friend of Brian's, refers to that point, three years after the leadership defeat, and says, "One day the terrible bitterness was gone. He simply stopped making disparaging remarks about Clark. He had also stopped drinking."

Journalists and commentators have often criticized Brian's lifestyle during this period of his life. The gossip later reached a pitch of intensity in the summer of 1991; the assumption was that the failure of the Meech Lake Accord was as wounding to Brian as the failure of his leadership bid in 1976 and that he had reacted to each defeat in the same extreme way.

Anyone in Canada (or, for that matter, Britain or Germany) who read a gossip column in 1991 read the revived stories from 1976 about Brian being depressed and drinking heavily after his leadership defeat. The drinking rumours told of wild nights in Montreal and lost weekends in the Laurentians, as well as long evenings drowning his sorrows in birdbath-sized martinis at the Beaver Club in Montreal's Queen Elizabeth Hotel. People claimed that his public behaviour was appalling, that his private behaviour was painful in the extreme for Mila. It has also been said that those were the years when Mila rescued him, that without her he couldn't have made it.

Sitting in an easy chair beside his desk in the downstairs study at 24 Sussex Drive, Brian Mulroney reflects on those years and on the stories about them that began to circulate after he became prime minister. "I don't know where people got the impression that I was depressed. Anyone who knows me will tell you that one thing I never do is get depressed. I get angry. I get upset. I can get a lot of things, but I never get depressed. I don't know where that nonsense started.

"If I were given to depression, I wouldn't be sitting here today. I'd have chucked it a long time ago. Propensity to depression and the job I am holding are two things that are profoundly antithetical. If that were the case—I've been under close scrutiny for eight years now—someone would have seen an indication of depression. I have had a helluva lot of reason to be depressed and anyone who has shown an inclination to despair would have taken a drink. I have not."

Brian doesn't deny that he did drink heavily in the 1970s—as most businessmen in his circle did. Judging his 1976 drinking habits by 1992 standards makes him look like an alcoholic. But this, says Brian, ignores the dramatic shift in attitudes toward healthy lifestyles that has taken place in the last fifteen years.

"If you went back to Montreal, say in March 1976, and you were to go to the Beaver Club for lunch, there would be 200 people in the dining room. Of the 200, eighty-five percent would be having martinis, fifteen percent would be having soda water. If you went to the Beaver Club today, eighty-five percent would be having soda water and fifteen percent would be having martinis. In 1976, six or seven out of ten of my friends smoked cigarettes. Today one, maybe two are smoking."

Attitudes have changed since the days when heavy
drinking in politics went almost unnoticed. In the 1860s
there were stories about Sir John A. Macdonald being
carried inebriated out of the House of Commons, and
all the way up to the 1970s the stories continued about
members being drunk at their desks. No one seemed to
be offended or surprised by such behaviour at the time.
The end of this era began, says Brian, with the revolution in healthy attitudes.

"It didn't just happen in Montreal, it happened everywhere. It was like the fitness movement. In 1965, if
you told people to go out jogging, they'd have told you
to jump off the wharf. Everyone is jogging now. There's
been a change in society's approach to life. People who
used to smoke don't smoke. People who used to drink
don't drink. And people who used to sit around and
become couch potatoes are out there jogging.

"In 1976, I did exactly what everybody did. I smoked
and I drank and I had a helluva good time. And I
worked hard and never missed a day's work and was
apparently successful at what I was doing."

Certainly he maintained a workload that would have
been impossible for someone incapacitated by drinking
or depression. "I ran a successful international fund-
raising campaign for St. FX University. The objective
was $7 million. We raised $11 million. I was chairman of
the United Way of Greater Montreal. I was on the board
of directors of eleven different corporations, including
the Canadian Imperial Bank of Commerce, Standard
Broadcasting, Provigo, and the Hanna Mining Company. I had a wife and three children. I did what everyone else did. If you were thirty-five or forty years of age
and successful, you did all these things.

"I can't speak for any other place than Montreal, but it was quite fashionable to drink a lot in those days. This was not something that got you scratched from the A-list. In fact the only good friend of mine who *didn't* drink was John Rae." (He was Jean Chrétien's campaign manager, the brother of the current premier of Ontario, Bob Rae.)

Brian also hotly denies that he was abusive, violent, or obnoxious when he had been drinking. "I'm sure someone would like to say that I punched someone out, that I got arrested for drunk driving, or got into a fist fight, or that I threw up at someone's table. But I did none of those things." He also categorically denies that he was unfaithful to Mila.

In 1979, the year he turned forty and the year Mark was born, Brian began to realize that it was time to change this hard-drinking, hard-living lifestyle. "When you're young, twenty-five or thirty years old, you can do all this. You can stay out late, have dinner until two or three in the morning and be back at work the next morning. The thing that dawned on me was the combination of the intensity of my work; my outside commitments, which I really enjoyed, from raising funds for the university to running the United Way campaign; plus my family; plus the fact that we went out a lot and we'd stay out late, as most couples did in Montreal. Well, I concluded that it would be just a matter of some years until this combination would get me into trouble. I didn't know if it would be two years or twenty years. You never can tell. But I wasn't about to find out."

Brian didn't intend to slow down at work, but he knew something had to give. "I decided that it would be a lot wiser for me, for my family, for my future, if I just cooled all this stuff. It was time for me to stop drinking and stop smoking. They weren't doing me any good. I stopped drinking and never drank again and never spoke to anyone about it. I have never directly or indirectly been to an AA meeting. I have never had a talk with anyone.

"Now let me make it clear that if I'd been associated with AA, I would tell you about it. I would be very proud to tell you because I think they do wonderful work and I'd be right out there proselytizing for them. But it didn't happen. I never told a single soul. I can still remember having lunch with Jean Bazin at the Beaver Club in September or October of 1979, and Bazin said to me, 'Let's have a bottle of wine.' I said, 'No.' And he said, 'You haven't had a drink with me in months.' Then I said, 'I'm waiting until Christmas, I'll join you at Christmas.'

"We all got together at Christmas in the Beaver Club, about ten or twelve of us at our Christmas lunch. Well, the place used to be floating in a sea of birdbath martinis. I just didn't feel like it. I've never had a drink since the day I stopped. This goofball stuff about me being involved in some secret organization to stop drinking is absolute fabrication."

He adds that he's no exception when it comes to world leaders and drinking. Today there are very few world leaders who will take more than a glass of wine. He says, "Kohl of Germany will take a beer and after a long day, George Bush may have a martini. Ronald Reagan never drank at all and Margaret Thatcher might take a glass of whisky now, but never when she was prime minister. None of them takes anything during the day."

Quitting drinking turned out to be a lot easier for him than quitting smoking, which he did about five years later. "I stopped smoking in February 1984. Mila and I were in Florida. We went out to dinner with Charles and Andy [Andrea] Bronfman. There were just the four of us at their apartment in Palm Beach. Andy smoked like a chimney. Charles smoked a pipe. Even Mila puffed occasionally. And I was putting back about three packs a day. I was a really big smoker. That night when we got home to our apartment, I thought I'd poisoned myself.

"I was the leader of the opposition at the time and it was getting harder and harder for me to smoke at the banquets and dinners we had to attend. I was forever trying to figure out how to get a puff. I'd pretend I had to go to the can or take an important phone call. I could hardly make it through Question Period. I'd sometimes leave and go behind the curtain in the House of Commons to have a smoke. That's how addicted I was.

"Mark was very young and watching anti-smoking ads on TV, and he was forever saying, 'Daddy, you know those cigarettes are going to kill you.' So the kids were working on me.

"Anyway, we got home that night in Florida and I decided it was time to stop. The next day, Mila had to leave to go to Bathurst, New Brunswick, for a function. I had to go to Vancouver or Toronto or someplace. When we met back at Stornoway a few days later, Mila walked into the room and said, 'What have you been doing? You're doing something differently.' I said I wasn't doing anything differently, and she said, 'I can't put my finger on it, but you are.' Then she realized what had changed and said, 'You've stopped smoking.' I said, 'I haven't stopped. I'm trying to stop. Don't tell anyone.'

"Nobody said a word until about two weeks later when someone on my staff noticed that I wasn't smoking and leaked it to the press. Then I was inundated with hundreds of letters of congratulation. After that I couldn't start again, even if I wanted to. I never missed having a drink from the day I stopped, but I still miss the cigarettes.''

In the meantime, Brian and Mila forged ahead with their new way of life. He was learning the ropes at the Iron Ore Company, while she entertained their friends and his business associates. He travelled frequently. He had to learn a lot very quickly and concentrate his time and energy on showing the board of directors in Cleveland how well he could perform. Mila decorated Brian's office with such pizazz, the furniture is still there today. ''We were financially secure and we lived well,'' she says.

Boba thought they were lucky. ''Everyone travels and everyone entertains, but their way was more lavish. I was proud of Mila, not just because she lived in a beautiful house, but because it was decorated with my daughter's own little hands.''

As glamorous as their lives became, Boba says they never thought of it as the lifestyle of the rich and famous. Mila certainly didn't. ''That sort of thing only works on TV,'' says Mila. ''I cooked. I cleaned. I picked my kids up at school and drove them to school. But we did enjoy vacations and travelling.''

The children travelled with their parents occasionally, but usually they stayed at home with a mother's helper. In 1982, the Mulroneys rented a cottage at the exclusive Hermitage Club in North Hatley, in the Eastern Townships. The children were three, six and eight. ''It was the worst winter in years,'' says Mila. ''It didn't snow, so there was no skiing. The lake didn't freeze, so there was no skating. There was just mush and wetness and brown grass everywhere. It was a nightmare. Guests kept dropping in. I spent the whole weekend stoking the fire and cooking for drop-ins.'' One of the advantages of being well-heeled is that you can walk away from nightmares. In February, they gave the place up and went to Florida.

When Mila gave parties, she hired caterers. Still, her mother would come to help, which was often disastrous since they're both bossy. With the two of them in charge, there would be chaos in the kitchen.

Mila says the lifestyle didn't change her because it wasn't that important to her. ''I like nice things but I can live without them. I *have* lived without them. Having material things is a cushion. It's a superficial need, not necessarily the most important thing in my life. I like moving furniture around, potting plants, arranging flowers. I'm happy doing that. If I don't have material things, I'll live without them.''

Their friends were as important to them as ever before. Cathy Campeau (who'd been married to one of Brian's law partners at Ogilvy, Renault) remembers it was Mila and Brian who helped her when her marriage ended in 1981. ''I'd been to Barbados with my three children. The night before I was to return, my husband Art called me and said he was moving out, but that I wasn't to say anything. He must have called Mila and another friend of mine called Imeka Vandenberg, because when we got off the plane at two o'clock in the morning, Mila and Imeka were there with my station wagon to meet me and the three kids.

''Mila called me every day and helped me through that dreadful period. But what amazed me was that

Brian helped me too, and those weren't easy days for him. He called me every day to find out how the children and I were getting along. And as time went on and events occurred that involved couples, Brian and Mila continued to include me. They never let me down.''

On June 1, 1981, Brian's agreement with the Iron Ore Company to stay away from politics for five years expired. There were rumblings about Joe Clark and a leadership review in the air. There were also rumblings from Iron Ore's head office in Cleveland about closing its plant in Schefferville, a town that the company had built in the 1950s.

By January 1982, Brian had a plan for both events. He planned to spend the spring making speeches and consolidating his Quebec base in case a leadership review was called. As for Schefferville, he'd work out the best deal the unions had ever seen. If this town was to go down, its demise would be eased by Brian Mulroney, who had grown up in a company town and knew the devastating effect a bad deal could have on the families who lived there.

His plan worked. In January 1983, the Tories met in Winnipeg for their convention. Even though Joe Clark received 66.9 percent approval from his party, he called for a leadership convention in June. Brian left the convention for Florida, where he put the finishing touches on his deal for Schefferville.

In February he had to face a Quebec parliamentary commission that René Lévesque had created to look into the plant closure. The government officials and the media assumed that his political ambitions would be buried with Schefferville. But when the hearings were over, Brian Mulroney had gained support, respect, and a higher profile.

With that behind him, Brian was ready for the job of winning over delegates, one by one across Canada. His team from 1976 was back in place. It was as though they were playing "This Old Gang of Mine." Only this time, Mila wasn't on the sidelines. She'd become a political force in her own right. She was not only part of the team, she'd become Brian's closest adviser.

Mila was working again on by-election campaigns and having dinner parties for the players in the new race. The names being mentioned belonged to heavy hitters from across Canada, such as Premier Peter Lougheed from Alberta and Premier Bill Davis from Ontario. She listened carefully to what her dinner guests said. She also listened to her own valuable network of friends. Andrée Beaulieu from the ballet group was one. Andrée tells a story that describes the network in action.

"Mila invited my husband and me to a football game. Four days before the game, we were in New York with our friends Peter and Jeanne Lougheed and Philippe and Nan-B de Gaspé Beaubien. Philippe and I were trying to convince Peter to run for the leadership of the Conservative party. He actually declined officially a few nights later when we were back in Canada.

"At the football game, we told Brian and Mila about spending the night with the Lougheeds, and Brian said, 'Do you really think Peter doesn't want to run? Because if he does want to run, I won't.' We assured him that Peter was not going to run. Both Roger and I wondered what the conversation would be about that night when Brian and Mila returned home.''

The Mulroneys had learned a lot—about people, about politics in Canada, and about how much pressure there is on elected officials. They'd had the time they needed to mature and to gain financial security. Mila says, ''Without those years between 1976 and 1983, we could never have done what we did after 1983.''

Andrée and the ballet group were there with Mila through thick and thin. They were there when she returned from Ottawa after the lost bid of 1976 and they were still there on the eve of the 1983 leadership race. It would be a race that they would help run, that they'd invest their hearts and souls in, even though the result would cost them the pleasure of the presence of their Yugoslav friend. But the distance between Montreal and Ottawa served only to strengthen the ties that bind these women. And after all, a sleepover at 24 Sussex Drive in lieu of ballet night was hardly an idea to lament.

Along with four thousand others, the ballet group was at the Queen Elizabeth Hotel in Montreal on March 9, 1983, for the unofficial launch of the 1983 leadership race. The event had been organized by Michel Cogger and Tory official Keith Morgan. It was billed as ''Friends of Mulroney.'' The purpose was to let everyone know that Mulroney still had drawing power, even though the upcoming campaign was going to be purposely low-key.

The party was at 6 p.m. on a weekday, so that everyone invited would come along after work. Big names in sports, the arts, business, and labour were invited too, and they turned up in droves. Bobby Orr was there, so was Martha Howlett of CTV and Pierre Péladeau of Quebecor and Paul Desrochers, who had been Robert Bourassa's right-hand man. Not surprisingly, half the Ottawa press gallery was there too. The send-off went on for an hour and a half. Throughout the speeches and the hurrahs, Mila stood beside Brian, watching, listening, checking the response. When the evening was over, they were filled with so much goodwill and energy and bold confidence, they felt they could have powered their own plane to Ottawa.

Eleven days later, on Brian's forty-fourth birthday, they flew to Ottawa together. The next day, March 21, 1983, Brian declared himself as a candidate for the leadership of the Conservative party. Round two was about to begin.

Chapter Five

We hadn't had anyone like this in generations. We'd
had two crazy old bachelors and Maryon Pearson,
who was a nice woman but not a political wife of any
kind. We've never had a thoroughly modern woman.

Craig Oliver

"Would Violet please come to the stage?" The
woman with the microphone in her hand
waited a moment and then asked again, "Violet, would
you come to the stage now, please." She leaned over to
the woman closest to her and whispered, "Her name *is*
Violet, isn't it?"

"I dunno," replied the other.

She tried again. "Violet Mulroney, if you're here,
would you please come to the stage."

That's when Mila realized they were calling her. She
rushed up to the front of the room to accept the gift the
South Western Ontario Conservative Party riding had
wrapped up for her, but before climbing onto the stage,
she corrected her name to the woman at the podium
and heard herself announced as Myla Mulroney. "It's
Meela," she said one more time.

She'll probably never again enjoy the anonymity she
had that wintry night of 1983 in southwestern Ontario,

but along with providing her friend Nancy Southam with a favourite nickname for Mila, the event did put life in the limelight into perspective for her.

She'd had some exposure to the world of politics seven years earlier, when her husband ran for the leadership of the Conservative party in 1976. But since she had been a full-time student with a toddler, and had been pregnant with their second child, her involvement in that campaign had been minimal.

The night before Brian Mulroney declared his candidacy for the leadership of the Conservative party in 1983, he and Mila gathered with a few old friends and Ottawa insiders—Pat MacAdam and his wife Janet, Michael McSweeney, Michel and Erica Cogger, and Allan Fotheringham—in Ottawa's Château Laurier Hotel. It was March 20, Brian's forty-fourth birthday. Over dinner, they discussed the role Mila would play in the campaign and concluded that she'd travel with Brian from time to time but that mostly she'd stay at home with the children.

The next day Brian declared his candidacy, and a few days later he and Mila travelled together to Vancouver for an appearance. From that moment on, Mila attended nearly every event. She knew she had a role to play. She felt Brian needed her, and furthermore, she enjoyed herself on the hustings.

Everyone who has ever travelled or worked with the Mulroneys knows that Brian's performance is better when Mila is there. He's more relaxed, more low-key. There's something about her presence that gives him a sense of confidence. When he's campaigning, his staff like her to be with him all the time.

Mila says that it was during the 1983 leadership race that their relationship really meshed. "It's lonely on the road when you and your husband and an assistant are travelling to one town after another, hoping to meet all three thousand delegates for the convention but finding maybe five delegates at each stop. There were long car rides, long waits in airports, and always the feeling that you had to be 'on.' We really got to know each other. We had never seen each other at work that close up before. When I saw my husband that focused, with that much discipline, my respect and admiration for him grew enormously.

"I used to carry what I called my Mary Poppins purse. In it there were oranges for potassium, Tylenol for headaches, alphagestine rub for neck aches. I'm a quick study, so I became a good sounding board for Brian." She also got used to staying in $30-a-night Travelodge hotels, eating chocolate bars for quick energy, ordering pizza just as a restaurant was closing, and using the bed and bedspread in the motel as a table and tablecloth. Although she is nervous about flying in small planes, she logged plenty of hours in four-seaters and six-seaters as she worked the small towns as well as the cities.

She could wade into a gathering of delegates at the Colliery Inn in Sydney, Cape Breton, or meet over lunch with six people in Caraquet, New Brunswick. These were party people—Brian knew a lot of them, but she'd never met them before. And wherever she was, she called the children three times a day. She worked one hundred hours a week for four months, her energy fuelled by an unshakable belief in her husband.

She recovered from the odd faux pas with panache. For instance, when they flew to Williams Lake, British

Columbia, their executive assistant, Michael McSweeney, got off the campaign plane and said, ''Welcome to Elliot Lake.'' Mila didn't skip a beat. She quipped, ''He never gets out of Ottawa. What does he know about B.C.?''

Brian won the leadership at a noisy political convention in Ottawa in June 1983. Pat MacAdam tells a story about Mila's instincts and how she learned to trust them during the convention. A deal had been made that if David Crombie didn't stay on the leadership election ballot, he'd release his delegates to Mulroney. If that happened, Brian was supposed to go to Crombie's tent and shake hands. Someone leaked the plan to the media and the event turned into a circus. Mulroney's people showed up with a band. Shirley Crombie was stepped on and pushed. The press were screaming. Crombie felt very offended. Before it happened, Mila, who was sitting in a suite with the campaign team, had begged Brian not to go. She said, ''The politics in this are wrong.'' But arrangements had already been made and Brian felt he couldn't let people down. After that, she trusted her instincts, and so did the people around her.

Soon after the convention, the family moved to Pictou Lodge, in Stellarton, Nova Scotia. Brian had to start campaigning again, this time to become a member of Parliament for the Central Nova riding, so that he could have a seat in the House of Commons.

A new test began for Mila as wife of the leader of Her Majesty's Loyal Opposition. Meeting delegates individually with Brian had proven successful. Now she'd have to meet voters on her own—a roomful at a time. It turned out she had an enviable ability to work a room.

She attended tea parties, auctions, lobster picnics, and corn boils. She discussed wildflowers like a native and learned to glance skyward in disgust and make a remark about the weather as though she'd been a maritimer all her life. Clearly, she was a hit. At one coffee party, when a horde of media people started crowding into the house, she realized that Brian must be on the way and quipped, ''Did I hear 'the voice'? That man was a female soprano when this campaign started.''

Many people in Stellarton remember an electioneering tea party that was held on one of those stifling summer days when the air seems to stand still and the humidity seeps into your bones. For Mila, this was party number twelve, day five of the by-election campaign. But it was an important event. And Mila knows better than anyone how to make important moments count.

About fifty women had gathered in the basement recreation room of a tidy bungalow in Stellarton. There were trays of egg sandwiches and jelly rolls, and pots of coffee and tea on old silver servers that still smelled faintly of the polish that had been rubbed into them a few hours before the guests arrived.

Mila leapt out of the car, whipped off her designer sunglasses, shrugged off her shoulder bag, and in mid-stride tossed them to Michael McSweeney, before swinging into the house and launching into an animated discussion with the guests. She was thirty years old at the time, and the people in the room remember to this day that she had a style, a way about her that made a difference. For instance, when she approached an elderly woman who was hard of hearing, instead of shouting at her the way most people do with senior citizens, she sat down beside her, moved up close, and spoke to her in a normal voice. The invited guests were surprised to see the Uptown Girl from Montreal sitting on the sofa, wearing a pair of culottes, discussing the amount of sugar in the cookies they were eating. These ones were good, she said. But hers were pretty good, too.

During that by-election, the Conservative backroom boys watched her the way farmers watch a spring crop, wondering what the harvest will bring. Early on, the consensus was that Mila Mulroney would be an enormous asset to the party. Hugh Segal, who's been a Conservative backroom expert ever since the Bill Davis days in Ontario and is currently the prime minister's chief of staff, says, "Mila can make anyone feel at ease almost instantly—kids off the street at Halloween, princesses, and Soviet wives on official visits. By comparison, some other prime ministerial wives, lieutenant governors' wives, and governor generals' wives could even make Dale Carnegie feel uncomfortable."

Ollie Bowan from the Conservative headquarters in Stellarton was assigned to ferry Mila from one coffee party to another. She remembers meeting Brian and Mila at the Halifax airport the day they arrived. "They were young, casually dressed, and eager to make their mark. Brian was worried about what they should wear. He had a diamond-pattern sweater on at the time and I told him that would be fine. He wore it almost every day after that.

"Mila was warm, you couldn't help but like her. She took the people of Pictou County to her heart and they took her to theirs. She's good with a crowd because she's so sincere. Whether she's talking to a young mother or a grandmother, she genuinely and easily relates to everyone. And as long as she's with Brian, she can make people love him. I was struck by the quick way she could size people up. After we'd been some place, she'd describe someone to me in a way that I always knew exactly who she was talking about.''

Another duty Ollie remembers with obvious affection and a twinkle in her eye is the tour of the local junk-food joints that Mila loved. ''The Pizza Delight was one place we'd go to and we always went to McDonald's for a bedtime snack. Then there was a Dairy Queen; she loved that place. But the place she loved the most was the Lobster Bar. They'd keep it open late if they knew she was in town.''

Michael McSweeney, who was also an alderman for Canterbury ward in Ottawa, remembers that August in Pictou County. ''The kids and a mother's helper had one cabin [at the lodge]. Brian, Mila, Pat MacAdam, and I had another. We were there from July 12 until August 29. Mila and I had a deal. I cooked and she washed dishes one night, the next night we'd switch. She taught me a lot. I'd never heard of fettuccine Alfredo before that summer. We were cooking for twelve to fifteen people a night. There was the family plus Pat and I, and always a few volunteers and local people. One night I was doing the dishes. I was wearing yellow Playtex rubber gloves. There were suds all over the place. Mila looked at me and said, 'There he is, the envy of Ottawa, in living yellow Playtex, serving the people of Canterbury.' ''

Life in the public eye took some adjusting to, but seasoned observers say Mila found her stride early and easily. ''She has superior people skills,'' says Bill Fox, who was later press secretary and director of communications to Brian Mulroney. ''She has a special sensitivity for new Canadians who are trying to establish themselves here. It seemed to me that everyone with a long name made a bee-line for her, often with problems related to immigration, education, aging parents, or children. She has the ability to make people feel that they are getting a hearing, but she doesn't cross the line into policy—she's a sympathizer rather than a policy maker.''

By the time the by-election was won on August 29, 1983, it was obvious that Mila needed a full-time assistant. By now Mila-mania was in full swing. All the major magazines and newspapers carried articles about her. She began receiving dozens of requests, particularly from the multicultural community, to speak at functions.

Bonnie Brownlee was hired as her executive assistant and quickly became her confidante and one of her closest friends. From September 1, 1983, to September 4, 1984, they spent twenty-five days a month travelling to hundreds of small towns in Canada, some of them as many as ten times. There were no Mounties and no staff and no motorcades; the two of them depended on volunteers and each other. They stayed in whatever hotel or motel the party made available. They wrote and typed speeches on hotel room coffee tables, usually with Bonnie kneeling on the floor, using a borrowed typewriter. Bonnie says, ''In those days when we'd get into a car with people who had organized the event, she'd whisper to me, 'You do all the talking, I don't know what to say.' Soon, I rarely needed to say anything.''

Despite the makeshift conditions, Mila was already being treated like a celebrity. On airplanes, Bonnie says,

''Everyone would rush up to Mila and say, 'Oh, Mrs. Mulroney, what can I get for you? Can I bring you something to drink? Are you comfortable enough?' She'd tell them what she'd like to drink, then they'd look at me and leave. Mila would end up calling after them, 'Oh, by the way, Bonnie would like...' It happened on every flight. I started to feel like the invisible woman. When the plane was landing, I would be holding up my coffee cup wondering if anyone was ever going to take it away.''

When Bonnie and Mila hit the road in early September, their plan was to eradicate the stereotyping of the political wife. They felt that leaders' spouses were almost prisoners of people's expectations. So they set out to broaden those expectations.

It started with an invitation to Mila to read *Peter and the Wolf* with the Victoria Symphony Orchestra. She'd received a series of invitations and she and Bonnie decided to accept as many as they could that fit around one interesting, new, or different event. *Peter and the Wolf*, they thought, would make a change from senior citizens' residences and Conservative party luncheons.

As Mila tells the story, ''It was December. I arrived in Vancouver wearing a fur coat. At worst, Vancouver is raincoat weather in December. At best, short-sleeve weather. When we arrive, there's a scrum. No one has ever told me about scrums. I end up jammed up against a wall with a dozen mikes in my face and questions being fired from every direction. It's pouring with rain. I'm in this thick fur coat. I take one look at Bonnie and I get a fit of the giggles. I can't stop laughing. Finally, we get into a two-door car with people I've never seen before. No one tells me their names. I try to signal Bonnie, 'Who are they?' She signals back, 'Search me.' "

The two checked into a hotel and worked on Mila's speech for a Conservative lunch party. After the luncheon, they came out to find photographers waiting for them. They got into the car, and Mila smiled and waved, expecting the car to move off after a moment or two.

"The person driving the car presses the wrong button. Instead of driving away, the hood of the car starts going up. I couldn't believe it. I thought I would die right there. Everyone is watching. The car doesn't move. The driver doesn't move. I'm sitting and waving. The hood is slowly rising. It was like something out of Monty Python."

Rehearsals for *Peter and the Wolf* began as soon as they arrived in Victoria. The conductor told Mila she was "fantastic," but asked to speak to her backstage after the rehearsal. Mila explains: "You have to remember that in those days my knees shook. I wasn't one of those lucky people who felt at ease on the stage. I mean, people were in pain watching me." Backstage, the conductor suggested she think about breathing once in a while. An overanxious Mila replied, "What? I wasn't breathing?"

Just before showtime, they discussed it again in the conductor's dressing room. "He told me to suck in a breath every time there's a period in the script, but while he's saying all this, the man is holding his shorts out and shaking talcum powder down his shorts. Maybe it's because I'm only thirty years old and haven't been around much, but I don't know where to look."

When the performance finally began, the hall was one-third full. Bonnie said, "Don't worry, Mila, you won't be able to see anyone because of the lights."

"Oh yeah?" Mila said later. "I looked up and saw four people sitting out there."

It wasn't exactly their finest hour, but Bonnie insists Mila's reading was great. She claims to have a tape recording of it in her car and even plays it once in a while.

Afterwards, at a restaurant, the maestro ordered a Pink Lady, his friend ordered a club soda, and another person at the table ordered a Shirley Temple. Bonnie and Mila looked at each other and then at the waiter and said, "A vodka martini, please."

The situation didn't really improve when they travelled with Brian's entourage that year. Mila was left to open her own car door so many times that she learned to kick an armoured limousine door open with her high-heeled shoe. She would step out in a ball gown feeling somewhat like Wonder Woman. Brian soon learned to sit still until someone opened her door for her. "It wasn't meant as a put-down," she insists. "It was just that people weren't used to having someone sitting next to him."

Wherever they were on Friday nights, no matter who was with them, they had a rule that stated, "The last event has to be over by 9:45." Friday night, a.k.a. Trash Night, was their time to unwind, to order junk food to the room and watch *Dallas* on television. "This was decompress time, time for watching something that had nothing to do with reality. Just time to stop," Mila remembers.

109

As their road show moved on, the players picked up valuable experience. The tea parties went off without a hitch. It was when they strayed outside the usual type of event that things got unpredictable. But together Bonnie and Mila felt they could handle almost anything.

In the process of criss-crossing the country they have drawn up a Ten Best Retirement Homes list. ''We've been to so many senior citizens' homes, we already know where we want to retire,'' Bonnie quips. Mila adds, ''It's going to be called the Mila Mulroney Home for the Aged. There are going to be plenty of Yugoslav workers and the bar is going to open every afternoon at five o'clock. And we'll serve Nanaimo bars since we've tasted every recipe in Canada and we know who makes the best ones.''

By now the Mulroneys had moved into Stornoway, the official residence of the leader of the opposition. Mila was learning as many lessons at home as she did on the road. Lesson number one: don't leave your personal belongings out in the open when you're having a party. One guest took her perfume, another was discovered checking out her bedroom cupboards and dresser drawers, and still another was caught sizing up Brian's closet, the same night his reading glasses went missing.

Stornoway, long considered the *bête noire* of the National Capital Commission (NCC manages the government official residences), had been redecorated three times in the previous seven years, by Maureen McTeer, Pierre Trudeau, and Maureen McTeer again. It's a barn of a house that probably deserves to be torn down. But as one leader of the opposition after another has occupied it since 1950 and it's one of two residences where Princess Juliana of the Netherlands lived with her family while staying in Canada during World War II, it has gathered historical associations the way ships gather barnacles. No one has the nerve to order it demolished.

Mila redecorated Stornoway too. Stevie Cameron, who was a lifestyles reporter for the *Ottawa Citizen* at that time, remembers, "Mila decided to have an open house to show off Stornoway to the press. She did it because in those days they'd said, 'When we spend government money, we'll show you how we spent it.' There'd been so much criticism and nonsense over the houses: 'The Trudeaus spent too much money. The Turners spent too much money.' Mila handed out press releases that explained who owned what in the house [which pieces of art and furniture belonged to the Mulroneys and which pieces belonged to the government]. It was also a chance for Mila to show everyone what a good designer she is. She'd hired this swanky designer called Giovanni Mowinckel. Giovanni wanted an old-money look to the house. But Mila wanted the bright colours that are her style. Even Giovanni admired her taste. She posed for photographs with him and showed us what she'd done to the house, including the child-size sinks she'd installed in the bathrooms on the second floor." The tour of the house was well received. Mila had passed the first test.

Now Stornoway was ready for its official debut. One hundred people from the who's who list in Ottawa were invited to a pre-Christmas party on December first. The house looked beautiful, with decorated Christmas trees and clusters of poinsettias. Mila had an engagement elsewhere, so Michael McSweeney went to Stornoway to make sure everything was in order. There are three fireplaces in the house: one in the living room, another in the den and a third in the foyer. Michael lit the fire in the foyer, closed the glass doors, and went to light the other two. He forgot to open the flue. "When I came back to the foyer, there was smoke billowing everywhere. The eight-foot white mantel was black with soot. It was five o'clock. The guests were coming at six. You could hardly breathe in the place." Michael dashed around opening windows, setting up fans to blow the smoke out, and asked three staff members to use toothbrushes to clean the soot off the carved mantel. "Just before six, Mila walked in," says Michael. "You could still smell the smoke. She wasn't one bit fazed. She said, 'Open the glass doors of the fireplace and the chimney will draw the smoke out.' She even commented that it was good to have the room cold with so many guests coming. The woman is unflappable."

They weren't in Stornoway long, because John Turner called a fall election. For Mila, it felt as though the campaigning never stopped. They hit the road again, but this time Brian had decided to run in his home riding of Manicouagan, which meant meeting and winning over a completely new set of voters. On September 4, 1984, the Mulroneys waited in a Baie-Comeau hotel room with their closest friends and advisers for the polls to close and the votes to be counted. Brian was slated to win, not only in his riding, but some pollsters had predicted a Tory sweep of the country.

They'd flown to Baie-Comeau on the Sunday, September 2, and were staying in the house beside the Manoir Baie-Comeau, the residence that had been built to accommodate the big bosses when they came to the mill town on business. The children were at home, in Stornoway, with the Pivnickis, who had come from Montreal to be with them.

Brian and Mila had been out campaigning on the Monday. On Tuesday, they went out early in the morning in the middle of a rain storm to vote. Press secretary Bill Fox remembers worrying that they needed an umbrella and realizing that whatever they used would be seen by millions of people on television. Someone produced a two-tone blue umbrella with the name Wilson (the sports equipment manufacturer) on it. Bill thought to himself, ''You can't get better advertising than that.''

That night, the gang from St. FX, the Laval Mafia, the boys from Baie-Comeau, and the campaign and constituency staff gathered in the living room of the old company house at 6:30, just after the polls had closed in Newfoundland. After eight weeks of frenzied activity, there was nothing they could do but sit and wait.

They didn't have to wait long. Phone calls to the Maritimes to find out about early returns suggested a Conservative sweep, and at 8:00, when CBC's Peter Mansbridge came on television, he announced a Tory landslide. The workers and backroom boys congratulated the new prime minister.

Mila slipped away from the crowd and went upstairs with Bonnie. She needed a few minutes to be alone, to reflect on what had happened and what was about to happen to her. She felt she'd never really known what to do on the campaign trail, although she had a gut sense of what not to do. Yet she'd helped in Brian's success and was ready to share it with him.

At one in the morning, the Mulroneys made their way to the local arena for the acceptance speech and the celebration. The place was packed. People were singing, balloons were floating above the crowd, music was booming from the loudspeakers.

Brian and Mila made their way to the stage, and the arena erupted with applause that lasted for ten minutes. They waved to their supporters, danced to the music, hugged each other. The noise was so loud they could hardly hear themselves think—but thinking could wait for the morning as they celebrated through the night.

The morning came soon enough—with additional RCMP officers, who had suddenly materialized in town; with a call from President Ronald Reagan; and with a trip back to Ottawa in the afternoon. Boba and Mita Pivnicki were due to celebrate their thirty-second wedding anniversary the next day, and Brian and Mila had to be home for the party.

Mila's next and critical test as political spouse was becoming the chatelaine at 24 Sussex Drive. The Mounties, the staff, the entourage became part of her life. Until then, Mila had been fairly accessible, particularly to the press. Magazines and newspapers easily obtained interviews and photography sessions with her.

On the day the Mulroneys were to move out of Stornoway (they moved into the Harrington Lake residence for several weeks until the Turners had made arrangements to leave 24 Sussex Drive), they obliged a journalist who wanted a family story for an upcoming Christmas edition of a magazine. Although the furniture had already been taken out of the living room, a fire was laid in the fireplace and a few chairs were left for the family to sit on. The family gathered in front of the fireplace for the photo. Just when all was ready, Brian with a copy of *The Night Before Christmas* in his hands, the kids around him, Mila leaning over the back of his chair, Brian was called away to the telephone. The family dispersed around the room while they waited for him to return. Suddenly, without warning, the overheated glass doors of the fireplace exploded, sending shards of searing hot glass streaking through the room. Had the phone call not interrupted the session, the children and their parents would surely have been badly burned and cut. Mila handled the explosion like one more event in the topsy-turvy world she'd begun to inhabit. The glass was cleaned up. The prime minister returned. The photo was taken. He went to ''the office'' and she carried on with the interview. It was business as usual.

Soon after Brian became prime minister, Mila took an office in the Langevin Block, where most of the Prime Minister's Office is housed, and staff was hired to handle the mail (about 10,000 pieces a year), the invitations (about a dozen a week), and the events she coordinated for the prime minister (for example, when the Prince and Princess of Wales visited Ottawa in fall 1991, Mila organized the black-tie gala for 2,100 people held in the National Arts Centre).

She wasn't the first spouse to have office space. In fact, every prime ministerial spouse had used secretarial help from the Langevin offices. Margaret Trudeau had an assistant designated to help her. Maureen McTeer had an executive assistant and an office in the South Block when her husband was leader of the opposition, and she had a staff of three and an office on the second floor of the Langevin Block when he was prime minister. Mila's style was different. She didn't skirt the issue of office space, she announced it. Not everyone approved. By now her spending habits, first at Stornoway, then at 24 Sussex Drive, were under scrutiny. Mila-mania was over and the snipers started taking potshots at her in the Ottawa papers for what they considered her White-House first-lady approach to the job.

Mila doesn't apologize for what she sees as essential services. She took 600 square feet of space that was not being used and set up four small offices and a receiving room. All of the Canadiana pine furnishings and most of oil paintings belong to her. Four paintings are rented from the Canada Council's art bank for $1,200 a year. Two computers were purchased for the office, and in 1984, carpeting was put down. A staff of three handles all the events at 24 Sussex Drive, the Cystic Fibrosis Foundation file, the gifts for visiting dignitaries, and Christmas cards. They also help the special events office with anything Mila Mulroney is involved in. Bonnie Brownlee oversees the operation of this office, but her title is executive assistant to the prime minister, so her duties include working on scheduling of events and planning tours for both Brian and Mila.

In a typical week, Mila spends three half days at her office. She arrives at about 12:30 p.m. and stays until 5:30 or 6. She reads the mail, makes a lot of phone calls, writes the thank-you notes that need to be hand written. She also works on her speeches. These are drafted by one of the government speech writers, but she invariably polishes the final version. She consults ministers when she needs to be briefed about an event she's involved in and keeps Brian in touch with the party.

Mila's stationery and stamps are paid for by the Conservative party. The correspondence done by Bonnie Brownlee is paid for by the government. The cost of running the office has never been made public, because the Prime Minister's Office claims that Mila's office is part of the PMO in the Langevin Block, and it isn't broken down as a separate cost. The cost of running the PMO is just under $5.83 million a year.

Some people object to Mila's office. At the White House, Barbara Bush has an office and a staff. But her set-up is different. The first lady in the United States has official status. She has a budget, the use of Air Force planes, and a recognized obligation to serve. The spouse of Canada's prime minister has no official status. She (so far there hasn't been a he) is a volunteer. She can be as involved or as removed from the Prime Minister's Office as she likes.

At the same time, the activities of the prime minister's spouse are strictly circumscribed. If she's a lawyer, she can't practise, in case of conflict of interest. If she ran an antique shop and gave a discount to someone, there would be hell to pay. For Mila, there is no question about her role. She is there to help her husband and she'll have staff to help her. The Mulroneys came to Ottawa as a successful team, and they're not about to change to suit their critics.

CTV parliamentary correspondent Craig Oliver says, "We hadn't had anyone like this in generations. She was breaking new ground. We'd had two crazy old bachelors and Maryon Pearson, who was a nice woman but not a political wife of any kind. Joe Clark wasn't around long enough for Maureen to get involved and Margaret Trudeau was in completely over her head. We've never had a thoroughly modern woman.

"As for her approach to an office, we've been moving toward a presidential kind of politics since Trudeau. The Mulroneys didn't start this. Television did this for the most part. In the 1960s, TV made the prime minister a major national figure in the country in a way he never used to be. So I can't fault Mila for becoming the major personality she's become. It's the system. The media want to see her. She's attractive and looks good on TV. You can't blame her for that.

"There may have been a concern that she was damaging him with a high spending style early on. But a lot of people began to realize it isn't public money she's spending on dressing well, and if she wants to look good—well, who doesn't? Mila got bad press initially regarding the White House office style, but I believe that was copycat journalism to some degree. I was working in Washington at the time and Nancy Reagan was being criticized for spending a fortune on new plates for the White House and on her clothes. There was a reflection of that in the Canadian papers."

Oliver remembers an incident in Washington that taught him how well prepared Mila is for the job she is doing. "Just after Mulroney became prime minister, they were in Washington for an event. Linda McLennan and I were down there doing *Canada AM* and the producer wanted an interview with Mila for the program. They asked the press office and were told, 'Yes, she'll do the interview. But only if Craig Oliver does it.' I think that was very clever. Linda might have been hard on her. But I would have looked like an old meanie if I'd slashed into this attractive woman who was the wife of the new prime minister. That tells you how carefully she thinks about what she's doing."

That's also one of the reasons people say she is ambitious and calculating. But Craig Oliver says, "I admire that. There's nothing unethical or dishonest about trying to be the best you can be. For Canada to have a prime ministerial wife who's as active and engaged as she is, is something new. In the United States they've been doing it this way since Eleanor Roosevelt. I think that on balance it has to be a good thing. It can be a very good pulpit if you use the job right, and I think she has."

Senator Michael Meighen, whose political campaign in 1972 was the first one Mila ever worked on, is afraid that "Canadians have a burr under their saddle right now, a warped and incorrect sense of what is appropriate about public spending by public officials. This is Canada at its worst. However, if you challenge this fixation, you're accused of covering up. I would guess that Mila's role is terrifically taxing."

Clare Hoy, a columnist for Southam News and Mila's biggest detractor, doesn't agree. "In the United States, the first lady is a formal office with a budget and a staff. Here it isn't. Whether it should be or not, I don't know.''

In one of Hoy's columns, he accused Mila Mulroney of asking the RCMP to salute her. His colleague at the *Toronto Sun*, Doug Fisher, was appalled at the accusation and wrote a column dismissing it as fabrication. The two men wound up in a shoving match at the Ottawa Press Club over the incident. While certain Ottawa journalists have questioned Hoy's sources, he says that he doesn't have to produce proof of his allegations. ''If I'm satisfied that something is true, I print it and I don't care if it upsets the Mulroneys or their children.

''If the view is that hers is a legitimate function, we should be up front about it. I'm not saying it shouldn't be, in fact maybe it should be. She's an important, much underrated cog in his political machinery. My complaint isn't that she spends money. I just want to know how much it costs to run her office.''

(Mr. Hoy claims he was fired by the *Toronto Sun* for columns he wrote about Mila Mulroney. The *Sun's* version is that he was recalled to Toronto from their Ottawa bureau and refused to return, so in their view he quit. ''You don't get the heat when you go after Brian nowheres near what you get when you go after Mila,'' Hoy says.)

There is no question that the role of the prime minister's wife has changed under Mila's tenure. Marjory LeBreton, the deputy chief of staff, has worked for four Conservative leaders—John Diefenbaker, Robert Stanfield, Joe Clark, and Brian Mulroney—consequently, she has been in a good position to observe four political wives in action.

"Olive Diefenbaker was stand-offish, serene, digni-
fied, and she certainly didn't do the things that Mila
Mulroney does," says LeBreton. "There was a lot of
criticism of the Diefenbakers and the stiff formal style
they used to entertain people. In fact, it was Olive's
strict Presbyterian upbringing that dictated their style
and made both of them look elitist. Olive Diefenbaker
doesn't come close to Mila Mulroney in terms of stature
within the party or for that matter with the public."

Olive Diefenbaker was fifty-five years old when she
and John moved into the prime minister's residence.
She was the first spouse to open 24 Sussex to the public.
She invited the press, members of Parliament, and dip-
lomats to garden parties, but the parties were always
dry and nobody wanted to go. She was known as a
judgemental woman who detested many people in Ottawa. But she was also a powerful supporter of John
Diefenbaker.

Mary Stanfield was a warm, down-to-earth woman
who always felt uncomfortable in the public eye. She
often confided to friends that she would have been
much happier back in Nova Scotia. Startling proof of
her gentle disposition (and, perhaps, proof of the lack
of power spouses really have) is the story about the time
the entire interior of Stornoway was repainted by the
Department of Public Works in an institutional-looking
green and pink. Though Mary Stanfield was living there
at the time, no one consulted her about the colour
scheme. The loveseats and curtains in her living room
were peach-coloured and clashed horribly with the pink
paint on the walls. She didn't make waves about it, she
made jokes. "She had a great sense of humour and was

a tremendous partner for Mr. Stanfield,'' says LeBreton. ''But she was happy not to have any profile at all. She was friendly and supportive, but she didn't travel with him very much.

''I worked with Maureen McTeer when she was a researcher for Bob Stanfield. She was a bright, young, bilingual lawyer and in fact, I always say I'm the honorary cupid in her match with Joe. (When Joe Clark won his seat as a member of Parliament in 1972, he was looking for a research assistant and he wanted to learn to speak French. I introduced him to Maureen in the fall of 1972. He hired her, and they were married in June 1973.) In terms of the party, the fact that Maureen kept her name was criticized a great deal. I used to hate the party's position on that and I argued vehemently against it. But there was an element in our party that blamed Maureen for the 'Joe Who' tag. Some of them were very unkind to Maureen and to Joe over that. There was also an identity problem on Maureen's part. I don't think that she ever decided in her own mind what she wanted to do or be in that role. At one point she was the 'spouse of,' the next an independent. It was very confusing.

''I used to travel with Joe Clark and run his tours. The party rank and file were always happier when Joe was by himself, only because Maureen wasn't sure where she wanted to fit in to all of this. Depending on what she was up to, we could wind up off-schedule. When she put her mind to it, she was terrific, but if she decided she didn't want to be there on a particular day, it was awful.

''So the relationship between the party and Maureen was not a particularly healthy one. I feel it was both their faults. They had a certain hostility to her. But she didn't always make it easy for them. She was moody at times and might all of a sudden decide not to go to something they had arranged for her.

''On the other hand, with Brian Mulroney, the opposite happened. Any time that Mila couldn't go on the road, for whatever reason, the party was always terribly disappointed. As for mood swings, if Mila has them, they're well hidden because I've never seen them, ever. The other thing with Mila is that she's very protective of the prime minister. She's like a rearguard, keeping her eye out for him. She's a good balance for him. She's very intelligent, watches what's going on, and is definitely an asset to him and to the party. She's by his side, but she's an independent thinker.''

While the continual comparison of spouses bothers Mila, the references to the days of Mila-mania irritate her more. She feels she touches people because they see a woman with kids, a mother, in her position. She says, ''I remember meeting a woman in Prince Edward Island who came up to me and said, 'I have four kids, I have to fit thousands of things into my days, too. It's nice to meet someone like you.' I felt I'd been paid a pretty nice compliment.''

Mila also finds the role-model tag to be a tricky one. ''I don't like being thought of as a role model, because I don't wear anyone else's shoes. I don't even tell my children how to think unless I feel very strongly that they're on the wrong track. If someone came here from another country and saw me as a role model, I think that would be nice. But I find it to be too much of a conflict to say I'd like people to emulate me.''

Her choices about the kinds of events and activities that she and Brian get involved in haven't always been shared by the people around Brian. But that has never stopped her from making suggestions. In 1989 David Foster asked them to play ball at the annual David Foster Foundation event for children needing organ transplants. ''Brian's advisers didn't want him depicted like that. But he's a great athlete. It's something Canadians don't know about him. He was a terrific hockey player, and you should see this man skate. He loves kids, and this event is to raise money for something valuable. He's always in a suit and tie. I wanted his advisers to get him out of that image.'' Brian did the event (she's a hard person to say no to) and the photo taken at the game was used and reused for publicity.

The very same thing happened when she asked him to become involved in the Missing Children Registry and with the opening of the AIDS Conference. His people said, ''Don't do it.'' Brian did these things because Mila asked him to.

''People say I influence Brian. It's not influence, it's corroboration. He'll come in and say, 'What do you think about—whatever?' I'll say, 'It sounds terrific.' He'll say, 'That's not what I'm hearing from my people.' If Brian is against something, I can't change his mind. But I can offer him a different perspective. I try very hard not to meddle in things I know little about, but in social things, which I've concentrated on, I try to show him why it's good for him. For instance, Brian loves children. He spends a lot of time with them. But when a literacy event came up, he was advised not to do it. I talked him into it and he loved it. I think he'd like to do more of these events, but I understand that time is scarce.''

Hugh Segal also feels she is the right counterweight to Brian the politician. ''When you are a Conservative, you are associated with values and positions that are viewed by some as old-fashioned. If he were married to a person who didn't have youth, attractiveness, or spunk or didn't embody some sense of relish about life, then the dowdiness of the collective image could be quite destructive. It could make you look not just old-fashioned in your values but fundamentally out of touch with reality. She makes them a thoroughly modern couple in the sense of both appearance and substance and the even-handedness of their relationship with each other. That's important to the sense of energy and sizzle of the party and to Conservatives. All of which is important when you have to sell ideas that are unpopular. She humanizes the party substantially.''

Although Mila is more practised at politicking than she had been in Stellarton in 1983, she's no less candid. At a recent cocktail party, her fourth public appearance of the day, she slumped into the corner of a couch and said, ''I had a twenty-minute nap before coming here—I think that was a mistake.'' It's that kind of off-the-cuff remark that endears her to the people she meets.

Whether she's at a head table, a conference table, or a cocktail party, Mila's expressive face gives her personality

away. She will tip her chair forward to pay more attention, then sheepishly look around the room and gently
ease the chair back onto all four legs with a "you caught
me" expression on her face. She's the vulnerable
mother who has to gulp water for self-control while
listening to a sixteen-year-old reformed drug addict talk
about wanting to die rather than see the disappoint-
ment on her mother's face. "I knew I was going to cry,"
she said later.

And she's the star who performs with all the trap-
pings of the office—red carpets, limousines, RCMP security guards (sometimes tuxedo-clad when opening a
path for her at gala receptions), and the photographers
and reporters who record her every move. But she's
down-to-earth at the same time, often wisecracking
with people in the crowd and putting pomp in its place.

Her sense of the appropriate is illustrated in a story
told by Bob Handforth, the senior citizen who plays the
piano at official functions at 24 Sussex Drive. Bob has
been playing the piano for the Mulroneys ever since
they lived in Stornoway, where his story took place. "I
always wore a business suit when I went to a function to
play the piano. Mrs. Mulroney asked me one day if I'd
mind wearing a tuxedo. I told her I wouldn't mind but
that I didn't have one and couldn't afford to buy one.
She bought the tuxedo for me. I wanted to find a way of
thanking her for that, so now, whenever she has a cystic
fibrosis function at the house, I play the piano, but I
refuse to accept any money."

In just one year after they moved into 24 Sussex, the
house had been changed; so had the style and so had
the family. Nicolas Mulroney was born on the first

anniversary of Brian's victory at the polls. It was a tough month for Brian. Two cabinet ministers (John Fraser and Marcel Masse) resigned and opposition members were crying foul. The media had developed a voracious appetite for scandal.

Mila knew the ropes. She'd mastered the balancing act. The question now was, would anyone trip her up?

Chapter Six

Gossip hasn't stopped me from being relaxed and
easygoing with people. I'll probably get burned again
but I'd rather live that way than always be paranoid.
                                              Mila Mulroney

In 1975, twenty-two-year-old Mila discovered that
"off the record" means different things to different
people. She and Brian had been in Baie-Comeau to
announce his first leadership bid. When Brian decided
to stay on, his friend L. Ian MacDonald suggested to Bill
Fox, a reporter with Southam News, that they take Mila
back to Montreal and perhaps go out for dinner.

Bill made the arrangements and invited Don Mac-
Pherson of the *Montreal Gazette* to join them. The four
dined at Ruby Foo's restaurant and spoke freely "off the
record" about the campaign and about Mila's life with
Brian. Several prominent Conservatives in the dining
room came over and to Bill Fox's consternation offered
to pay for Mila's meal. But that was only a minor annoyance compared to the commotion that erupted two days
later when the entire conversation appeared in the *Ga-*
zette. Bill says, ''Perhaps Don didn't know it was off the
record, but Mila sure thought it was. I was afraid she'd
never speak to me again.'' The article started:

It is late in the Year of the Woman and the Candidate is about to start his campaigning for the day with a policy statement on that very subject.

Though the day has just begun, the first low-angled shafts of light striking quiet Devon Avenue in close-to-uppermost Westmount, the Candidate is already up and dressing and is worried about missing his flight.

"Mila," he shouts irritably at his dozing wife, who is to give birth to their second child two months later on, if he's lucky, the day of the vote, "where are my shirts?"

His wife, a real living human being and not simply another model of the basic wind-up doll that most politicians take out of the box when the presence of a Wife is required, confides that the campaign is "driving Brian crazy."

Still, she accepts the craziness, the pre-road downs and the demands they put on her, rising early to help the Candidate find his shirts in the same place she has always put them since their marriage three years ago.

She does it because that is what her husband expects from her. She wants what he wants and what he wants is to be leader of the Conservative party.

Mila could hardly believe her eyes when she read the story. She called Brian in tears and asked, "How could this happen?"

The situation Mila had walked into was a new one, not only for her but for all public figures. Though many observers say that Watergate was the event that triggered the change in journalism, the shift actually began in the 1960s. The first election campaign to reflect the new power of the media was that of 1968, when Pierre Elliott Trudeau defeated Robert Stanfield. All the paraphernalia of modern campaigns had arrived: media gurus to analyse every word spoken, public relations firms to groom the candidate and manipulate the event to the advantage of the party, and a campaign that focused on the candidate's personality rather than on the party's policy.

The style had percolated up from the United States at the same time that television technology developed sufficiently to handle the demands of up-close electioneering. The spouse became much more visible, and children were brought into the campaign as well. The American concept of a good politician with an attractive family became important and was carried into Canadian politics. Miriam Stanfield campaigned with her father in 1968 and often received more attention than he did because it was so unusual to have a young woman campaigning alongside the leader.

Then, in 1973, *Washington Post* reporters Bob Woodward and Carl Bernstein had broken a story of corruption, double-dealing, and theft that implicated the White House and finally toppled the president of the United States. For the reporters' hard work and dogged determination, there was fame and fortune in the form of contracts for a book, a movie, and speaking engagements.

131

For politicians everywhere and those close to them, there was the heat of a much brighter spotlight and an intensified scrutiny.

The post-Watergate style of journalism that emerged brought out the best and the worst in reporters. Today, investigative reporters are more skilled, more analytical than ever before. But the blow-the-whistle-and-become-a-star style of journalist has also flourished. Although the public is beginning to question the propriety of a media that sets itself up as public prosecutor, they retain a taste for the sensational: the *National Enquirer* sells more copies than any other weekly magazine in North America except for *TV Guide*.

Hartley Steward, who has been an editor and publisher of major Canadian newspapers as well as a magazine journalist and is currently the publisher of the *Ottawa Sun*, says, ''The post-Watergate style has given birth to a lot of good investigative journalists, but also to a lot of men and women who are relentlessly attacking politicians and celebrities without a lot of research. The feeling that you can write anything you like in a harsh, intemperate style wasn't there a decade ago.''

Mila Mulroney has, for the most part, had good press. She's been on the cover of most major magazines, she's been the subject of newspaper stories, and she's been interviewed extensively on television. And yet she says that in the eight years she's been in Ottawa, she's read almost nothing in print about herself that's wholly true, which is one of the reasons she prefers television interviews.

To the uninitiated, her life in the political limelight is viewed as a haven of privilege and protection. But the red carpets, limousines, and police escorts come with a price: a high-tech, hungry media looking for scandal, waiting for a slip-up, prepared to publish at a moment's notice intimate details that satisfy the public's seemingly insatiable appetite for the inside story.

Item: During the Commonwealth Conference in Vancouver in 1987, Mila hosted two lunches for the spouses of the summit leaders, the Vancouver philanthropic crowd, and a handful of celebrities. One was at Bridges, a popular restaurant with a view of the city, the other was a dim sum meal at a Chinese restaurant. Two hundred people attended these lunches. She ordered flowers for the tables from Thomas Hobbs Florist Ltd. and afterwards had them delivered to several hospital wards. A few days later, a story carried in the *Globe and Mail* said that Mila had spent $5,000 of taxpayers' money on purchases that included the flowers and items such as garden furnishings for herself and the house in Ottawa.

"I called the florist and asked him to fax a copy of the bill to me," says Mila. "The bill was $2,000 for flowers. He was in a frenzy. He felt he'd been had."

Thomas Hobbs explains, "When [journalist] Stevie Cameron called me, I didn't even know who she was. She didn't tell me she was writing a story. She said she was calling about her sister's wedding, that she wanted to discuss flowers with me and that she was an old friend of Mila's. She asked me what Mila was doing in the store and I told her. Then she made up a bunch of stuff to put in the paper. She said Mila bought lawn furniture here. We don't even sell lawn furniture. The bill wasn't $5,000, as reported in the *Globe and Mail*, it was around $2,000. I felt I'd really been burned. I wrote a letter to the *Globe and Mail* saying they should check things out before they print them. The *Globe and Mail* didn't print a retraction, but they did print my letter.''

Mila functions in a highly visible way. She decided in 1983 that she would be available to perform on behalf of her husband on the public stage. She knew that if she stepped on the stage, she would invite personal criticism and that some people would dislike her performance. She knows, for example, that her shopping habits are an easy target for columnists. ''I've had people write things that aren't particularly favourable. I don't dismiss them because I recognize the fact that they are probably right. You don't always do everything well. I know that sometimes I may not have done the right thing. My feeling is, I have no problem if you want to get the goods on me. If you want to hear what I did or where I shop, phone the office.

''Once we got a call from a gossip columnist in Montreal who wanted to know where I shop. Bonnie Brownlee said, 'Read your list to me and I'll tell you if she shops there. I promise.' The reporter mentioned a place and Bonnie said, 'Nope, she doesn't shop there.' The reporter said, 'Well, my sources tell me she does.' I'd never been to that store.''

Mila says she has no problem with telling people the truth about her clothes and her lifestyle. ''But if you're going to pull punches and you've got an audience and a pulpit to preach from and you don't have to give the other side of the story, well why should I be

134

interviewed? If you're going to distort what I say, it's a waste of my time. If you're going to write a smear story about me, you can write it without me.''

Item: The great Giovanni Affair that occupied our newspapers for weeks on end in 1987 involved interior decorator Giovanni Mowinckel, who was hired by Mila to decorate Stornoway and later 24 Sussex Drive. Every minute detail of the decoration plans and prices was dissected in the daily news.

''Closets designed to hold hundreds of pairs of shoes, including dozens of pairs of the Prime Minister's loafers, and custom-finished pads for the baby's crib are among the lavish furnishings at 24 Sussex Drive,'' began one front-page article in the *Globe and Mail* by Stevie Cameron and Graham Fraser. The article went into tedious detail about the dimensions of the closets (three and a half metres of hanging space for evening dresses), the fittings in the bathroom (a whirlpool tub and double vanities), the cost of the hall wallpaper (sixty rolls at $100 a roll), even the source of the sheets and towels (the Duvet Shop in Ottawa).

The article made the furnishings sound as ''lavish'' as possible. More than a hundred pairs of shoes became ''hundreds of pairs.'' Mila's evening gown collection sounds enormous, but it's not outlandish when one considers that she has to attend several events a month in a long gown. Plenty of modern houses have double vanities and whirlpool tubs. And good-quality wallpaper *is* expensive, particularly if you have a very large hall.

Subsequent articles examined the payments for these renovations and the use of PC Canada funds. Since contributions to PC Canada are tax-deductible, the *Globe and Mail* called the method of paying for the renovations a "scam."

In March 1987, Giovanni Mowinckel went broke and left Ottawa, leaving stacks of unpaid bills behind him. His company, Colvin Design, went into receivership. There were several reasons for his cash-flow problems. He usually charged a hefty markup (of about 60 percent) on supplies and furnishings ordered for his clients, but he charged Mila only the costs and a design fee. His other clients felt he was neglecting them while he worked on the official residences. At the same time, he spent heavily on cars and real estate, importing an antique Bentley from England and buying condos in Toronto and Florida, a country house in the Cotswolds, and a farmhouse in the Gatineau Hills.

Reporter Stevie Cameron went through Mowinckel's finances with a fine-tooth comb, listing the dates and amounts of every single cheque paid by the PC Canada Fund in one of her articles. Later, she located his files in a warehouse and entered the warehouse with a photocopier to copy the invoices in the Mulroney transactions. The *Globe and Mail* even flew her to Italy to find Giovanni and interview him about the unpaid bills. (Giovanni refused to be interviewed.)

After all this investigation, Stevie says that the accountant she hired to go over the invoices and receipts concluded that the only item unaccounted for was a necklace purchased by Giovanni for Mila. In a 1988 article, under a headline that announced that the Conservative party paid for Mila's jewellery, she wrote that

Danielle Letarte, a temporary bookkeeper working for Giovanni, had used a cheque from the PC Canada Fund in August 1985 to buy a bank draft for $3,237 to be sent to Bulgari, an exclusive jewellery store in Rome, to pay for the steel, gold, and topaz necklace Mila had ordered during a private visit to Rome in May.

Ms Letarte says that the cheque was for $5,000. She was instructed to get a bank draft for $3,237 and put the rest in Giovanni's account and return the bank draft to Giovanni. She does not know where the draft was sent, or what was done with it.

Mila says, ''I saw the necklace in a store in Italy. They didn't have one for sale, but promised to get one for me. Giovanni said he'd pick it up when he was there the next time. He did and brought it to me in Ottawa. The necklace was listed as an item on his invoice. It cost $2,400. I paid him for it. I didn't say, 'Can I have a receipt, please?' You can't be always looking over your shoulder. This was a man I worked with on two houses. You can't be suspicious of everybody. Gossip hasn't stopped me from being relaxed and easygoing with people. I'll probably get burned again, but I'd rather live that way than always be paranoid.''

In fact, Derek McSweeney, who worked as a driver for the Mulroneys at the time, says he personally delivered $2,400 in cash from Mila to Giovanni at his Ottawa office. Also, Brian issued a cheque to the PC Canada Fund to cover personal expenses on the Giovanni invoice. The cheque was for a substantial amount that he prefers not to disclose.

There is a tendency for a journalist to become a popular psychologist in the course of writing a profile. Profiles are supposed to capture the personality of an individual, but often the journalist has only an hour-long interview in which to find out about a complex character. That leaves room for a lot of conjecture and a lot of assumptions.

The profile Robert Fulford wrote for *Saturday Night* magazine in April 1988 called "Imagining Mila" illustrates the problem with the pop-psych approach. Although the article is long on information about other prime ministerial wives and American first ladies (Fulford compared Mila to Jacqueline Kennedy) and rather short on information about Mila, Fulford managed to reach a number of fairly sweeping conclusions about her, based on a single interview. After explaining the contradictory expectations that the Canadian public has for a prime minister's wife, he summed her up as "an actress playing her role without a script, watching for cues from the audience." Remarking that she does not attack her critics or the enemies of the Conservative party, he concluded that hers was "a curiously muted personality, contained and rather predictable... She gave me the impression of a carefully edited public persona."

Mila says, "I think he's a good writer, but in this case he had a preconceived idea about me and he didn't need to interview me for the story he wrote. I often find that the people who write that they know a lot about me actually know the least."

Clare Hoy is also happy to speculate about Mila's personality in public and in private. "Mila Mulroney is friendly, really nice in public. She makes people feel good. I think it's a card she plays that's helpful to her husband. My guess is that when the door closes, she puts the card back in the deck. I'm not saying that's a bad thing for her to do, and I don't have any way of knowing that is what she does. I just think journalists should keep that in mind.''

Robert Fife, Ottawa bureau chief for the *Toronto Sun*, is more leery of snap judgements. ''We [journalists] often have a mindset of operating in a pack. You form opinions of people based on that. It hinders you from taking a broader look at people.''

Item: When Caroline Mulroney was thirteen years old, she walked into a book store at Christmas time and saw a new book with her mother's photo on the cover. Excited at the prospect of reading about her mother, she started thumbing through the book. It was *Political Wives*, by Susan Riley, who stated in the preface, ''Real prostitutes work much harder for their money than political wives do, under much inferior conditions.'' She likened Mila to Imelda Marcos and then referred to her as ''Evita of the frozen pampas.''

Riley didn't interview the women she wrote about. She didn't ask for interviews and makes no apology for that in her introduction, stating, ''This is not a book of reportage.'' Lucille Broadbent, who is also featured in the book, says, ''A lot of spouses wondered who had been interviewed. If one is going to write about people, one should do them the courtesy of interviewing them. I feel that if you're going to comment on people's personal lives, it should not be superficial comments that you can't back up.''

Susan Riley says it was enough that she watched the political wives in action. But Hartley Steward's first lesson in journalism school twenty-five years ago taught him that observing isn't enough. ''I remember my first day at Ryerson. There was a terrible fight in the classroom. No one knew the professor had scripted the fight. When he finally threw the two culprits out of the class, he turned to the rest of us and said, 'Write what happened.'

''The result was amazing. No one had the story right. In fact, one of the fighters was wearing a brilliant red tie (part of the script) and no one even had the colour of the tie right. The professor explained that whenever an incident happens you think to yourself: 'How is this going to affect me?' In this case, 'Is the guy going to hit me next? Am I going to have to worry about this guy all year? Is it going to be okay?' The professor went on to say, 'If you want to be a journalist, you have to stand back from those things. You can't let your personal feelings interfere.' That lesson in objectivity isn't taught today.''

The latest development in journalism seems to be an alarming tendency to report rumour as fact. When rumours appeared in *Frank* magazine and a few British and German tabloids about marriage problems between Brian and Mila and about Brian drinking and abusing Mila and Mila leaving, Maureen McTeer says, ''There was a level of viciousness that was quite devastating. People across Canada repeated this rumour back to me with no amount of denial. I even had phone calls from friends in Europe who wanted to know if it was true. How would I know, anyway? And why would people mention it to me except to be mean? If people can lower themselves to start or repeat that kind of rumour, it can affect all of us. Everyone should know that although they're talking about them this week, it'll be someone else next week. We're all vulnerable.''

She assumes that the rumour was started as a way to ''bring them down when the party is down in the polls. In this business, when you're down, people give you lots of kicks.'' It also enraged McTeer that a rumour about a woman being abused would be repeated with glee, in some cases by feminists who would fight to open a shelter for any other woman who was in danger.

In fall 1991, John Sawatsky's biography of Mulroney, *Mulroney: The Politics of Ambition*, flatly stated that the man hadn't had a drink in twelve years. This statement finally put to rest the stories about drinking. But the rate the original rumour spread across the country and the credibility of the people who were spreading it gave rise to yet another rumour: that a smear campaign had been started by someone who wanted to bring down Brian Mulroney.

CTV Ottawa bureau chief Craig Oliver says, ''The viciousness of the campaign somebody engineered against the Mulroneys was really something. I believe it started in Toronto, because that's where most of the calls were coming from. It actually became so intense that I had a call from one of our editors asking, 'Why is your bureau covering up the fact that he's drinking and she's left him?' It was that widely believed in Toronto. I even got a call from ABC News in New York saying, 'We have solid information that Mulroney was seen being admitted to a drug abuse clinic in California.' I said,

'Okay, find me the person who saw it.' They couldn't.
No one could ever nail down the person who saw these
things. The last call I had was in July [1991], and the
person confided to me that he'd just seen Mulroney in a
clinic in the United States. Well, I'd just seen him in
Ottawa that same day.''

In Oliver's experience, these attacks were unprece-
dented. ''The gossip about Pierre and Margaret Trudeau
was wild, but at least you could track the rumours down,
and Margaret *was* acting nuts in public. But this was
different. There was no source and we were all under
terrible pressure to do these stories on Mulroney.''

One day in late July 1991, a news crew from CJOH
television in Ottawa arrived at the gates of Harrington
Lake, the official summer residence of the prime minister. The crew told the RCMP at the gate to carry a
message to the house that they were going live on the six
o'clock news with the story that the prime minister had
checked into the Betty Ford Clinic the week before,
unless they could produce the prime minister at the
gate. Brian Mulroney was inside the house. The story
was denied. The message was sent back via the RCMP,
''Produce him or we're going on the air with the story.''
It was now fifteen minutes to news time.

Finally, Brian Mulroney called the station and asked
what they thought they were doing. The story was
dropped. Actually, a little research would have solved
the problem at the outset. The prime minister had been
seen on television news, including CJOH's own news
program, a few days earlier, during a meeting with
Ontario premier Bob Rae at Harrington Lake. The two
had been filmed walking together around the grounds.

The problem with rumours is that the victim's hands are tied. If he or she denies the allegation, the accusers claim to have touched a nerve, which ''proves'' that the story is true. If the victim doesn't fight back, the accusers can say, ''You see, she didn't say a word, so it must be true.'' Moreover, the victories and the excesses of investigative journalism have encouraged readers to believe that negative news is more likely to be true than positive news.

Maureen McTeer knows how the victim feels. ''We've had many hurtful and false things said about us. It's unfair, which you can expect in politics, but it's also untrue, which you shouldn't have to accept. It's not so much that ugliness and falseness exist. It's the glee with which people spread the ugliness and falsehoods that bothers me. People who know better go around repeating rumours to the point that the lie takes on a life of its own.''

Rumour is a valuable commodity in Ottawa, as it is in any other capital city. Important decisions are being taken and there's a lot at stake. So the political ''spin doctors'' go to work on the media, trying to put a favourable twist on the outcome. The politicians, adept at using media stories as red herrings, suggest that the problem isn't their record of government, the problem is the media communicating it. This further confuses the issues, sometimes making it hard for the media to get at the facts.

At the same time, party PR people like to march the families of politicians out into the limelight, trying to show them as squeaky-clean, with perfectly behaved children and an unblemished past. There's something hard to swallow about all that perfection, so members of the press begin to scrutinize the propaganda. Invariably they find fault with the laundered dossier on the family. The smallest eccentricity is regarded with deep suspicion, and minor discrepancies are treated as evidence of a murky past.

Soon after the Schreyers moved into Rideau Hall in 1978, there was a story in *Today Magazine* about the family. The story was a collection of put-downs, including an ugly crack about Lily Schreyer's housecoat, which, according to the reporter who was relying on comments made by the maids to someone else, was tattered. Ten years later, the Schreyer offspring still remember the slight. It seems a trivial matter, but it was the very pettiness of the remark that stung.

This bitchy reporting style has intensified to the point at which Geills Turner was described as a woman who "can make Imelda Marcos look like Mother Teresa," in a 1987 *Chatelaine* article. Geills is certainly sharp-tongued and impatient. But like all the other spouses, she seems to be lined up by the print paparazzi and set on a scale that always ranges from Mother Teresa at one end to (take your pick) Imelda Marcos, Evita Peron, or Nancy Reagan at the other.

Item: Clare Hoy was a columnist for the *Toronto Sun* when he wrote that the Mulroney children's French teacher had jumped the immigration queue because of personal interference by Mila Mulroney. He stated that she had made a call and immediately secured landed immigrant status for the teacher. Mila says it's true that

144

the teacher approached her for help. She asked Brian his advice and he said, ''Is he a good teacher?'' She said that he was. Brian felt it was appropriate to send a letter of reference, and so Mila asked Bonnie Brownlee to write to the immigration office. Nine months later, the teacher received his papers. In his file was a letter from the office of another prime minister, Pierre Trudeau, requesting help five years earlier.

''I get a dozen requests every day,'' Mila says. ''Some of them are inappropriate for me to handle, others I give to Bonnie and she responds. I think it's what anyone would do. It's just that this arena is different.''

Marjorie Nichols was a highly respected, well-known political columnist. Eight weeks before she died of cancer just after Christmas 1991, she did an interview on the business of public personalities and private lives. ''The whole world has turned on its axis in the last five years,'' she said. ''The only way to describe the political culture is everyone has become mean and ugly. It's not journalism, it's scandal-mongering. The wives, children, and husbands and the rest of the political personages are regarded as targets in the same way elected spouses are. You have the *Globe and Mail* going after Mila's spending habits and spending enormous amounts of money finding out how many times she's ripped up the carpets. Frankly, I don't care.

''There used to be limits when the press was dealing with people in public life,'' she said. In 1967, John Burns, then of the *Globe and Mail*, now of the *New York Times*, wrote that Queen Elizabeth had arrived in Canada looking pale and wearing what appeared to be a plastic hat. The newspaper was deluged with hostile letters. As Nichols remarked, "You couldn't speak the truth about the Queen even if she looked like she'd powdered her nose with flour." In 1979, Nichols wrote a column about Margaret Trudeau dancing in Studio 54 the night Pierre Trudeau lost the election, and her editor threatened to pull the column (eventually he buried it at the back of the paper) because he felt it was inappropriate to talk about the prime minister's wife that way. "All I'd said was that her behaviour was embarrassing to the prime minister."

"Now there are no limits," said Marjorie Nichols. "There's no right to privacy whatsoever for public people and that's a fact. The wives of Diefenbaker and Pearson would never have tolerated this. Maryon Pearson hated politics. She probably would have moved out."

A story told about Maryon Pearson illustrates her feelings about political life. It was the night of the 1958 Tory sweep. Apparently she had hoped that her husband would lose his own seat, since that might force him to leave political life for good. But when victory was clear she groaned, "Oh no, we've lost everything. We've even won Algoma East"—which meant her husband was going to have to continue after all.

Maryon Pearson had a drinking problem, but no one would have dared to write about it in those days. In fact, as late as 1988, when Pam Wallin (then CTV bureau chief in Ottawa) asked John Turner on television whether it was true that he had a drinking problem, there was a great hue and cry about the unfairness of the question. Wallin says she asked the question because rumours about Turner's drinking were rife on Parliament Hill, and she felt he should have a chance to quash them. Parliamentary reporters often assume that everything said on the Hill echoes across the country, but it's doubtful that the people in Revelstoke, B.C., or Sydney, Nova Scotia, would have been aware of the rumour. Mel Sufrin, the executive secretary of the Ontario Press Council, says, "By asking the question in public, she accused him." Three years later, however, when rumours about Brian Mulroney's drinking circulated, people simply passed them along.

Item: In summer 1991, even members of the media were stunned by the publication of a full-page advertisement about Caroline Mulroney in *Frank*. The headline announced a "Deflower Caroline Contest." The copy was basically an invitation to rape the seventeen-year-old girl. It even included a coupon to clip and mail as proof of conquest. Later, the editor of the paper tried to explain it away as a failed attempt at satire.

Even though the Advisory Council on the Status of Women wrote a letter of protest to the editor of the paper, there wasn't another remark made in the House of Commons by members of Parliament, or by feminist organizations across the country, or by the women, some of them in the House of Commons, who are presumably battling violence against women. "If they can do that to the prime minister's daughter—condone violence and rape on her body—what can they do to the rest of us who have no power, no Mounties to protect us?" asks Maureen McTeer.

The change in what was acceptable and what was not in reporting degenerated rapidly when magazines such as *Frank* began printing outrageous stories that continually went unchallenged. This isn't the *National Enquirer* with its celebrity diets and Elvis sightings, a tabloid that is so far-fetched that it's become a parody of itself. Nor is it like the scandal-hungry British tabloids, which are still taken seriously enough for politicians and public figures to challenge the more offensive stories. *Frank* is a curious hybrid that calls itself a magazine of satire. Although the magazine has been sued, people seem to be generally reluctant to respond to untrue allegations because of *Frank*'s capacity for mischief.

Journalists recently have done a lot of hand-wringing about "libel chill," and about how wealth seems to entitle one to privileged treatment from the press. At the same time, the line separating fair comment from libel when it applies to a politician is becoming blurred. It may no longer be financially feasible to make openly critical remarks about Albert Reichmann or Conrad Black, but it appears that you can say what you like about the prime minister and his family.

Nichols likened the Canadian press to a gang of roaming wolves. "There are exceptions, of course, but there are others whose copy you can't trust at all. They aren't looking for news. They aren't looking for information. They're looking for error, contradiction, anything they can twist to make someone look stupid and silly." One illustration of this is a photo that ran in the Canadian papers in early October 1991. The shot captured Mila with one leg in the air, her head back, laughing uproariously, unattractively. The caption read, "Mrs. Mulroney attends convocation ceremony at Stanford University in Palo Alto, California."

Seconds before the shot was taken, George Shultz had introduced Mila formally, and then he called out to the crowd, "Hey, this is a woman who's been lucky in love; look at her; she must be a Stanford girl," while trying to get her to stand up and take a bow. The 7,000 people in the audience cheered their approval. Without the story, the photo made Mila look foolish. But there isn't a news photographer who wouldn't agree that this is the kind of shot the papers want. It's the reason that people like Mila Mulroney learn to sit for long periods without moving. They know very well that one embarrassing pose or misplaced foot or mistimed remark will make the front pages.

Nichols blamed the scandal-seeking on a lazy and ill-educated media. "They'll hang out of a tree to get a photo of someone in the bathroom, but they won't go to the parliamentary library and do any research on a story," she says. And she wonders what reporters are being taught in journalism schools. "John Sawatsky wrote a book, *Mulroney: The Politics of Ambition*, that doesn't have a single footnote, and he's a journalism teacher. That wouldn't pass muster in an introduction to junior journalism, so why is this book taken seriously?"

The gap between reality and comments in the news concerns Maureen McTeer. She believes the media do not allow public figures the fair trial private citizens get. For instance, she feels that her position as a feminist was never understood by the media. She points to the major social changes that took place in the 1970s and 1980s, changes that affected not only her life but the lives of the people who were writing about her. "If they could be so wrong, such dinosaurs on issues of equality, on changes in people's relationships, when they were living those changes themselves, what are they going to do with the major changes in process we're dealing with now? We are living through a revolution in our demo-cratic institutions and in how we look at ourselves as a nation. The media are the people whose eyes these changes are filtered through. If they couldn't see the difference in how we treated women in the 1970s, I'm worried about how they'll deal with the fundamental issues at stake today."

While Mila is portrayed as the opposite of McTeer, a stay-at-home mother and stand-by-your-man wife, she suffers from the damned-if-you-do-damned-if-you-don't syndrome. When she was accused of spending too much time away from her children, she took them along to her public engagements—and was accused of using them for political gain. When she left the hospital with newborn Nicolas, she held him up to the window of the car so the photographers could get the shot they'd been waiting for. The next day's papers chastised her for not putting the baby in a car seat.

Item: Stevie Cameron wrote a column criticizing Mila for charging $5,000 to people who wanted to attend a gala fund raiser for cystic fibrosis that included a hockey game between the Edmonton Oilers and the Montreal Canadiens at the Ottawa Coliseum, cocktails at 24 Sussex Drive, and a benefit at the National Arts Centre.

Regularly priced box office tickets were also available for the game.

Stevie defended her column, saying, "A lot of charities in this country are starving and she was lending her name to some charity—multiple sclerosis or something—at $5,000 a ticket."

The Cystic Fibrosis Foundation was flabbergasted at what they saw as a mean-spirited attack. Almost every charity in the country depends on celebrities to raise funds. CF was far behind many other charities in both funding and hope for help in a deadly disease. They couldn't imagine why anyone would criticize their efforts to raise their profile.

Times for political spouses have changed. But so have the media. It used to be you could settle an argument by saying, "I read it in the newspaper." Not any more. What's off the record is suddenly on the record because someone needs a story that will sell newspapers or magazines.

This is not to suggest that the press should not cover private behaviour when it involves misuse of public funds or the privileges of the office. There's no doubt that the limelight invites a searing scrutiny and that public figures need to be prepared for the searchlights the moment they step onto the stage.

Stevie Cameron has written a lot about Mila Mulroney and says she has eighty files on her that range from the Giovanni accounts to who pays for her dry cleaning and what she does with leftover food after a party. A lot of the files have loose ends—people who won't be interviewed, denials, stories that no one will publish. Stevie says it's because people have been told not to talk. Bonnie Brownlee says it's because the stories are unfounded. Says Stevie, "People think I have a personal crusade against this woman, but that's not true. I think she's an extra-ambitious woman. She's one of the smartest women I've ever met and one of the most charming. I don't believe any of the rumours about her family—I believe she adores her husband and is a terrific wife and mother. My concern is simple. It's money. I want to know how they live like Palm Beach millionaires on the prime minister's salary."

Mila has no intention of responding to allegations about her spending. She says Brian's years at the Iron Ore Company guaranteed them financial security and that her personal spending is nobody's business but her own.

Chapter Seven

When there's a lot of protocol going on and everyone is
elbowing you out of the way to be first in line, she
steps back with me and giggles about it.

Barbara Bush

The badge read "Spouse Canada." Mila pinned it on at the Commonwealth Conference in Nassau in 1985 and proceeded with the other "spouses" to lunch. On the way, she passed through half a dozen metal-detector security checks and at each one had to dump out the contents of her purse. She smiled, obliged, and thought to herself, "This has to change." It did, when the Commonwealth Conference came to Canada two years later and Mila was charged with entertaining the spouses for the week-long program.

Although she's not prepared to play her role as "Spouse Canada" without a name, the fact is, she likes the international stage and enjoys the work it entails. And by all accounts, she's good at it. She maintains telephone contact with G-7 and Commonwealth spouses throughout the year. When a hurricane hit the home of George and Barbara Bush in Kennebunkport in fall 1991, she telephoned Barbara Bush to share her concerns. When the son of German chancellor Helmut Kohl and his wife Hannelore was seriously injured in a car accident in November 1991, she telephoned to offer her sympathy. When Sally Mugabe, the late wife of President Robert Mugabe of Zimbabwe, needed a kidney transplant, she called to find out how she could help. And then, in typical Mila fashion, she remembers to follow up, to make the next call two weeks later, to make the Mila connection stick.

She's been called everything from Mother Mila (by Nancy Reagan) to Sunshine (by Sally Mugabe) to a glamour girl (by the British press). One of her biggest fans is Barbara Bush, who says if the wives of the summit leaders were to take a vote, Mila Mulroney would get the Miss Congeniality award. "She's the most fun, the most interesting, and she's always the one who makes everyone else, especially the spouses of leaders from the Third World, feel at home. You ought to see her work one of these diplomatic crowds. She never walks by a group of women who are not entering into the conversation without trying to bring them in.

"I particularly noticed that at the Bicentennial Celebration in France, where there were women from countries all over the world attending the official functions. Some of the ones from the Third World are very shy. They huddle together and look like they really don't want to mix with people from other countries. Mila was right over there bringing them in, or bringing me over to them.

"When you're the new girl on the block, you're a little nervous in the big world of the summit. But she made me immediately feel all right. I'd met her before, of course. But when there's a lot of protocol going on and everyone is elbowing you out of the way to be first in line, she steps back with me and giggles about it. One time when we were all at the Versailles Palace, some people seemed to think it would make a difference if they were first in line. All these big shots were stepping on each other to be first. Mila was so funny, we stayed behind and laughed together. We didn't feel we had to be first.''

Mila isn't awed by the international circuit and she doesn't change her style for it. When a reporter in Zimbabwe asked her if she believed that behind every great man there is a great woman, she replied, ''In my country, we say *beside*.'' When she was asked, ''Have you always been interested in politics?'' Mila answered, ''Yes, even before I met my husband.'' And at the Geological Survey Offices in Harare, when the man guiding her through the rock samples said, ''Your husband would know a lot about this,'' she quickly replied, ''Our whole family knows a lot about this.''

Mila has had dozens of entertaining experiences on the international circuit. There was the time in Nassau at the Commonwealth Conference in 1985, when the motorcade left her behind on the sidewalk. (They returned a few seconds later when they realized she wasn't in the car.)

In Harare, Zimbabwe, the car she was in kept getting hopelessly lost (the driver was from Zambia and didn't know the area). One morning, when she was on her way to visit a children's hospital, the chauffeur got so confused that he eventually had to park the car at the side of a dirt road in the country. Mila sat in the back seat making small talk with the ambassador's wife, as the driver shouted into a two-way radio that the "city" was lost. The RCMP responded and, like air traffic controllers, kept him on the radio while they gave him directions and brought him in to the hospital.

At the survey office in Harare she had to cut a ribbon to officially open the new Martin Konings Work Station, a laboratory named after a Canadian scientist who had died in a car crash the year before. Since there had to be a dozen official photos, she ended up holding the ribbon, which had already been cut, together with her fingers. She quipped to the dignitary beside her, "Really, the things you have to do in this job."

The Boeing 707 the Mulroneys fly on is also the source of many stories. The inside temperatures are impossible to control, the fittings are ancient, and it is often delayed for repairs. It even leaks. On one flight, the prime minister was sitting in the forward compartment working with government documents when water started dripping from the ceiling all over him and his papers.

The plane usually carries forty or fifty people: the prime minister and his family members, advisers, aides, staff, and Mounties take up about twenty-five places; the other passengers are journalists. There are two forward compartments. One is fitted with two single beds, two seating areas for eating or working, and a bathroom for Brian and Mila, and a second has chairs and tables for the staff and advisers. The rest of the plane is fitted with regular seats. At the back there is a bar and a table with fruit and chocolate bars on it. The decor reflects the vintage of the plane: the brown and blue fabric on the seats recalls the early 1960s, as do the noise and pollution level. In fact, the government of

Canada must secure special permission for the plane to land at civilian airports because of the noise and air pollution it causes.

On most flights, the prime minister likes to wander back and chat off the record to the journalists, but Mila usually stays in the cabin in front. Five crew members serve average airline meals.

On one occasion, Brian and Mila were flying home from a state visit to Germany with the staff from the Prime Minister's Office and members of the media. A sudden noise in the cabin scared PMO staffer Anne Marie Doyle almost out of her seat. The steward came by, looked out the window (which scared her even more), and announced, ''It's probably a change in temperature, which would change the pressure in the cabin.'' He didn't sound very convincing. A few minutes later, he returned and said, ''If you notice the plane is a bit jerky, don't worry. The automatic pilot is broken.'' Doyle vowed she'd never fly on the government 707 again.

The Challenger aircraft isn't much better. On one flight, the handle to the bathroom door fell off and every time the prime minister (or anyone else) used the bathroom, the staff had to stand by and use a letter knife to reopen the door. The telephone doesn't work either. Passengers on Air Canada flights can use a telephone, but the prime minister of Canada cannot.

According to Hugh Segal, the prime minister's chief of staff, Air Force One, the plane used by the president of the United States when Ronald Regan was in office, was noise-polluting, vapour-polluting and unsafe at any speed. ''The last thing Ronald Reagan did before he left office was order a new plane for George Bush. Reagan knew Bush's presidency could not stand the heat from the public over such an expenditure. And he knew Air Force One needed to be retired. Since he was leaving office he felt he could absorb the public outcry. So George Bush has a thoroughly modern Air Force One.''

Despite the inconveniences of the plane, the rest of the arrangements are first class. If the Department of Health and Welfare deems their destination to be one that could pose a health problem, there is always enough plasma for the prime minister and Mila, their staff, and the media on board, in case of an injury in which a blood transfusion is required. Bottled water is provided for them by the embassies when they are visiting countries that don't use the same water purification system as Canada. And there is usually a doctor on board for long trips.

Mila's wardrobe for these trips is carefully coordinated and packed. She likes to have a different outfit for each day of the trip. Although she prefers to stay in the same ensemble all day, she often has to change into a long gown or cocktail dress for evening events. That requires shoes and bags to match each outfit. She also takes several coats, as no one can be sure of the weather. At the Francophonie summit in Paris, she needed a winter coat as well as a rain coat, since the temperature was changeable in late November. Her luggage includes two large suitcases, two large tote bags, and wardrobe bags to hang her dresses in.

Although the prime minister doesn't sleep on the plane, Mila does. He suffers from jet lag, she doesn't. She credits her good fortune to drinking lots of water to avoid dehydration and exercising when she arrives. Even if it's been an all-night flight, when they arrive in the early morning, Mila goes fast walking.

They usually stay in five-star hotels, paid for by the host country. They stay at the Plaza Athenée in Paris or the Inn on the Park in London. Occasionally they stay at the residence of the ambassador, as they did in Zimbabwe, or in a government house, as they did in Moscow.

Although their hosts try to make sure that their reservations are perfect, from time to time, unforeseen problems crop up. When they were in Speyer, Germany, they were booked into a hotel next to an ancient cathedral. The village square outside was gorgeous. Unfortunately, the cathedral bells rang every half hour throughout the night. The prime minister didn't sleep a wink. Mila said the next morning that she had fallen asleep, but Brian woke her up when he couldn't sleep because he wanted someone to talk to.

Occasionally the arrangements made to honour the Mulroneys' arrival are a little alarming. In one small nation, the plane was greeted by a ragtag band of men in uniforms with loaded guns. The display of military might was rather disorganized and some journalists wondered whether the Mulroneys should take the salute or hit the dirt to avoid a stray bullet. Brian was ushered into a bullet-proof car with the head of state, and Mila got into another one with his wife. The motorcade raced through the streets with sirens wailing, past soldiers with machine guns at every street corner. Mila swallowed her apprehensions, smiled, and concentrated on asking polite questions.

The programs for the spouses at international meetings usually include a tour of the city, luncheons, and fashion shows. Mila tends to add to or substitute for the planned activities with her own priorities. She is there primarily to support her husband, and when the program excludes her from an important event, she insists that changes be made. At the opening of the Francophonie summit in 1991, Brian was due to give a speech, but Mila had been left off the guest list. It took a few phone calls that morning, but when Brian Mulroney stood up to give the opening address, Mila was sitting in the first row.

She also visits the local cystic fibrosis association if there is one, and looks for events in areas that interest her, such as literacy. Acting on behalf of bureaucrats at home, she may present a cheque or deliver a gift from a Canadian organization. In Zimbabwe, for example, she presented thirty pairs of binoculars to a group of children at an environmental awareness centre. The ceremony went off without a hitch. But when it was over, the binoculars were still sitting on the table and a roomful of kids were eyeing them. The centre was out in the country on an animal reserve, and Mila wanted to take the kids to the lookout to try out the new binoculars. It had been raining. A trip to the lookout wasn't on the agenda. But Mila prevailed.

Mila, the dignitaries, and the children sloshed along a muddy path to the lookout. When they arrived, the view was magnificent. Two elephants were taking a sand bath (sucking sand up with their trunks and blowing it over their backs to get rid of ticks) and a herd of zebra were running across the fields. It was a satisfied, if somewhat mud-splashed, Spouse Canada who said goodbye to the children and returned to her waiting car that day.

Her trips also include arranged visits to local artisans. Silversmiths, furniture makers, and antique dealers are always happy to stay open when she comes to visit. But her major shopping trips are in the cities.

Although Mila loves Paris, her favourite city for sight-seeing, eating and shopping is New York. She feels it's the most cosmopolitan city she knows. It's only an hour from Ottawa, she can go down there and be anony-mous, but at the same time she can visit the art gal-leries, theatres, shops, and restaurants she loves.

Part of Mila's international role is to encourage, pro-mote, and publicize charities, institutions, and projects that she feels she can lend support to. For instance, in Harare at the Commonwealth Summit of 1991, she visited the Jairos Jiri Handicap Centre.

When her motorcade pulled off the Northway Road in Prospect Waterfalls, about an hour's drive from Harare, she was met by Chiwanda Mira, the director of the centre, who was standing in a yard criss-crossed with clotheslines covered with tiny pieces of coloured cloth. The children had cut the bits of cloth and hung them on the line as a sign of "happy greeting" to Mila. They were surprised and pleased that she'd travel so far out of her way to see them.

Sandra Bassett, whose husband, Charles, is the Ca-nadian ambassador to Zimbabwe, had written to Mila about the centre and the brave work they were doing and had suggested the visit. The only centre of its kind in Zimbabwe, it is home to twenty-eight disabled children between the ages of two and eight. It contains dormitories as well as an exercise and therapy room and a classroom. Fifteen non-handicapped children from Prospect Waterfalls also attend the school.

Inside, the place is dark, so dark it's hard to see. There is little equipment. The children have made their own walkers out of papier mâché. The wooden tables they sit at for meals have semicircles hand-carved along each side so that they can swing themselves into the table and sit without falling over. The two dormitories have child-sized cots, seven lined up on each side of the room.

Most of the children have cerebral palsy, many of them are mentally disabled, and some are totally immobile. The children come from all over the country and are referred by urban and rural doctors regardless of family income. In an against-all-odds situation, the staff are making remarkable progress with their tiny charges.

Mila walked among the meagre furnishings in the house to the playroom where the children were waiting for their visitor from Canada. She looked very white in this room, her chic suit and sparkling jewels setting her apart. But she plunged in, using hand and facial gestures to bridge the language barrier. When she says hello to children, she often extends both arms to them and bends her hand at the knuckle as though she's squeezing a tennis ball with straight fingers.

The kids responded enthusiastically. One of them used his walker to move across the room and stand beside Mila. Another slid along the floor on her hips to lean against her. When she said goodbye, twenty-eight little pairs of hands mimicked her distinctive wave.

Outside the centre, Mila looked at the therapy pool, a large swimming pool used for exercising children with damaged, withered limbs and swollen joints. But the pool was covered for the season.

"How can it be out of use when it's supposed to be so useful?" Mila asked. Chiwanda Mira explained that the rainy season was beginning, and although the daytime temperature heats up to thirty-four degrees Celsius, Zimbabwe is sixteen thousand metres above sea level, so everything cools off rapidly in the evening, making the water too cold for the children to have therapy. The rainy season would last for four to five months.

Mila suggested they put a roof over the pool. Mrs. Mira told her that it would cost the equivalent of $25,000 Canadian to do the job. Mila said quietly, "Are you telling me that for twenty-five thousand dollars those kids could have double the therapy? This is ridiculous."

Mila is not the sort of woman to helplessly wring her hands about the plight of these children. She's action-oriented. On the drive back to Harare, she was quiet. Planning who to call. Back at the residence of the Canadian ambassador where she and Brian were staying, she made a few notes before joining Sandra Bassett for tea. Three days later, just before her departure from Harare, Mila secured the funds for the roof from CIDA, the Canadian International Development Agency. She presented the cheque for $25,000 to Mrs. Mira at the Canadian embassy.

People are often amazed at the way children take to Mila. The secret to her success is that she understands kids and what makes them afraid of or attracted to a stranger. When she toured the children's ward at the Harare Hospital, she dressed in a bright green and white dress with big red spots on it. She had two chubby gold frog brooches pinned to her collar. At one point, however, when she approached a little boy, he began to cry. She knows when to approach and when to leave children alone. ''I move toward the child once. If there's no response, I move again. If the child doesn't react to me on the second move, I stay away. You can tell if a child is afraid.''

Mila walked through the ward trying to keep a cheerful face. But the overcrowding appalled her. Babies were two to a crib, and some were on mattresses on the floor. About half of the children in this ward had fractured limbs, but there was no equipment for traction, so the kids lay on beds tipped up at one end, with their limbs tied to a stick at the end of the bed. Their own body weight acts as the traction, keeping the limb straight while it heals. Kids with gaping wounds and kids with AIDS shared space with children who had tracheal and abdominal infections.

Mila would have liked to be able to tell the hospital staff that a cheque for $5 million for a new children's hospital was on its way, but she couldn't. The announcement would have hurt her husband politically, because on the same day he'd been criticized for giving funds to African nations with poor human rights records. So the news had to wait until the following week, when Foreign Affairs Minister Barbara McDougall presented the cheque to the administrators of the hospital under a slightly less glaring spotlight.

Although the international spotlight is more intense than the one at home, it sometimes sheds a more sympathetic light. When Mila visited the refugee camps in Malaysia while attending the Commonwealth Summit in Kuala Lumpur in October 1989, several reporters went along to write about the visit. Mila had asked to visit the camp of seven thousand Vietnamese refugees who lived behind high barbed wire fences. The reporters expected she would arrive at the camp in her usual array of diamonds and designer clothes. They thought the display of wealth would be inappropriate.

Mila didn't change her style of dress for the visit. But she was obviously moved by the plight of the camp's residents. They crowded around her from the moment she arrived, and she was nearly mobbed by children waving Canadian and Malaysian flags. They told her through a translator of their experiences crossing the treacherous China Sea: being robbed at sea by pirates, or watching their loved ones die of illnesses or drown in storms.

Robert Fife, the Ottawa bureau chief for the *Toronto Sun*, wrote of the visit: ''Mila Mulroney is often derided at home as a lavish spender. But the thousands of Vietnamese boat people that lined the Sungai Besi refugee camps don't care about her reputation as a clothes horse. To them, Mila is a symbol of a country that has opened its heart to more than 32,000 boat people from Malaysian refugee camps alone since 1975. A small group of often cynical reporters who accompanied Mila to this refugee camp yesterday were proud to be Canadians.''

Mila was supposed to tour the camp and meet some of the people. At first, that's all she did. She shook hands with the adults and picked up the children to hug them. They smiled back at her and clapped as she walked through the squalid surroundings in sweltering heat. Then she walked into the open-walled dining room; more than a thousand people jammed in after her. Blinking away the dust blowing in from the dirt walkways, she started to talk. "I'm pleased that every year we accept more refugees, but it is still not enough. We're going to do more."

There was a brief pause while her comments were translated into Vietnamese. Then the crowd broke into thunderous applause and cheers. Says Robert Fife, "Mila, fighting back tears, was left speechless and so were the reporters. The pomp and circumstance of the Commonwealth Conference paled into insignificance."

Protocol at international conferences is very important to all concerned. It's also, on occasion, the source of some amusement to Mila. At one evening event being held in a garden while they were in Kuala Lumpur, Mila decided to wear a new silk scarf over her shoulders. She explains that the scarf was definitely too expensive and that she really shouldn't have bought it, but she couldn't resist. The sultan of Brunei, one of the richest men in the world, was there with the younger of his two wives. The young woman complimented Mila on her scarf, telling her it was the loveliest scarf she had ever seen. Mila thanked her for her generous comments and was about to move on, when to her astonishment the woman asked, "Can I have it?" Mila, realizing she had no choice, handed over the scarf.

On the last night of the October 1991 visit of the Prince and Princess of Wales to Ottawa, staff members wondered if a similar incident was about to occur. There had been a black-tie gala at the National Arts Centre for twenty-two hundred guests. A dinner party for forty at 24 Sussex Drive followed, with guests that included David Foster and his wife Linda Thompson Foster, Michael J. Fox and Tracy Pollan, Allan Thicke, Rich Little, Céline Dion, and André-Philippe Gagnon.

When it was time for the royal couple to leave for the airport, staff members heard Diana say, ''My coat was sent ahead to the plane. I'm going to be cold.'' Mila immediately reached into the closet and pulled out a black mohair wrap. ''Here,'' she said. ''Put this on, you'll be warm.''

Suddenly a voice from the back of the crowd wailed, ''That's *mine*.'' The voice (and the wrap) belonged to Lady Anne Beckwith Smith, the lady-in-waiting to the Princess of Wales. Someone else might have been horrified by the faux pas, but not Mila. Leaving the wrap for Diana to return to her lady-in-waiting, she said, ''Wait right here.'' She raced up the stairs two at a time and returned with a black velvet double-breasted coat of her own (she and Diana are about the same height). She helped the Princess into the coat and said, ''There, you'll be all right now.'' Diana murmured, ''Ah, I may keep this.''

At the airport, journalists who had seen Mila in the black velvet coat before, asked if the princess was wearing Mila's coat. A staff member said she was and wondered if the coat was about to go the way of the silk scarf in Kuala Lumpur. Moments after the royal couple boarded the plane (the same one that flies the prime minister around the world), the coat was returned.

When the Mulroneys arrived back at 24 Sussex, they abandoned protocol for the rest of the evening. A few of the guests were still there, and Brian immediately suggested a sing-song. David Foster played the piano. Céline Dion, Linda Thompson, André-Philippe Gagnon, Allan Thicke, and Mila sang back-up. And Brian, the crooner, led the group in golden oldies such as ''Shine on Harvest Moon.'' When the singing was over, Allan Thicke remarked, ''I learned something new tonight. The prime minister of Canada works so hard he hasn't had the radio on in thirty years.''

The Mulroneys' travels to the summits and international conferences have given them the chance to establish personal relationships with world leaders. The Bushes and the Mulroneys met while George Bush was vice-president. ''We were instant friends,'' says Barbara Bush about Mila. ''I'm old enough to be her mother, and yet I feel like a great friend of hers. That's a wonderful quality she has.'' She says their friendship is also based on the fact that they agree on so many things. ''We both adore our husbands and neither of us feels insecure because our husbands' lives are a large part of our lives.''

Barbara Bush feels that the spouse of a head of state must represent her or his country. ''And Mila presents Canada very well, especially artists and writers and certainly fashion designers. She's a great salesman for Canada.''

Barbara Bush has her own perspective on the job she and Mila Mulroney do. ''On the positive side, you get to meet everyone you want to in the world. Writers, artists, musicians, and people you admire will come when you invite them. You meet heads of state from all around the world. If they aren't extraordinary, good, wise, and kind, they are at least extraordinary. You get the best of the world. I also think you feel you can make a difference by helping to feed the hungry or take care of people who are suffering. I think that's one of the best parts of this job.

"The worst part, and I suspect it's harder for Mila, because my children are older, is when your family, your children are hurt. Our boy Neil was really persecuted. After a lengthy trial [for fraud while he was president of Silverado Banking, Savings and Loan Company, which went bankrupt] he was found guilty of bad judgement. It cost a lot of money and caused a lot of problems. It took his job, his house. That hurts. Anything that hurts your children hurts you. So I think when you are the mother of teenagers, it has to be difficult in public life because you really have to protect your children."

For Barbara Bush's predecessor, the spotlight has been even more difficult to bear. "It's a high and very hurtful price you have to pay to be in politics," says Nancy Reagan. She feels that Mila "can probably take it in her stride. It hurts, though. To live in the public eye is never easy, but she does it extremely well."

Another couple the Mulroneys became friends with are George and O'bie Shultz. George and Brian met briefly in the 1970s when Brian was on the Cliche Commission and the company George was running in the States was doing construction work at the Baie James project in Quebec. Shultz says, "He was playing a

critical role in stabilizing things and I had a little ac-
quaintance with him on that account.''

Almost a dozen years later, President Ronald Reagan
sent Secretary of State George Shultz to Canada to try to
improve relations with the neighbour to the north.
''That's when I met Mila,'' George says. ''She's such an
asset to him. She's beautiful, outgoing, capable, engag-
ing with people, and it shines through.'' At a dinner
party they had when Brian and Mila visited Palo Alto,
California, where George is now a professor, Mila sat
opposite two Nobel laureates, one a chemist, the other
a physicist. ''Mila immediately plunged right into the
conversation,'' Shultz remembers. ''She's sort of fearless that way. Things strike her and she's curious and
interested and she sails right into it. She followed the
conversation very closely, she engaged the intellectuals
on subjects that ranged from developments in chemis-
try to the problems facing Yugoslavia. She's a person
who makes an effort to understand what's going on. I'm
very impressed with her.''

The characteristic that really won George Shultz's admiration was the way Brian and Mila keep track of the
people they care about and take note of the events in
their lives. ''When I was testifying at the Iran-Contra
hearings in 1987, I received a telephone call from them
one night. They said they'd been watching the proceed-
ings on television and just wondered how I was getting
along. That's typical of them. They give out credit and
remember you. Every so often, I'll hear from them because something has happened that is related to something I had worked on, something important to me.''

Nancy Reagan treasures her friendship with Mila Mulroney. She says Mila has bailed her out on more than one occasion at international events because "she speaks French and several other languages and can understand what the others are saying." She says they have the sort of friendship that can go years without contact and "then we get on the phone and it's as though no time has passed at all, as though we left off yesterday. We always seem to have so much to talk about—children, families—you know, all the things women talk about.

"Mila is the sort of woman who knows what is real and what isn't. She handles everything very well. I don't think it's a skill you can learn. You can learn a certain amount, maybe, but a sixth sense is something else. Either you have it or you don't."

Mila plunges into a crowd or a conversation because she wants to, because she's good at it and she isn't easily embarrassed by slips or faux pas. Perhaps as the youngest of the international "spouses" she knows she will be indulged and forgiven for the odd lapse.

Her first solo outing on the diplomatic scene was to the First Ladies' Conference on Drug Abuse held at the White House in April 1985, when she was thirty-one. It was quite a performance—seventeen "first ladies" attended (although Mila explained to the others that the governor general, if a woman, or the governor general's wife, is Canada's first lady). Many of them came from drug-producing countries, such as Bolivia, Jamaica, and Mexico. This was Nancy Reagan's opportunity to showcase her "Just Say No" campaign and to offer support to the other countries so that they could adopt her program and begin drug education for their citizens.

How would "Mulroney from Canada" respond, the international press wanted to know. After all, Canada had had drug education programs since 1971. How could Mila Mulroney accept Nancy Reagan's idea as a new one? On the other hand, how could Mila insult her by refusing the offer?

Mila handled the situation with aplomb, thanking Nancy Reagan for inviting her, applauding her for her efforts to tackle a difficult issue, describing the Canadian program, and acknowledging that the problem was not easy to solve.

Suddenly the international gathering of reporters wanted to know every titbit about Mila—her dress size, her height, weight, the origin of her name. They'd watched her in action at the discussion table and noticed the combination of sensitivity and practicality which allows her to be emotionally giving and at the same time politically astute.

Although she almost always attracts attention when she travels to a foreign country, the trip to London, England, for the G-7 summit in July 1991 turned her into a celebrity. All seven daily newspapers featured her on the front page almost every day of the week-long conference. The headlines screamed: "Mila: Smashing in Yellow." "Gee! It's Mila with a Show of Fashion Power." "Glamour Girl Mila Plays the Diplomat." "Mila Is the Summit of Style." She put on a dazzling display of haute couture, and the newspapers called her "Brian's chic wife who stole the show."

Helen Fielding wrote in the *Sunday Times*, "Picture the scene in Downing Street. It was the start of the G-7 summit and the world's hacks were assembled for a photocall of the 'G-7 spouses' as they were officially dubbed. They were in a frenzy, worrying about how to distinguish one politely dressed middle-aged lady from another. Finally the spouses appeared all together. And a voice piped up from the throng, as if speaking for us all: 'Who is that stunning woman next to Norma [Major]?' "

The paparazzi went crazy, snapping up photos and following her around. Caroline, who had accompanied her mother, was pestered at the hotel when reporters called there wanting to do a story on her too. They asked if she was jealous of her mom, who was getting all the attention. She refused the interviews and wondered how they'd managed to get her telephone number.

Mila says, "It wasn't pleasant. I felt like a prisoner in my hotel. They were downstairs waiting for me at the front and back doors. Caroline and I couldn't go out for a walk, we couldn't be tourists, we couldn't do the normal things people do in a city." But she did manage one solo outing. Ignoring the photographers lurking in the hotel lobby, she tied her hair up in a pony tail, put on a head band, her jogging clothes, and a pair of dark glasses and went out fast walking. She strutted right past the photographers in the lobby without being recognized. One of the PMO staff remarked, "That's Mila Mulroney. Playing with fire. And never getting caught."

By the time Mila left London, the papers summed her up this way: "International power dresser Mila Mulroney emerged last night as the undisputed star of the G-7

summit wives' fashion stakes. She strode into the limelight at Buckingham Palace wearing a ritzy lace and
satin gown with a dazzling smile to match. But the
world's youngest and most glamorous First Lady had
already grabbed the spotlight on the day she arrived in
her Chanel suits and mini skirts."

The British papers dwelt heavily on the shopaholic
angle, and reckoned she'd spent more than $200,000 on
her summit wardrobe, citing her Chanel bags, her Bulgari
jewellery, her love for Ralph Lauren, Gucci, and French
designers. The *Sunday Express* even did a full-page story
describing the wives and estimating the cost of their
ensembles. They estimated one of Mila's outfits at £5,000,
contrasting it to Norma Major's "recession chic" (£380),
Hannelore Kohl's German elegance (£1,500), and Sahiyo
Kaifu's "minimalist" stylishness (£800).

Not even close, says Mila. The dress and jacket she
was wearing cost about $800 Canadian when she
bought them. The fake amber bracelets she wore that
day were from Bulgari and cost $100. However, the
Chanel purse she carried was $1,000, expensive indeed.
Still, the total for her outfit was nowhere near the
$10,000 estimated by the wags on Fleet Street.

Mila was amused by their conclusions, but says, "I'm
sorry to disappoint them, but I don't walk into a Montreal couturier and say, 'I'll have a week of clothing for
the summit, please.' " In fact, the only new piece of
clothing she had at the G-7 was an evening gown from
Holt Renfrew that she paid $1,500 for. The rest of her
wardrobe had not only been worn before, it had all been
photographed before, some of it three months before,
some of it two years before, some of it seven years before.

The glitter of the international stage doesn't seem to turn Mila's head. According to Madeleine Roy, wife of Brian Mulroney's former chief of staff, during a visit to Paris, "I was going to get my hair done one afternoon. Mila said, 'Are you crazy? It'll take the whole afternoon and cost you a fortune. Go put on your bathrobe. I'll do it.' She washed it and we sat in her room while she styled and dried my hair. When she was finished she said, 'Go look in the mirror, you look gorgeous. And think of all the money I saved you.' "

Staying put in the hotel room is not only easy (and inexpensive in Madeleine's case), it's often the only way to avoid the complications of security. When the Mulroneys travel, they must respect the security considered necessary for them by the host country, whether they're there on business or a holiday. In the United States, secret service agents are assigned to them (the Mounties who accompany them, to the RCMP's annoyance, aren't allowed to carry guns in the United States). When they vacation in Florida, the secret service sets up camp outside their house or hotel in a black van called the war wagon.

The fuss is so intense, it's often difficult for the Mulroneys to rent accommodation in Florida, as neighbours complain about the oppressive security. Simply leaving the house or the hotel becomes a complicated operation. One night when they went out to a movie in Jupiter, Florida, there were eight secret service men sitting in the row behind them. After that, they decided to rent videos and watch them at home. For the same reason, they tend to order in instead of going out to dine.

There's something camp-like about doing this job. You have to be a good sport and a participant. You have to get along with a lot of people you didn't know before. And, if you're married to Brian Mulroney, you even have to sing campfire songs occasionally.

On the plane on the way home from Zimbabwe, Mila entertained the passengers with a recently acquired skill. It was a staff member's birthday, so a cake had been prepared. Everyone was clapping, except Mila. Earlier that day she had attended a literacy event women had put on in Harare. Every time one of the women shared her accomplishment with the group, they would all break into an African-style cheer. The women ululate, making a noise almost like a bird call. During the day, Mila had watched them intently and several times commented that she wished she could do it. Clearly she had been practising, because during the birthday celebration in the plane she gave the gathering a whoop they won't soon forget. (She can also put her fingers between her teeth and let out a whistle so shrill, her kids say she could stop a train.)

The kids come along on some occasions when she pins on her "Spouse Canada" tag. But usually they stay at home. She calls them every day and tries to stay up to date with the important events in their lives. But she's aware of the cost to her and to them of her being away so much. Invariably, when the Boeing 707 taxis to a halt at Uplands Airport in Ottawa, Caroline and one, two, or all three boys are there to meet their parents. They scramble up the stairs into the private cabin at the front of the plane. When they emerge, they're all talking at once, trading stories, ready to go home together.

Chapter Eight

*I used to love to read about myself in the paper. Now
when I open it up, I just hope there's nothing bad in it.*
                                                    Benedict Mulroney

At eleven o'clock on a Sunday night at Harrington
Lake, Caroline Mulroney realized that she'd left
her paints at school. Caroline's art assignment was due
in the morning, and she couldn't finish it without the
paints. The class had been told to create a cartoon about
any subject they liked. Caroline had done twelve vignettes about a boy and his grandfather who were being
punished for not doing what they'd promised to do.
She'd finished the drawings, but when she reached for
her paint set, it wasn't in her school bag. And she was
stuck in the country on a freezing cold night in February
1988.

When her mother went into her room to say goodnight, she found a very distraught Caroline worrying
about her homework. Caroline felt it was bad enough
that the work was crude and amateurish—she com-
plains that she inherited her father's genes in art—but
that it couldn't even be painted meant she was sure to
get low marks for not having finished the project.

Mila turned the house upside down looking for paints. She checked every drawer of the old cottage. She woke the boys to check their rooms for anything Caroline could use, but to no avail. Finally she went into the attic where she keeps half a dozen old trunks filled with the children's toys and memorabilia from their bedrooms on Belvedere Road in Montreal.

There are bats and mice in the attic of the Harrington Lake house, and in the winter months it's unbearably cold up there. But Mila climbed the narrow stairs and crawled around the rafters in her nightgown, searching through trunks of Barbie dolls and Tonka toys for the strips of paints she was certain she'd stored there. At last, in trunk number four, she found several strips and a few small paint brushes. She returned triumphantly to Caroline's room.

At one o'clock in the morning, Mila checked on Caroline again, to find that she'd painted only two of the twelve vignettes. Mila told Caroline in no uncertain terms that it was much too late for a thirteen-year-old to be awake. Exhausted, Caroline started to cry and protested that she had to finish the assignment. Mila was adamant. Caroline went to bed. Then Mila went to work. When Caroline woke up the next morning, the cartoon was propped up on her desk, finished.

Caroline left Harrington Lake for the drive to school feeling particularly happy. It wasn't just that she knew she'd pass her art assignment. It was knowing that although her parents are away a lot and they're extraordinarily busy when they are at home, when she needed her, her mother was there for her.

Garth Pritchard

"I used to think that if people were coming over, the baby should be upstairs," says Brian. "But Mila said, 'No, our children have to be used to being around people.'"

Andy Clark

"The Conservative backroom boys watched her the way farmers watch a spring crop, wondering what the harvest will bring. Early on, the consensus was that Mila would be an enormous asset to the party."

"Mila wanted to eradicate the stereotyping of the political wife. She felt that leaders' spouses were almost prisoners of people's expectations."

"Whether she's at a head table, a conference table, or a cocktail party, Mila's expressive face gives her personality away."

Bill McCarthy

Bill McCarthy

With Mark at the David Foster Celebrity softball game in 1989. ''Her choices about the kinds of events she and Brian get involved in haven't always been shared by the people around Brian.'' Inset: time out with Nicolas.

Bill McCarthy

''To live in the public eye is never easy, but Mila does it extremely well.'' Nancy Reagan

Bill McCarthy

''I'm old enough to be her mother, and yet I feel like a great friend of hers.'' Barbara Bush

Entertaining royalty is all part of the job: with the Prince and Princess of Wales (above) and the Duchess of York (below)

Andy Clark

Wherever she goes, children seem to gravitate towards her. Visiting schoolchildren in Nassau during a Commonwealth Conference in 1985, and meeting refugees at the Sungi Besi transit camp in Kuala Lumpur in 1989.

Bill McCarthy

The travelling never stops. Mila and Brian share their delight at an anniversary card from their children on a flight between Hong Kong and Tokyo (top). Mila, Brian, Caroline, and Benedict on a helicopter flight in Ireland (bottom).

"Mila is a very hands-on parent, constantly correcting, showing, teaching, reminding."
With Mark (above) and Nicolas (below).

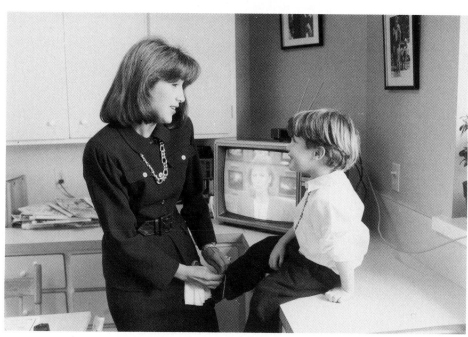

Mila has a particularly close relationship with her daughter, Caroline, whom she calls Lali.

The children lean on each other for support. As Mark puts it: ''Nico has me, I have Ben, Ben has Caroline, Caroline has Mom, and we all have Dad.'' Ben is holding Nicolas; Mark stands in front of Caroline.

Mila with John and Julia Herbert. Julia was the Cystic Fibrosis poster child in 1988. She died in April of that year, aged thirteen.

Mila and members of the Pivnicki family. Beside Mila is John's wife Manuela, with Ben behind her and Nico in front. Caroline has her arms around Mita. Brian is standing behind Mark and Boba, and John is on the right.

Mila with Bonnie Brownlee, her assistant, and Irene Mulroney, waiting for Brian, who has been caught in a media scrum after a speech in the House.

Bill McCarthy

Bill McCarthy

In Brian's office in Centre Block on Parliament Hill. ''They share information, trade compliments, reinforce their bond.''

Mila chats to Nico just before going out for an early-morning fast walk. ''So many people have been cajoled into walking with her that she says she'll get T-shirts made with 'Bodies by Mila' written across the front.''

''She calls him her buddy. He calls her a teenager. She quips back, 'That's why I married you. You're so much older than me, I'll be forever young.'''

At Baie-Comeau on election night, 1988. Brian says, ''I would never have won the leadership without her. I mean that in crass, vote-counting terms.''

Mila makes no bones about the fact that Brian is her number-one priority, but the children come ahead of everyone else but him. ''I never choose the children over Brian. There is no second-guessing. There is a pecking order. This is a commitment we've made. I'm not saying I don't feel guilty. We've missed piano recitals, but someone attends in our place. We go to parent-teacher meetings, but the principal schedules all the teachers at once.

''When I get home at night, I always go up to their rooms to see them. I don't think a single working mother doesn't feel guilt on a regular basis. I'm this committed because I'm married to someone who's doing something very important.''

The children of immigrants are often raised with great expectations, since they have opportunities their parents missed. Mila has always had high expectations for her children, and she was determined to realize them. Nothing was too much for her to do for them. They would be schooled in social graces and benefit from international experiences. They would have the love of an extended family. They would learn early and well the value of doing your best and being your best.

While their neighbours in Westmount were registering their children for private school education at The Study and ECS and Selwyn House, Mila and Brian were investigating French schools, looking for one with a curriculum they approved of. Their children would be bilingual, well taught, and exposed to children from around the world, not just other rich kids. They would meet children from various cultures who spoke several languages and who had plans for the future. Children, in fact, like the child Milica Pivnicki had been. She drove across the city to the suburb of St. Laurent to check out Notre Dame de Sion, a school that had a reputation for solid French-language education. She sat in on classes and interviewed the principal. Eventually she chose Villa Ste. Marceline for Caroline and Notre Dame de Sion for Ben. Later, in Ottawa, all four children attended the Lycée Claudel.

Mila is a very hands-on parent, constantly correcting, showing, teaching, reminding. "Mark-o, fix your hair. Caroline, if you arrange the crudités this way, they look nicer. Ben, don't put your desk under your window—the room doesn't look right that way. Nico, we don't use words like 'I can't.' " When she really wants to get her children's attention, she switches to Serbo-Croatian and makes her point with a little more gusto. When she is travelling with Brian, she calls the children every day and expects a full report of their comings and goings. Even from the other side of the Atlantic, she is instructing them, polishing their behaviour, guiding their decisions.

She gets involved in whatever her children are doing. On Halloween, first Mark and then Nico stood in her peach-coloured bathroom while she dipped into paints and blushes and creams and created the Grim Reaper for Mark and Captain Planet for Nicolas. She's the sort of mother who always has the materials for a project (who else keeps white face paint for goblins in the bathroom drawer beside the Chanel cream?) and the imagination to improvise.

On another occasion, the night after the 1988 election, when both Brian and Mila had collapsed into bed exhausted, Caroline crept into their room and in a sheepish voice said she had an English essay due the next day and needed some help. Her mother started to read it. After a while, she nudged Brian and said, "Here, correct this sentence." He sat up and helped out, suggesting Caroline add more information here and there. Two hours later the essay was finished. And the prime minister of Canada went back to sleep.

At the same time, Mila is a no-nonsense mother. When the family moved to Ottawa, Caroline was enrolled in the Lycée. It was tough at first for a nine-year-old to get used to a new school, a Parisian accent that she was unaccustomed to, and a classroom full of kids she didn't know. "I felt totally lost," says Caroline. "Later on in the year I started faking sick a lot so I could go home from school. Mom finally said, 'Look, we're going to be in Ottawa for a while. You're not sick. You don't have to go back to school today. But I want this to stop.' I stopped."

Mila is also quick to correct inappropriate language or comments. One afternoon when the kids returned from school, they gathered in the sunroom at 24 Sussex to catch up on each other's day. Caroline complained about a teacher who, she said, "just got off the boat." Mila reacted immediately. "Now wait a minute. Watch the way you describe that man." She never forgets that she was once an immigrant and she won't let her children forget, either.

Not all children would adapt to this kind of parenting. Someone else's kids might consider Mila's approach interfering. They might rebel or sulk or refuse to fall in with their parents' plans. Not the Mulroney kids. They adore the woman who acts like a head coach and expects a world-class performance from her team. ''We can talk about anything with her,'' Caroline says. And she quips, ''At the dinner table we talk about sex, boyfriends or girlfriends—as long as Dad isn't there.'' Caroline wonders if she can ever match her mother's energy and style. Ben says, ''She's as close to perfect as a parent can be.'' Mark, the irrepressible Mulroney, calls his mother a star.

The kids are invariably included in whatever their parents are doing. As a new father, Brian may have thought that the arrival of guests at their home would signal the disappearance of the children, but Mila always insisted that the children meet their parents' friends and even Brian's clients, and accompany their parents to restaurants and the theatre. Today at 24 Sussex Drive, the presence of the four Mulroney children is very evident at functions from business breakfasts to formal dinners.

When the Prince and Princess of Wales came to dinner in October 1991, the forty dinner guests were just starting their second course when Nico flew into the room in pyjamas and a dressing gown to say goodnight to his parents. Ben and Mark had mingled with the guests earlier before going to their rooms to finish their homework, and Caroline attended the reception and the dinner.

The children also know that they're expected not just to attend events but to participate in them. At the gala in honour of the visit of Charles and Diana, Ben did the voice-over announcing the performers for the show at the National Arts Centre. Mark helped out backstage. When they all took a bow after the performance, Caroline (who hadn't worked on the show) applauded from the audience while her brothers stood in the limelight with the celebrities. At cocktail parties at 24 Sussex, the guests' coats are likely to be taken by Mark and Nicolas. Caroline, who drives her own car—a 1986 Honda—is expected to drive the other kids to school every morning. And when the family is making a meal, everyone is expected to kick in and help with the preparations. They set the table and clear the dishes. As well, they have to make their own beds, tidy their rooms, and pack and unpack their own things whether they're going to Harrington Lake for the weekend or away with their parents on a trip.

Mila believes in what she calls the Japanese style of parenting. Keeping the children very busy is, in her opinion, the way to build bright, interesting adults. "I didn't have a schedule as a kid. I think that kids can take a lot when they're young. Boredom is a tragic word for kids. Schedules teach them to stimulate themselves." The children are not allowed to watch television during the week. They tape their favourite programs and watch them on the weekend. (Ben always tapes *The Simpsons*, and Caroline tapes *Murphy Brown*.)

Nico, six, has something scheduled every day after school: judo, Beavers, music classes, reading lessons. (Mila wants him to learn to read in English, but at the Lycée, all the lessons are in French, so she has a tutor come in for English-language reading lessons after school two days a week.) Caroline, seventeen, plays piano and attends dance and aerobic exercise classes. Ben, fifteen, is an excellent pianist who insists that he doesn't have an ear for music, he just practises hard. For the grade ten Royal Conservatory examination that he'll complete before his sixteenth birthday, he needs to play one of the two grand pianos at 24 Sussex for three-hour practice sessions several times a week. He also works out in a gym and plays tennis four days a week.

Mark, thirteen, is the hockey player in the family. He started to play later than most young Canadian kids, since he had to persuade his mother to let him do it. His father (who isn't a bad hockey player himself) had bemoaned the fact that hockey is Canada's biggest sport yet his boys weren't even playing the game. The truth is, Mila was worried that they would get their front teeth knocked out and she didn't encourage them to play. Mark says that when he asked if he could play, she tried to discourage him. Then Ben went to work on her and finally she relented.

Mila may have lost that round, but she isn't a sore loser. Mark joined the B-team of the peewee league as a right winger in the fall of 1991. At the first weekend tournament in Embrun, Ontario, Mark was sent off with a Mountie and he figured he would be on his own. At about eleven o'clock that Sunday morning, Mila suddenly had pangs of guilt. She said to Ben, "Mark is out there playing hockey in the country and here we are sitting at home. We should be there, cheering for him." She roused the rest of the family and mustered them all, including Brian, into her jeep for the ride to Embrun.

Once there, she realized the other team not only had supporters, they even had a proper "cheer." She insisted that Caroline and Ben get into the spirit of the game and yell for their brother. She cheered for each player who touched the puck and whistled with her fingers in her mouth every time Mark went on the ice. "She isn't exactly a hockey expert," says Ben. "She was yelling defence when it should have been offence. When the goalie on Mark's team made a good stop, she yelled out 'Great—puck stop!' It's not exactly the cheer of a seasoned hockey mom."

It's hard for the Mulroneys to attend everything the kids are involved in, but they know the value of parental or at least family support and try to make sure that at least one family member is in attendance for important events if they cannot be there themselves. Like many a working mother, Mila feels that guilt drives her to music recitals, hockey games, and ballet performances.

One night, Mila thought Caroline was performing in a dance recital. She convinced Brian that the two of them really should attend. They arrived at the modern jazz studio to find a class made up of women between the ages of sixteen and sixty. "Here were all these women dressed in black leotards and tights dancing around the floor. Brian and I were sitting in the first row. In fact, we were sitting in the *only* row. It wasn't really a recital, it was an invitation to observe the class. I don't know who felt sillier, Brian or the women in the class. In any case, Brian suggested that we exit—fast."

Sometimes Mila's insistence that family members attend each other's performances makes for extremely complicated arrangements. For instance, just before Christmas 1991, there was a first ministers' conference on the same day as Nicolas's investiture in Beavers. It also happened to be Slava, the Yugoslavian feast day that is strictly observed by the Pivnicki family in Montreal. The prime minister went to the afternoon conference. When it was over, he picked up Nicolas and attended the investiture with Mark and Ben. Afterwards, Mark and Nicolas were driven to Montreal, where Mila was waiting for them at her parents' home. (Caroline had flown to London, England, and Ben stayed at home finishing some end-of-term school work.)

It sometimes requires a score card to know who is where, but the family members usually manage to balance their official functions with their private lives. And no matter where they are, the command from the head coach is that they must keep in touch at least by telephone every day. The children also lean on each other for support. As Mark puts it, "Nico has me, I have Ben, Ben has Caroline, Caroline has Mom, and we all have Dad."

Mila has a particularly close relationship with her daughter. She calls her Lali (pronounced Luli). When Caroline was a baby, Mila spoke only Serbo-Croatian to her. There's no diminutive for the name Caroline in Serbo-Croatian, so she nicknamed her Lali. Caroline tells a story about her favourite birthday celebration. She was only seven. Mila announced that they were going to have a Girls' Day, that the boys had to stay home. "I remember we went to the Crêpe Bretonne, my favourite restaurant, for lunch. Then we went to Place des Arts to see *Madame Butterfly*. We went shopping to buy a birthday present for me, but I don't even remember what we bought. The powerful memory for me was having my mom all to myself and feeling like one of 'the girls.' ''

Summer vacations are spent, for the most part, at Harrington Lake. Twenty-four Sussex is closed from July 1 to September 1, and the entire family moves to the lake. The children keep their bikes there. They invite friends from school or camp or the Montreal friends they're still in touch with up to the lake for weekends. The Pivnickis go to visit; so do Irene Mulroney and Ivana. It's a relaxed family time they all savour.

Ben and Mark go to a mixed camp in Vermont for part of the summer. Caroline used to go to camp but decided to stay at home in summer 1991. She worked as a volunteer at a literacy centre three days a week, teaching a senior citizen to read.

The Mulroneys usually try to visit Florida for a vacation once a year. They used to stay at the St. Andrews Club near Boynton Beach when the children were younger, but now the family rents (from friends or an agency) a house on the east coast, usually near Jupiter or Palm Beach.

One year when they spent Christmas in Florida, they arrived too late to buy a Christmas tree. Christmas without a tree was inconceivable for Mila. So she and the kids found a craft shop, bought green and red construction paper, and created their own tree. They cut out the tree, pinned it to the wall, then cut out red balls and pasted them onto the cardboard branches.

Caroline says, "We put all our presents under the tree against the wall. I thought she was the most creative person in the world."

If an opportunity to travel with their parents comes up in the summer months, the family tries to take advantage of it. In summer 1991, the family travelled together to Ireland to the area the Mulroney ancestors came from. In September, Ben had a few days of school holiday, so he joined his parents in Palo Alto, where his father gave the convocation address at Stanford University. But when classes are in session, Mila is adamant that her children attend school. She's often asked to take them out of school for the kick-off to a campaign, such as the Easter Seals campaign. She says she'd like to oblige because she wants to help, but school days are off-limits.

Perhaps because of Mila's rules, all the Mulroney kids are good students. All of them are trilingual. Caroline has decided she wants to study international law and history when she graduates from high school in spring 1992 and has applied to several universities in Canada, the United States, and Britain.

Although friends from the Lycée often come home with them after school, evenings are strictly reserved for doing homework in their rooms. They each have a bedroom on the third floor, and all four share a playroom. They don't have phones or television sets in their rooms, but they have a computer, which is kept in the playroom.

Caroline's room is decorated in pastel shades of green, yellow, and pink. Her shelves are filled with framed photos of her parents and brothers, and teddy bears sit on her bed.

Ben's room is blue and white. "Ben's room smells like sweat socks," Mila says. Ben shoots back, "Hey, I'm only fifteen." He's too long for the bed at present, but even so, he leaves enough room for the family's standard poodle, Clover, who likes to sleep at the end of his bed. Ben likes to think that his growth spurt (he's six foot two) and the weight gain he'd been hoping for are due to eating cereal by the boxful. "*Slurping* cereal by the boxful," his mother amends.

Mark's red and blue room houses every souvenir he's collected in the eight years he's lived at Sussex Drive. His mother calls it "a challenge, or a time warp, depending on where you're standing."

Nicolas has a blue and white room that's filled with stuffed animals and features a much-prized photo taken of him showing his room to Barbara Bush. Mrs. Bush autographed the photo and Nicolas asked to have it framed.

The children have inherited their mother's style and her beautiful-people standards. Their jeans are ironed. Their hair always shines. They have straight teeth (braces helped with Caroline and Ben) and good bone structure. Together they look like a Ralph Lauren advertisement. They also know exactly how to behave with visiting dignitaries. They bear a remarkable resemblance to the little girl in Sarajevo who entertained artists and scholars with "pretend tea." But the Mulroney kids are still kids, and they do what kids do. Messy rooms drive their mother crazy, as does whining. And, like children everywhere, they get into scrapes.

When Nicolas was only three, the family attended a centennial celebration in Trenton, Nova Scotia. The entire entourage—provincial Tory party bigwigs, executive assistants to the prime minister, RCMP security officers, and local dignitaries—were strolling through a park and circling a duck pond. Nico was fascinated by the ducks and moved closer and closer to the water's edge. All of a sudden, he slipped on the mossy rocks and went head-first into the water.

Before anyone else, including several burly detectives, had time to react, Mila jumped into the pond and hauled her youngest out of the muddy water. Although the water was only two feet deep, Nico had been submerged. When Mila climbed out of the pond, her white suit was wet and filthy. No harm done, she insisted briskly, before rushing off to the hotel for a change of clothing and a short chat with Nicolas about wandering away. She didn't let go of his hand for the rest of the day.

The kids describe their mother as a "clean freak" and howl with laughter when they recount her cleaning stories. "She got us up at three o'clock in the morning one time to move furniture," says Ben. Caroline adds, "She and I went to New York recently. We were sitting in our hotel room, talking. It was one o'clock in the morning when she said, 'Caroline, go over there and fix that curtain, it's out of place.' I tried to fix it, but it wasn't right. So here she is, in New York at 1 a.m., standing on a chair, fixing the curtains. It really annoys her when something is out of place."

Olive Elliott, her sister-in-law, has often seen this side of Mila in action. "I brought a present to Mom while she was staying with Brian and Mila at Harrington Lake. She opened my present and after thanking me for it, she put it on the floor beside her chair. Mila asked Mark to take it up to Grandma's bedroom. She really keeps everything in order.''

''She's always rearranging our rooms and cleaning the house,'' says Ben. ''She really takes pride in her home. Everything she has means something to her.'' One night, Caroline woke up and vaguely realized her mother was moving around in her room. The next morning, she awoke to find the room spotless. ''All the junk in the corners had been retrieved and sorted and put away.'' Another time, Ben came home, looked into his rearranged room, and yelled, ''What happened?'' The other kids yelled back, ''Mom had a day off.''

The Mulroneys protect their children fiercely and keep the family relationships private. No interviews. No stories. They fear for the safety of the kids, but mostly they fear for their privacy. This isn't easy in the glare of the public spotlight, with Mounties in constant attendance.

When the family moved to Ottawa and Mounties became a regular part of their lives, the children's code names were Angel Three, Angel Four, and Angel Five. (That was before Nicolas was born.) Fortunately, the Mountie who was assigned to the children—Corporal Forest Dunsmore—was a good-natured man who not only understood children but understood the position these kids found themselves in. He used to tell them their code names ought to be Rug-rat Three, Rug-rat Four, and Rug-rat Five.

Mounties go everywhere with the Mulroney children. Mila insists that they accept this as a fact of life and not complain about the restrictions on their freedom. In fact, she says, their lifestyle at 24 Sussex is not hugely different from the lifestyle they had at the Belvedere Road house in Montreal. The family also had a fairly high profile in the city because of the notoriety their father received as commissioner on the Cliche Commission. They were picked up and delivered wherever they went then, either by Mila or by Joe Kovecvic, the handyman who worked for the Mulroneys. (He had worked for Boba Pivnicki before going to Mila's house, and today he still works at 24 Sussex Drive.)

As far as being followed by Mounties is concerned, the kids say it's simply a matter of making plans slightly ahead of time and calling the RCMP to say something like, "My friend and I are going to the movies. Then we're going for a pizza. Then I'm coming home." In about ten minutes a car shows up and the outing begins. The kids don't complain about it, and in fact have lots of funny stories about being under surveillance.

One day Caroline was driving home and going a little over the speed limit. She suddenly saw a red flashing light on top of a car across the road and groaned at the thought of being caught speeding and facing her parents with the news. The officer wheeled his car around, crossed the road, pulled alongside Caroline's car, and said, "Slow down, will you? The corporal assigned to you today can't keep up." Caroline says, "I got his point. It was a nice way of telling me to watch out."

Another time, Caroline was visiting a friend in Toronto. Her friend was driving down a major street, talking to Caroline and some other friends in the back seat. Suddenly the car in front of them stopped. The friend didn't. While Toronto police investigated the accident, the Mounties following Caroline were there in seconds to check on the kids in the car. The next day, Caroline had a call from her mother, who was in Germany on a state visit. Mila wanted to know how she was getting along. Not wanting to worry her mom, Caroline said that everything was fine and she was having a great time. "So when are we going to discuss the accident?" Mila asked. Caroline had forgotten about the deal the Mounties have with her mother to report everything.

Although she'd been reported, Caroline says she understands the situation she and the Mounties are in. All the kids admit that having Mounties following them around has gotten them out of more jams than it's ever gotten them into.

Brian Mulroney loves to talk about his children, whether he's chairing a cabinet meeting or dining with heads of state. His best friend of more than thirty years, Bernard Roy, says, "It always amazed me that the children would come into his den to see him when they came home from school, even if he was conducting a meeting. And he would always stop the meeting to say something to whichever child it was. For instance, if it was Caroline, he'd say, 'Look at that lovely daughter of mine.'

"He's so proud of his children. I think I know them as well as anyone and they are a family that is strongly bonded. Mila obviously exercises a strong influence over the children and they adore her, but they have a genuine empathy and sense of love and affection for their father. I sometimes felt guilty as his chief of staff that I didn't have enough time for my son—I'd come home late, feeling exhausted—but with all the problems he had to deal with as prime minister, he would always take the time to stop for his children.''

Brian describes Caroline as ''the nicest person I've ever met. She's an absolutely wonderful girl. She's hard-working, disciplined, bright, and affectionate. She's all the things you'd ever want to be. Mila asked me once why I loved the kids so much and I told her it's because they're such an improvement on me.''

Brian describes Ben as ''a real gentleman. He's almost naive in his lack of malice. There's not a malicious bone in his body. He's always helpful. He's a great kid.'' Benedict is the family storyteller. He entertains everyone with his imitations of rock stars and country bumpkins. And he creates scenes the way other people discuss the weather. ''There was this old guy, eh...'' he'll begin, stooping over and putting on a McKenzie Brothers accent. Part of his schtick is stroking his chin, which he says he's proud of because it's a Mulroney chin. (Actually, it isn't exactly like his father's chin. When he was five years old, Brian Mulroney went headfirst off his tricycle and almost impaled himself on a fire hydrant. He broke his jawbone and required several stitches under his chin to close the gaping wound. So while Ben has the long wide chin of the Mulroneys, his father's is even broader.)

Ben also has a ''Ben's in trouble with Mom'' routine. ''They call me Ben or Benzoid when everything is okay. But if I'm in trouble, it's 'Benedict.' I'll hear Mom's voice on the intercom saying, 'Benedict, will you please come down to my room?' When I go past Caroline's room, she'll say, 'Boy, are you ever in trouble.' Mark will explain it much more elaborately. Even Nicolas will lecture me. Then I'll hear about whatever it is from my mother and that's the end of it.''

The Mulroney children's reaction to their mother's brand of discipline closely resembles Mila's attitude toward her parents when she was growing up. It was hard for Mila's adolescent friends to understand why she didn't argue with her parents, why she accepted their decisions. Mila's children follow the same pattern; they don't argue or talk back. Unless their mother has the facts wrong, they simply agree when she corrects their behaviour.

Ben is his mother's biggest fan. ''My mom makes speeches. She's taken cystic fibrosis from number twenty-seven to number two in terms of fund raising. She's raising four kids. She gets I don't know how many pieces of mail every week. She entertains heads of state. And yet people seem to think that because she's married to the prime minister, she has nothing to do other than shopping and redecorating the house as many times as she likes. It's incredibly frustrating to read that all the time. People just assume that because she's good-looking and stylish, she doesn't have any depth. They don't try to see her for who she is. She can relate to anything. She's lived through a lot in Yugoslavia, in Montreal, here. We have great conversations with her. Our friends can tell her what's going on in their lives. They all confide in her.''

Mark is ''the most partisan one of the four children,'' says Brian. ''He came home one day and said, 'You were good in Question Period today, Dad. But Mr. Mazankowski was really excellent.' '' His partisanship has seen him get into some difficulty from time to time.

He's been known to ''put kids at school up against the wall'' to explain to them why they shouldn't say rude things about his dad.

If Ben is the storyteller in the family, then Mark is the showman. When he helped out at the gala for the Prince and Princess of Wales and stood on the stage with the stars of the show during the finale, the prime minister laughed heartily and said, ''That's Mark. Having the time of his life. He and Michael J. Fox up there on the stage. That's just it for him.''

He's the one who will spend time with a cystic fibrosis patient who is visiting at the house. An hour later, when another visitor pops into the basement room he's in to say goodbye, he'll be in a less angelic pose. Sitting on a chair tipped on its back legs, with his feet on a wicker side table, he talks on the phone. When he notices the visitor, he covers the mouthpiece of the phone and mouths the word ''girl'' while pointing to the phone with glee.

He's also the entrepreneur in the family. During one of their many visits to Boba's house in Montreal (Mila says it takes days afterwards to de-program them from a visit to Boba's), he found his Uncle John's hockey and baseball cards from the 1960s. With permission from Boba, he took them home, cleaned them up, and now says proudly, ''They're worth a fortune.''

Mark will happily walk for hours with Irene Mulroney around the property at Harrington Lake. ''I love to hear stories about my dad when he was a little boy and how my grandfather was with him.''

Nicolas is the child Mila and Brian planned to have soon after Mark. ''But we had a leadership convention and an election instead,'' says Mila. He's the baby of the whole family and sometimes the diversion they all need. When he was born, Brian says, ''It was like black September in the House of Commons. Everything was going wrong. The rat pack was busy. John Fraser had just resigned over the tuna fish business. I used to go home at night and Mila and I would watch Nicolas on our bed. I wouldn't watch the news or read the newspapers. Nicolas would entertain us. Then the other kids would come in and they'd entertain Nicolas. I remember those days. Nicolas got us through some tough times.''

Nicolas has been attending international functions since he was four weeks old and sitting through speeches since he was three years old. One of Brian's favourite stories about him took place in British Columbia in the summer of 1988. Nicolas was three. ''The press was going crazy about when there would be an election called. I was carrying Nicolas onto the plane and the media called out, 'What about an election?'

''I said, 'Well, what do you guys think?'

''They replied, 'No, no, Prime Minister, it's what you're thinking that we want to hear about.'

''I told them, 'I'll think about it tonight. I'll talk to Nicolas about it and I'll let you know.'

''I thought that would be the end of it. But the next morning they were all waiting by the plane and said, 'Well, what about the election?'

''I said, 'I'm still thinking about it.'

''Then they said, 'Did you talk to Nicolas about it?'

''I said, 'Oh yes, I talked to Nicolas,' and they wanted to know what he'd said. One of them yelled out, 'Nicolas, did you tell your daddy to call an election?'

"Nicolas looked up and said, 'No comment.' "

Nicolas has a special relationship with his dad. One day when an argument was raging in the House of Commons about free trade, the prime minister slipped out the side door and phoned Nicolas. "When did you say you wanted to see *Bambi*?" he asked. "Today," shrieked an ecstatic Nicolas. And the two of them went off to the cinema, bought big bags of popcorn, and sat through *Bambi* twice. Meanwhile, the Ottawa press gallery reported that the prime minister was in high-level strategy meetings. When asked what he'd do if he could take a day off, Brian replied, "I'd pick up Nicolas and go over to the governor general's [the grounds of Rideau Hall]. We'd take Clover and chase squirrels and tell stories and have a great old time."

Clover is the successor to Gucci, the dog left behind in Montreal. Although she is better behaved than Gucci was, she still gets into the odd scrape. At Harrington Lake one day, while Mila was involved in a meeting, Nicolas decided to make his mother a necklace out of noodles. With help from the kitchen staff, he cooked the noodles in green and blue food colouring before stringing them together. He presented the dripping arrangement to his mother, who made an appropriate fuss about the beauty and delicacy of the necklace and suggested that he lay it on the kitchen table to dry so that she could wear it later on in the afternoon. About half an hour later, he returned to the room obviously close to tears.

"What happened?" Mila asked.

Nicolas didn't speak. He just pointed at Clover.

"What do you know about this, Clover?" Mila demanded.

The remnants of green noodles were hanging out the side of Clover's mouth.

"You ate my necklace!" Mila roared.

Even Clover seemed to know it was funny. Her tail wagged. Nicolas started to laugh. And the pair were dispatched back to the kitchen to make a new one.

All four children have a very close relationship with their mother's mother, whom they call Babi. "We love to go there because there's always food cooking, always people there, always guests staying," Ben says. "And when we were little, there were lots of kids to play with on her street, way more than on Belvedere Road where we lived."

Boba gives the kids the run of the house. She sends them to the corner store to buy something she claims she forgot. Even though the Mounties follow close behind them, the kids love running the errands. She cooks with them, and Mark says her "moon" cookies are "the best."

When Mark was a baby, Boba would arrive at the house on Belvedere early in the morning. While Mila slept, she'd dress Mark and take him to the park and have him back to the house before Mila was out of bed.

Now, at 24 Sussex, she does the same thing with Nicolas. He knocks on Boba's door early in the morning (when he was very small, Boba would go to his nursery and get him out of his crib). They go for a walk or take a swim in the indoor pool or make cookies together in the kitchen. "Sometimes, when the kitchen staff arrived, the kitchen would be full of flour and broken eggs and there would be a few raised eyebrows," says Boba.

For Nicolas's sixth birthday, Boba organized a barbe-
cue party at her house in Montreal. There were nine
kids in the backyard, all of them older than Nico. Nico
thought it was a terrific party.

They all feel the heat of the spotlight from time to time,
yet the Mulroney kids agree that being the prime minister's kids also has its advantages. The night before the
prime minister was sworn into office in 1984, Mila drove
to Montreal with Caroline, Ben, and Mark because there
was a Michael Jackson concert at the Olympic Stadium
and she had promised to take them. When the concert
was over, a messenger appeared at their seats with a note
from Michael Jackson. He'd invited them back to his
hotel suite. It was a long drive back to Ottawa and the
next day was an important one. But this was an opportunity not to be missed. Mila gave in to the kids' pleading
and watched while Michael Jackson dazzled her children with small talk and autographs. It was three o'clock
in the morning before they got back to Ottawa.

In 1991, when David Foster arrived in Ottawa to
rehearse for a gala he was doing, he picked up the four
children and took them to see *Little Man Tate*. But the
children's favourite story is about Barbara Bush.

In 1989, Mila hosted the Sixty-five Roses fund-raising
gala for cystic fibrosis in Ottawa. Celebrities from all
over the country were either attending the performance
or taking part in it. Barbara Bush was coming to show
her support for the work Mila was doing with the Cystic
Fibrosis Foundation.

All the Mulroneys were dressed up and ready to leave
24 Sussex for the National Arts Centre—all except

Nicolas, who was just four years old at the time. He was in tears, not because he wasn't invited, but because everyone in the house had a name tag except him. There were about a hundred people having cocktails before the performance and waiting for Barbara Bush to arrive. Nico was sure that no one would know his name.

The doorbell rang. Nicolas answered the door and found Barbara Bush standing there. She smiled and said, ''Well, Nicolas—hello.'' He was so pleased she knew who he was, he invited her upstairs to his room to see his hockey card collection. Mrs. Bush obliged and while a hundred people waited in the foyer, Nicolas and Barbara Bush went up the stairs to ''do hockey cards.''

Such memories help to offset the disadvantages of being the prime minister's kids. Having insults hurled at you because of the job your father does is tough. Reading things about your parents in the papers—that your father drinks to excess, that your parents are on the point of splitting up, that your mother is a shopaholic—is also tough. Finding out that you're powerless to protect your parents, to stop the gossip and the innuendo, is also a painful learning experience.

The Mulroney kids have heard it all, but they've survived relatively unscathed. They're cynical about the media and more worldly wise than most children their age. The publicity that raged around Caroline after the Economic Summit in London, England, in 1991 simply made them laugh. ''It was pretty hard for me to understand that all of England was interested in my sister,'' says Ben. ''She had paparazzi chasing her all over the place. Then they did a double-page spread in the newspaper called 'Princess Caroline.' Now my sister is as perfect as they come, but she isn't what I would consider a double-page spread story. I mean, what are they going to ask her? 'How's high school, Caroline?' "

They agree that the good news is that it wasn't negative publicity. They have seen too much of that. Ben admits, "I used to love to read about myself in the paper. Now when I open it up, I just hope there's nothing bad in it. I didn't use to see it in terms of bad or good reporting. Now I see newspapers from a different angle. Our parents say something and the next day it's in the newspapers, but it's turned around in a bad or negative way."

When *Frank* magazine ran a full-page advertisement inviting "young Tories to deflower Caroline Mulroney," Caroline commented, "They crossed the line, but I was more insulted from a woman's standpoint than anything else. If it had been a credible magazine, I might have been hurt. But it isn't, so I wasn't."

Some of their childhood has been sacrificed for the job their parents do and the times they live in. But they see themselves as lucky. Brian and Mila feel that their children have an unparalleled opportunity to learn new things, to gather experiences, to visit places they might otherwise never see. And as for the guilt they feel about the amount of time they must spend away from the children, Brian says, "You can look at that another way too. Most working parents can't suddenly decide to take one of the kids or all of the kids along on a business trip. We can do that, and we're very grateful that we can."

Nevertheless, the cost is high. Their father has aged visibly over the eight years he's been in office. He often returns home exhausted yet with hours of work still to do and little time for his family. Mila is away a lot, and although she's always in touch with them by phone, a telephone doesn't replace a mom's lap. They have close relationships with the staff at 24 Sussex and a host of loving relatives. But Nicolas says it for all of them: "Daddy, when we no longer be prime minister..." They all have plans for the day when they can have their parents to themselves.

Chapter Nine

*Very few people could watch a child suffer in such a
senseless, terrible way without wanting to do
something.*
                                          Mila Mulroney

"I think it was the cruellest thing I ever heard," says
Barbara Herbert. "It was in a book about prime
ministers' wives. The comment was that Mila Mulroney
had managed to attach herself to a disease with photo-
genic children. If you want to pick an easy disease,
cystic fibrosis isn't the one. It's got to be terribly hard
meeting with children who are so incredibly sick. She
didn't pick us because we're an easy one."

Barbara's daughter Julia lost her battle with CF in
April 1988. She was thirteen years old and weighed fifty
pounds when she died. Julia was one of many CF patients who have had a special relationship with the
woman who vowed in 1985 that she'd make everybody
aware of cystic fibrosis so that she could raise money for
research to help defeat this child-killer disease. At the
same time, she made it clear that she was in it for the
long run: "until we beat CF."

Mila and Julia first talked after Julia had been named
the Cystic Fibrosis poster child in 1988. Although Julia

and her parents had decided to go ahead with the poster publicity, they had in fact been advised in January that Julia's disease had reached the terminal stage.

When Mila called her on February 5, a nurse came into Julia's room and said, ''There's a woman on the phone who wants to speak to you. She says her name is Mila Mulroney.'' Julia was wheeled to a telephone with her oxygen bottle trailing along behind her. They talked about the hospital, Julia's family, and how Julia was getting along. Julia told Mila about her dog and the visit she was going to have with him when she was allowed to go home for an overnight stay. They promised each other they would stay in touch.

Five weeks later, Julia got a message that Mila and Brian would be in the London area and would come to the Victoria Hospital to see her. Barbara Herbert was worried. Julia had lost a lot of ground. She'd been asked to present flowers to Mila, but Barbara didn't think she was strong enough even to reach up and give the bouquet to Mila.

On the day of the visit, the motorcade was late. It seemed as though everyone who worked in the hospital had been in and out of Julia's room saying ''Aren't you excited?'' all day long. Julia was so frail, she wasn't sure she wanted to go through with it. Then there was a sudden commotion in the hallway and Mila walked in.

Mila sat very close to Julia and smiled at her encouragingly. Julia perked up, sat on the side of her bed, and talked to Mila about the animal collection she had all over her hospital room. When Julia presented the flowers to her, Mila said, ''Oh, I should have something for you.''

When it was time for the reception organized by the hospital, everyone was surprised when Julia asked if she could go too. ''At that point, she hardly ever left her bed and just wanted to lie still,'' says Barbara. ''A child so ill wanting to go along to the coffee room—I couldn't believe it. But she was in awe of Mila.''

A few days after the visit, a gift-wrapped box arrived at the hospital for Julia from 24 Sussex Drive. Inside was a toy rabbit with floppy ears. At the bottom of the box there was a letter, which read:

Dear Julia,

It was great to see you the other day during my visit to London at the Children's Hospital. I was truly looking forward to this special moment— chatting with you was indeed the highlight of my day! Thank you for the lovely flowers!

I want to take this opportunity to extend my warmest regards to your parents. Keep in touch and take good care of yourself—give a big hug to your brother, mom and dad for me!

With every good wish,
Hugs,
Mila Mulroney

Julia was very ill by the time the package arrived, but she took the rabbit out of the box and tucked it in her hospital bed beside her. She died the next day. The nursing staff at the hospital, students from Julia's school, and all of her London, Ontario, neighbours joined Julia's parents in mourning the loss of the little girl. So did Mila and Brian Mulroney, who telephoned just a few hours after Julia died and talked with Barbara for ten minutes. Barbara says she was surprised that Brian cried when he was talking to them on the telephone.

Mila certainly touched Julia's life, says Barbara. And when it was over, Mila continued the work Julia had begun. There was to be a cystic fibrosis fund raiser at Julia's school. The students there were shocked to learn that Julia had died; none of them had known how sick she really was that winter. Mila wrote to the students and congratulated them for going ahead with the fund raiser. Her letter said, in part: "In addition to bringing comfort to Julia's family, you have helped to keep her spirit alive by lending support to the battle Julia fought so bravely her entire life. On behalf of everyone who knew and loved Julia, I thank you very much."

Mila Mulroney announced that she would be the honorary chairperson of the Canadian Cystic Fibrosis Foundation on March 20, 1985. She knew that she'd find herself in the spotlight as the wife of the prime minister, and she wanted to find a charity that would benefit from that spotlight. The story about how she chose CF started nine years earlier.

During the 1976 leadership race, Ian Thompson was a reporter for the *Halifax Herald* who met Brian and Mila Mulroney and kept in touch over the years. In 1983, when the Mulroney leadership team published the book *Where I Stand*, Ian asked if the royalties might be donated to the struggling cystic fibrosis foundation. His two children, Robbie and Jane, both have the disease. Later, when Brian was campaigning in Nova

Scotia's Central Nova riding, he told Ian that he hadn't forgotten the suggestion. (In the end, the book did not earn any royalties.)

Soon after, Brian became prime minister and Ian Thompson became president of the Canadian Cystic Fibrosis Foundation. Ian wrote to Dr. Claude Roy, a CF researcher in Montreal and the brother of the newly appointed chief of the prime minister's staff, Bernard Roy. He also wrote to Mila. "We reflected a long time about the value of having a prominent person as our spokesperson," says Ian. "A person who doesn't have a connection to the cause isn't the best person to choose. We'd already had governors general and athletes and hadn't achieved the results we wanted. I'd read that Mila wanted to play an active role with children, and I thought her interests and energy and enthusiasm fit our foundation like a glove." Dr. Claude Roy pitched the case to her and she accepted. Ian Thompson's children became the first poster children she worked with.

"Whenever people ask me why I got involved in the fight against cystic fibrosis," says Mila, "I wish they could meet our campaign poster children like Robbie and Jane Thompson from Halifax, or Valerie and Benjamin Mouton from Quebec, or any of the kids with CF I've met all across the country. Then they'd understand.

"When I saw a child suffering in the hospital, I thought to myself, here's a kid who never caused pain to anyone. He's sitting in a hospital bed struggling to breathe. It doesn't seem fair. Very few people could watch a child suffer in such a senseless, terrible way without wanting to do something.

"After Brian became prime minister, I was approached by a number of very worthwhile organizations and charities. I wanted to get involved in something, but I wanted an organization where I could personally make a difference.

"When I read the devastating details of cystic fibrosis and learned that these kids look healthy and bright, then get terribly sick and die, I thought of my own healthy children and felt that maybe I could help. Because of the high profile that comes with being the wife of the prime minister, I thought I could increase awareness of and interest in a killer disease that most people don't even know exists.

"I spend about one day a week working with the foundation. There are letters to write, meetings to attend, and fund-raising galas where I usually deliver a short address. (This is a source of great amusement to my friends, because they know that I once vowed I'd never make speeches. The first time I did was when Dinah Shore asked me to be guest speaker at her annual golf classic in Palm Springs and offered me $15,000 for my favourite charity if I'd accept. I thought being paid to have people listen to me could be quite an experience.) And whenever I travel within Canada or outside the country I try to visit the CF clinics or volunteer association chapters in that area."

On one such visit, to the University of Stanford in Palo Alto, California, when Brian was there to deliver a speech at the university's centennial convocation, Mila met Professor Jeffrey Wine, a researcher in the cystic fibrosis laboratory.

"I was bragging to people about meeting her," Wine recalls, "and someone remarked that she'd got into this because it's such a fabulously progressive area. At first I wondered if that was true, but then I found out that she became involved in 1985 when we were really in the wilderness with our research. I know there's a tremendous animosity toward people in public life, but this was a bad rap. Her contribution came at a time when the Canadian researchers were bucking the accepted style of research. It's very difficult in the scientific community to refuse to go along with the trend in research, because you tend to lose your funding. But the Canadians did. She got the funding for them. As it turns out, the research the others were following for all those years was totally wrong. When the gene responsible for cystic fibrosis was discovered by researchers at the Hospital for Sick Children in Toronto, the Canadians got the credit they deserved. That reflects on Mila Mulroney too."

The four Mulroney children are also involved to some extent in the campaign. Caroline is pen pals with a child with cystic fibrosis. And Mila takes her kids with her to some of the events for children. As well, the family rule is: when you come home from school, if something is going on, you're expected to come in and say hello (although you don't have to stay unless you want to). During a recent tea party to honour the fund raisers from the Quebec Cystic Fibrosis Association, Caroline arrived home from school, so she joined her mother in the living room and was introduced to the gathering of about a hundred guests. Mila was obviously delighted to have her by her side and tucked her arm through Caroline's during the introductions.

Shortly thereafter, thirteen-year-old Mark arrived home. After kissing his mother hello, he made a beeline for Benjamin Mouton, a twelve-year-old with cystic fibrosis who was the only other youngster in the room, and suggested they escape to his room or, better still, check out the swimming pool. When it was time for the Moutons to leave, Benjamin was carrying a poster. His mother inquired about it and Benjamin said shyly, "Mark gave it to me." It was Mark's Wayne Gretzky poster, signed by Gretzky himself. When they left, Mark said to his mother, "Benjamin really likes hockey. The next time we're in Montreal can I have the Canadiens tickets so I can take him to the game?"

Mila has been the honorary chairperson of the Canadian Cystic Fibrosis Foundation for seven years now. In spring 1992, her title will change to "chairperson," in recognition of the hands-on nature of her work for the foundation. She says it's been exciting, heartbreaking, and educating all at once. "Exciting because on August 24, 1989, the news everyone in the CF family had been waiting for arrived—the discovery by the Toronto research team headed by Lap-Chee Tsui of the gene that causes cystic fibrosis." The finding holds out the prospect of an assault on cystic fibrosis because researchers now understand that its cause has to do with a basic genetic defect. With the discovery of the gene comes a new scrutiny of the role the gene plays in the body when someone has cystic fibrosis. Scientists will identify what is missing and may learn how to replace or correct the basic dysfunction.

Dr. Jack Riordan, who is a colleague of Dr. Tsui's at the hospital, says, "Mila Mulroney provided the focal point for fund raising that made this research happen. She certainly could have chosen an easier cause." He also feels that her involvement with the researchers has been a valuable boost to people who usually never see the limelight. "Scientific research can be a lonely and non-rewarding business. Having someone with public visibility pointing to what you're doing helps a great deal."

Although the first breakthrough had in fact occurred in 1985, when Dr. Tsui and Dr. Manuel Buchwald found the DNA linkage to the gene, Riordan says, "From our point of view, Mrs. Mulroney attracted the attention to the cause to get the job done."

When Mila heard the news, she telephoned Ian Thompson in the middle of the night at a hotel in St. John's, Newfoundland, where he was on a business trip. The discovery was encouraging, of course, but for her, it's not enough. Finding the gene wasn't enough to save the children who died last year, and that is the heartbreaking aspect of the work.

She sees her work as an educating opportunity because, like many Canadians, she had a lot to learn about cystic fibrosis. "People tend to confuse CF with multiple sclerosis, muscular dystrophy, or cerebral palsy. I'm still amazed at some of the questions people ask: 'Is it contagious?' 'Can you get it as an adult?' 'Is it a muscle disease?' The answer to all three questions is no."

She explains in her speeches that CF is a life-threatening, hereditary disease. You're either born with it or you aren't. You cannot get it later in life. The disease attacks the body's exocrine glands—the ones that secrete sweat, saliva, and mucus. In the lungs, mucus that is fifty times thicker than normal—it's almost like glue—makes breathing difficult and creates an ideal environment for bacteria. Respiratory failure caused by repeated lung infections places a burden on the heart. In the digestive system, thick mucus blocks the flow of pancreatic enzymes necessary for normal digestion. Without treatment, the body's growth is slowed and the child suffers from malnutrition.

The double whammy in CF is that parents suffer first of all because their child has a killer disease and they suffer again because they know the child inherited the disease from both of them. Mila's understanding of that pain impresses Robbie and Jane's mom, Donna Thompson. "When you're in the hospital with your child and she comes in, you feel special. That she makes the time to see you and that she's so cheery means a lot to the parents of kids with CF. She also organizes coffee parties so the moms can get together just to talk and support each other. My gratitude to her is enormous. She's done things for us that no one ever knows about."

All the kids who meet Mila have a favourite story. For Robbie Thompson, it's the time he was selling shorts and Mila agreed to buy two pairs—one for herself and one for Brian. When he received the cheque Mila sent to pay for the shorts, he couldn't decide whether to frame it or cash it. For a while, it was in a frame but then, alas, it became cash.

For his sister, Jane, it was feeling that she would be shy and embarrassed and wouldn't have anything to say when she met Mila and then finding out that Mila is so talkative, it is easy to have a conversation with her.

For Benjamin Mouton, it was the day he met her when they were preparing a commercial for CF in Toronto. He thought she was a princess. For his sister, Valerie, it's the time Mila asked her to present flowers to Queen Elizabeth when she was visiting Montreal.

But Mila's involvement is not just with young children. At Mila's first fund raiser in Toronto in 1985, Mila sat at the head table with twenty-six-year-old Karen Lackey, who'd travelled to the event from Regina. The two women hit it off immediately. They kept in touch, exchanged gifts, and talked openly with each other about the future. In 1985, most CF patients did not live as long as Karen had. Her prognosis was very poor. She wanted a lung transplant and she discussed it with Mila over and over again.

At last, Karen received word that she could go to England for the transplant. She'd had a very difficult year. Her health had been poor, and while she was in hospital in Winnipeg, her father had died of a heart attack in the hospital cafeteria shortly after visiting her. Her mother said that it took a lot of courage for Karen to go ahead with the transplant, but she was determined to try it.

"Mila gave her a real pep talk about going to England," says Gladys Lackey. "She told her she was going to get the best gift of all. Saskatchewan Medicare helped us get Karen to England in a private plane. She needed a nurse and a doctor to travel with her and was on oxygen constantly. We stopped in Ottawa to refuel and had a two-hour dinner with Mila and her assistant, Bonnie Brownlee, at the airport.''

Karen left Canada on January 17, but she was so ill by then that the surgeons in England felt the transplant was too risky. She died in England on February 25, 1988. Mila still speaks of the brave, high-spirited woman she made friends with at her first fund raiser and vows that future research will focus on transplants to help adult patients like Karen.

Dr. Jack Riordan is the Mila Mulroney Cystic Fibrosis researcher at the Hospital for Sick Children in Toronto as well as being a professor at the University of Toronto Medical School. He gets his title from a fund-raising gala that provided a trust fund for the hospital to do CF research. It's not the usual way of funding research, but the gala was an unusual event.

It took place in Ottawa in 1989 and was called Sixty-five Roses—A Gift of Love. The name Mila chose for the gala set the tone for the evening. It was a phrase coined by four-year-old Ricky Weiss more than two decades earlier. Ricky's mother, Mary, had moved from Montreal to Palm Beach in 1965 with her three little boys. All three had cystic fibrosis, but the youngest, Ricky, who was four at the time, hadn't been told that he had the same disease his brothers had. Mary noticed that there was a lot of charitable activity in Palm Beach, and she thought it was time someone did something to raise research dollars to solve the puzzle of the disease that was killing her children.

Mary says at that point the Cystic Fibrosis Foundation had a lucky break—she fell and broke her foot.

While waiting for the injury to heal, she got on the phone and called every civic, social, and service organization she knew of. She spent the entire day on the phone and with each call, she began, "I'm calling about cystic fibrosis."

At the end of the day, Ricky came to her and said, "Mommy, I know what you're doing." She was horrified. Had he somehow figured it out from her phone calls? Cautiously, she asked him, "So what am I doing?" Ricky smiled at her and said, "You're working for sixty-five roses."

The story touched everyone who heard it. The rose has become the symbol of the foundation. Mary adds, "Today, my three boys are living and working independently, developing their careers and interests. Important advances in science indicate that today's prayers may be tomorrow's reality, when cystic fibrosis will be a fading memory."

The Sixty-five Roses Gala was an extraordinary night when the stars came out to shine for the CF families because Mila Mulroney asked them to come. Barbara Bush accepted her invitation. David Foster, of Tears Are Not Enough fame, responded to her request to write a song for the gala because, he says, "Being in the public eye allows you to do the things she's doing. You're in a position to make a difference." (He knows what he's talking about. The David Foster Foundation for children who need organ transplants started two years before Mila called him to help with cystic fibrosis.) The song he wrote was called "Don't Let Me Walk This Road Alone," and it was sung by Céline Dion at the gala.

David says it surprises him when Mila asks him to call singers like Céline Dion and performers like Dan Aykroyd to help out with a gala. He feels she underestimates her ability to attract people to her causes.

While David Foster's song made a sensational contribution to the Sixty-five Roses Gala, Douglas Bassett, the owner of CTV in Toronto, made a remarkable contribution of his own. Bassett was there because Mila had called him to ask whether the gala could be a national television event. He thought it would make great TV. He had been involved in CF for years through the CFTO telethon operated through the CTV network. The cause is close to his heart because the son of a friend has cystic fibrosis.

During the show, Doug Bassett, George Cohon, and Albert Reichmann decided to raise half a million dollars to establish the Mila P. Mulroney fund for cystic fibrosis research at the Hospital for Sick Children. They each pledged $50,000, and they needed seven more people. The three of them circulated around the crowded ballroom in search of seven more donors. Everyone wondered what they were up to. Soon they were calling themselves the three musketeers. "Not one person turned us down," says Bassett, "but in the end one person did stiff me, so we had to find an eleventh."

When it was time for Barbara Bush to leave, Mila got up on stage. She was beginning her thank yous when David Foster came rushing out on the stage yelling, "Excuse me, excuse me. Aren't any of you wondering what the three Musketeers—Bassett, Cohon, and Reichmann—have been doing? They've raised half a million dollars for CF research!" No one could believe it. They'd done it in twelve minutes.

Recently Doug Bassett was invited along with President Bush, Barbara Bush, and a number of other celebrities to watch a Blue Jays game at the SkyDome in Toronto. "At the end of the game, Mila hands me a baseball signed by the president and the prime minister. Under their names, she'd written, 'To Chris, warmest regards, Mila P. Mulroney.' She said, 'Would you give this to Chris for me? It's his birthday.' Chris is the boy I know who has cystic fibrosis."

Bassett says he's still struck that, with all Mila had to do that day, she remembered Chris's birthday, and in such a spectacular way. That is, for him, the essence of the woman. He first met her when she was in London, England, on her honeymoon and they were all attending the wedding of a mutual friend. "She made an immediate impression on me," he says. Today he sees Mila as a woman who came here from another country, someone who knows how tough it was, and is giving back a lot more than she's taking out.

The Sixty-five Roses Gala was enormously successful, yet it wasn't the biggest fund raiser Mila has ever staged for CF. In fall 1987, she brought together the reigning and immediate past Stanley Cup champions for a showdown hockey game in Ottawa. There were 9,000 general admission tickets that sold for between $15 and $30 each. As well, there were 232 pairs of VIP tickets that sold for $5,000 a pair. These tickets included an invitation to cocktails at 24 Sussex, seats at the game, and afterwards, entertainment at the National Arts Centre featuring Dinah Shore and Céline Dion (who had donated their time for the cause). The event raised $1.5 million for research.

Clearly, raising money with galas and hockey games is a controversial approach. In a recent *Chatelaine* editorial, Mildred Istona commented, ''By all accounts, Mila gives unstintingly of her time to charities, including cystic fibrosis, but her style is insular, and one is left with the impression that she circulates mostly among the elites.'' Istona complained that Mila was ''inaccessible to the Canadian public'' and compared her charitable work unfavourably with the work done for deaf children, the elderly, and AIDS patients by the Princess of Wales.

Those who work with her have a different view. Linda Kinnear, director of communications and planning at the Canadian Cystic Fibrosis Foundation, says, ''We've been phenomenally lucky that Mrs. Mulroney got involved with us. We couldn't have dreamed how far she would carry us. And although she lends her name to the organization publicly and campaigns for funds, privately she works behind the scenes all the time, visiting patients in the hospital, telephoning them at home, keeping everyone's spirits up. People not only like the heart she brings to the organization, they like the glamour too.''

However, the researchers and fund raisers realize as well the perils of the spotlight that Mila brings to their cause. Going from number twenty-seven on the list of charities (in terms of the amount of money raised) to number two attracts attention. Life expectancy for people with cystic fibrosis has gone from twenty-one to thirty in the last seven years, and that also brings attention.

''It's been hard for us in some ways to be pulled into this spotlight,'' says CCFF executive director Cathleen

Morrison. "If we fall on our faces, it will be seen. We have to deal with the spotlight much more than we would have and none of us were trained for public exposure. But we just have to handle the spotlight. You can get into trouble as a charity if someone tries to muddy the water where a political person is involved. But Mila seems to be able to separate the two with ease."

The people who work with her say she's had a dramatic effect at every level. As a fund raiser, she brings creative, daring ideas to the table and makes them happen. She goes out of her way on her travels to visit CF clinics, facilities, and families. But it's her personal commitment to the cause that impresses the patients. They see her as a source of support, a shoulder to cry on, someone to talk to.

Mila says, "I feel very close to these families. I have witnessed the urgency with which they live their lives. I hope that my participation can help them. If a letter or a visit will bring a smile to a child's face or take the family's mind off the situation even for a minute, it's the least I can do.

"They're all waiting for the magic words that a cure has been found. So am I."

Chapter Ten

The first impression you get when you walk into 24
Sussex is this is a family home, it's warm, kids in
jammies are coming downstairs to say goodnight.

Hugh Segal

M ila thought she'd poisoned one of her guests. The
woman had looked all right a moment before.
Then suddenly she slumped forward. As twenty invited
guests looked on, paralysed by what was happening at
the dining room table, the woman's head bowed forward
into her soup bowl. She had passed out cold.

It was Mila's first dinner party as chatelaine of 24
Sussex. Brian and another man rushed to the ailing
guest's side. They each took an arm and tried to carry
her out of the dining room. But the guest was like a rag
doll, arms and legs flopping every which way. After a
minute or so she came to her senses and murmured
something about being sick. The sofa was so new no one
had even had a chance to sit on it. Now, Mila thought,
someone's going to throw up all over it. Well, she rea-
soned, at least the woman isn't dead. She rushed away
to the foyer to call a doctor.

On the way back to her guests, who were now gathering around the patient, she pondered a worse calamity.

What if an ambulance with screaming sirens arrived at the door? The press might get hold of that and assume the prime minister had keeled over. Rumours would fly around, the dollar would fall... She quickly made a second call. No ambulances, please.

When the doctor arrived, he asked discreetly if the lady had been drinking. Mila looked at the creamed soup in the woman's bangs and thought to herself, "What was your first clue, Doctor?" As it turned out, the woman had felt a cold coming on and had taken a couple of antihistamines before boarding the plane to Ottawa for the occasion. Once there, feeling a bit nervous about the dinner engagement, she had had a few drinks, with predictable results.

The doctor confirmed that the woman would be all right. So would Mila's new couch. The dinner party resumed. The guest even returned to the table and enjoyed the rest of the evening.

Welcome to 24 Sussex Drive, the nation's fish bowl. The place runs like the stock exchange—all smooth order in the outer offices and a hive of activity behind the scenes. Tonight, dinner for twenty. Tomorrow, lunch for forty and a five o'clock reception for one hundred. The next day, a breakfast cabinet meeting and lunch for a visiting head of state plus entourage.

In a normal week, Mila shakes three hundred hands, hosts two or three dinner parties and two or three luncheons, one big reception (she doesn't like the guests at these to exceed 110, the number the house comfortably holds), and half a dozen meetings over coffee or tea. Outside 24 Sussex, she attends an average of five public day events a week and two evening events.

Months like December are particularly hectic. More than seven hundred guests attend a variety of Christmas brunches, teas, and cocktail parties at 24 Sussex. Days on the road with the prime minister are packed with meetings, receptions, and dinners.

And that's just her job as the prime minister's wife. Add to that the typical duties of a mother of four, such as a Beaver meeting with Nicolas, a parent-teacher evening at the Lycée Claudel, a fitness class with Caroline, and a piano recital for Ben, and you have a life that is anything but restful.

When the family arrived at 24 Sussex, Mila began her infamous redecorating program, which got her into hot water with the media for spending too much money. Mindful of the place's history, she proceeded carefully. The house had been built in 1866, though it didn't become the official residence of the prime minister until 1950. Its continuing renovations and their costs have been a thorn in the side of every prime minister who has lived there.

Louis St. Laurent was the first to be called spendthrift, for the $557,319.86 it cost to buy the place and get it ready for him. Since then it has been decorated and redecorated, designed and redesigned by a succession of prime ministers and their wives and families. Like Stornoway, it is too historic to be demolished, but anyone with even the slightest knowledge of construction agrees that it would be much more cost-efficient to tear it down and build a new residence. (The same could be said for the residence at Harrington Lake.)

Despite renovations, there are endless problems with venting, heating, and electricity. The temperature from the front to the back of the house can vary by as much as ten degrees on extreme days. That's because of the granite walls and the difficulty of installing insulation. When Margaret Thatcher visited, the power in the house went off. On New Year's Eve 1991, while Mila was preparing a dinner for seventy people at Harrington Lake, the power went off there too, and for some curious reason, two inches of water gathered on the basement floor.

Upstairs at 24 Sussex, there are seven bedrooms, four bathrooms, a den, and a family room. Downstairs are the formal rooms: dining room, living room, and another den, as well as a men's washroom off the foyer and a ladies' powder room near the den. The kitchen is smaller than one would expect for a place that entertains several hundred people a week. There are numerous passageways and hallways that intrigue little kids who want to play hide and seek. The swimming pool in the basement that Pierre Trudeau had installed is reached through one such passageway. The staff quarters at the west end of the house is home to five live-in staff members.

High on a shelf in the cupboard of the master bedroom at 24 Sussex is a red phone. There's one on the shelf in the bedroom at Harrington Lake as well. The phones are to be used in case of a war, a grim thought for the family that's growing up in this place.

The Mulroneys have their meals in a little alcove off the dining room. Brian frequently uses the den on the first floor. And of course the kitchen is a bit like a command post for the family. But most of their living is done upstairs, "above the store."

"Sometimes I feel the house is an extension of the office," says Mila. "You become a manager. I feel that

I'm expected to be creative, that since this is 24 Sussex, the meal or the event or whatever has to be special and interesting. I'm constantly leafing through magazines and looking for new candlestick ideas or interesting new ways to line bread baskets. I feel I have to always one-up myself.

"The worst part is that you are a tenant. You can't phone someone and say, 'I want the jute matting put down today or the storm windows put on this week.' Everything has to go to tender. You have to wait for everything. But the best part is the heavenly view and the spacious house that's big enough to hold most of our furniture. As well, you never have to worry about snow removal or cutting the grass. All that is done for you here."

There are some peculiar built-in restrictions to living in a government residence. One weekend, when the family was leaving for Harrington Lake, Mila picked a dozen roses from the garden to decorate her cottage table. When she returned on Monday, she received a note reminding her that the roses belong to the National Capital Commission and that she isn't to touch them.

The much-discussed renovations, which included putting hardwood floors in some of the rooms where there had been carpeting over plywood, cost a reported $97,500, paid for by the government. The decorating was an additional $308,000, initally paid for by the Conservative party; later most of this was paid back with a personal cheque from the prime minister. Canadians may complain about the expense, but the result is, admittedly, stunning. The residence had a cold, empty look about it before and was often described as an extension of the Langevin Block. Though it had been redecorated many times before, there is a difference between making the house look like a museum and creating a family home for the leader of the country. Twenty-four Sussex has become a warm, attractive residence that reflects a family lifestyle and a nation's history.

The house is built on shale rock, so it shifts occasionally and cracks are forever appearing in the walls. For that reason, Mila used wallpaper in a warm orange to decorate the front hall. She selected salmon-coloured carpet for the floor. There is navy blue fabric on the dining room walls for a rich dramatic effect (the cloth is lightly padded to muffle sound). The living room walls are sponged in a yellow-beige paint. The floors are covered with beautiful wool rugs in pastel shades of peach, yellow, and green in the living room and striking blue with off-white in the dining room. There are huge flower arrangements in every room and family photos on almost every table in the house.

Her friends in the ballet group insist that the decor is typical Mila. Giovanni Mowinckel, the famous Ottawa decorator, may have helped to locate and order the materials and furnishings, but the bold statements and the warm colours are Mila's own choice. Says Shirley Corn, "She really has nerve. When the painter comes to my house, he says, 'What colour, Mrs. Corn?' and I say, 'The same. Maybe a little lighter.' Not Mila. Orange. Navy blue. She's not afraid."

Although Mila chose her furnishings with care, she often has to find house room for official gifts that heads of state present to them during visits to Canada or the Mulroneys' visits to other countries. Some are so peculiar that Mila has threatened to open the Brian Mulroney Believe-It-or-Not Museum. Most of these things are stored in the basement at 24 Sussex. They include an antelope coffee table with matching end tables. "Where would you put your coffee? There are antlers all over the thing," says Mila. Another item is a tar-oil-soaked jacket for Brian that is supposed to keep bugs away. The smell is so strong, it's even a problem in the storage room. There are ornate trays and useless plaques by the dozen. The gifts they receive aren't all bizarre, by any means. "I could fill a library with the wonderful books we have received on every subject from settlers and small towns to Inuit life. I bet I have a book on every small town in Canada," Mila says.

The Mulroneys have to declare all gifts they receive to the Receiver General's Office. Therefore, some of the items from anonymous senders (a pair of skis arrived for Caroline, for instance) are refused at the gate. Other items are tagged for the National Archives.

Keeping an accurate inventory of the contents of 24 Sussex Drive is a complex job. There are tables and chairs coming and going. For the bigger parties coat racks are rented. There are donations of Canadian art that need to be placed in the residence. And with seven staff members, four children, and two parents, not to mention numerous family visitors, there are plenty of deliveries to keep track of.

The fish bowl is home to Mila—at least for now. Moments before heads of state or dinner guests arrive, she's calling down the grand circular staircase to one of the kids, "Are you ready? Come here and let me see you." She races down the stairs with two belts in her hand and says to Brian, who's usually ready before she is, "Which one shall I wear? The fancy one or the plain one?"

Although she has staff to cook and clean and maintain 24 Sussex, Mila occasionally, and unexpectedly, takes charge of cleaning the fish bowl. Whether it's a window that looks dirty or a mess their dog Clover has left on the floor, she doesn't hesitate to get down on her hands and knees and clean up. Everyone who knows her tells funny stories about her obsession with cleanliness. Helen Vari, a friend from Toronto, remembers the day she arrived for a visit and was greeted by Mila in a jogging suit, an apron, and rubber gloves. "What on earth are you doing?" asked Helen. Mila said, "Come in, but don't come with me. I have to go downstairs. I'm cleaning the furnace." Helen was flabbergasted and said, "Are you out of your mind? Call the service." Mila explained that the service was busy. The furnace had backed up and had to be cleaned immediately. She felt she couldn't ask the household staff to do it. "So I'll do it myself," she said. "And as soon as I'm finished, we'll have a cup of tea." With that, Helen says, she disappeared down the basement stairs. She returned about fifteen minutes later, pulling off her rubber gloves and saying, "There. It's fixed."

She's the first occupant to treat 24 Sussex as her home. Margaret Trudeau felt so uncomfortable there that she created what she called "the freedom room," where she could get away from everyone. Maureen McTeer says the chef told her to stay out of the kitchen and she did, even though she loves to cook. Maureen felt intimidated in the house. Not Mila. The house itself seems to have changed personality, as Hugh Segal has remarked: ''Anyone who's ever been to 24 Sussex at even a quasi-official event when Trudeau lived there knew it was cold and austere. The first impression you get when you walk in there now is this is a family home, it's warm, kids in jammies are coming downstairs to say goodnight.''

Everyone in this house knows who they're working for. Most of them enjoy their work, but there have been times, such as the departure of chef François Martin, that have created heartache for Mila. ''It's not like we're living in the old days when the staff were separate from the family. I couldn't live in a house like that. I know everyone who works here. I know about their troubles and their families. That's important to me. If I get too close and get burned, well, I just have to take that chance.''

François Martin left 24 Sussex after four years of managing the kitchen and creating spectacular menus for the Mulroneys. He then wrote a kiss-and-tell book about the upstairs-downstairs experiences he'd had there. Although he couldn't get a publisher to take the book, the *Globe and Mail* front page ran a few gossipy items from the manuscript.

François said that the staff called the Mulroneys ''Mr. and Mrs.'' (true). He also says that boxes of food, including staples and cleaning supplies, were sent to the Pivnickis in Montreal every month (false, though if her parents have been staying with Mila, she'll often send them home with a care package—the remains of a meal,

flowers, a bottle of wine—the kind of thing most daughters do for their mothers). He said that the food for John
Pivnicki's wedding was prepared by him (true, and it
was paid for by the Mulroneys).

Mila doesn't know why François wrote the book. "He
was a terrific chef. I felt we'd done a lot for each other."
Helen Vari says she could write a kiss-and-tell story
about François. "Mila asked me if he could come to our
home in the south of France and stay with me for a
week. She asked me to arrange for him to apprentice
with Chef Roger Verget at the famous four-star restaurant Moulin de Mougine. I had to work very hard to
convince Chef Verget to take him. But finally he agreed.
Then François Martin arrived, with a woman, to stay in
my house. Furthermore, he went to the restaurant for
half an hour one day and returned only once more to
have dinner. I felt awkward for having asked the chef to
do a favour for me. I felt François had behaved inconsid-
erately and inappropriately."

John LeBlanc is the chef who presides over the dazzling banquets and superb dinners now. He is accus-
tomed to preparing lunch for eight visiting dignitaries
or five extra kids at a moment's notice. He doesn't have
time to spare and seems to be always on the run. But the
trays that come out of that kitchen in the hands of
waiters and waitresses hired to serve at special events
are wonderful to behold.

From the day she moved into the residence, Mila's goal
was to entertain as many Canadians as possible. Consequently, the guest lists are usually a mix of artists and
business people, entrepreneurs and professionals,

occasionally students and often senior citizens, from all across Canada. She tries to invite out-of-town people to weekend or Friday events so that they have a better chance of attending.

First-time visitors to the house often have some odd notions about how to behave. Some people think you're supposed to curtsy to the prime minister and his wife, the way you would to the Queen and Prince Philip (you are not). A lot of people don't know what to call Brian Mulroney—Prime Minister, Sir, Mr. Mulroney, Brian (all are correct, but most people call him Mr. Prime Minister). Some people call Mila "Mrs. Prime Minister" (wrong; it's Mrs. Mulroney or Mila—most people call her Mrs. Mulroney). Many people refer to her as the first lady (also wrong; at present, that title belongs to Gerda Hnatyshyn). Mila usually corrects people, but she feels that sometimes it is more embarrassing for her guests to be corrected than for her to overlook the faux pas.

Not everyone is thrilled to go to 24 Sussex Drive. There has been the occasional boorish guest who feels a social occasion is the place to lecture the Mulroneys about a particular interest or concern. And some people steadily refuse all invitations: Karen Kain, for instance, has been invited numerous times but never obliges, although she has participated in fund-raising events for Mila. But for the most part, Mila says Canadians are pleased to accept, and well behaved when they come.

Invariably the guests are surprised at how friendly Mila and Brian are, how tall she is, how relaxed he is, how beautiful the house is, how the children are so much a part of the goings-on. Some of them enjoy themselves so much that they feel the need to take an unofficial souvenir away with them. Mila's colognes in the downstairs bathroom disappear regularly. The odd coffee spoon goes missing. And a few times, the tiny lacquered boxes that Mila loves to collect, and have at times been gifts from heads of state, have found their way out the front door.

At most functions, there is an official souvenir to take home, a small china coaster with 24 Sussex Drive printed on it or a jar of jam made in the kitchen. For distinguished Canadian visitors, Mila had porcelain replicas of the house made by a Quebec artist. One hundred copies were made at a cost of $250 a copy.

Days like Halloween are special events. Eight hundred trick-or-treaters turn up at the front door. The porch is turned into a graveyard of ghoulies and ghosties. Eerie music is piped out the window. A cauldron of dry ice puffs fog out over the tombstones (cut and spray-painted by Mark) stuck in the ground. A six-foot witch stands guard. Tufts of cotton wool cling to the ivy on the stone wall around the front door. Thirty pumpkins, sixteen of them carved, decorate the steps. The glow from their candles adds a spooky look to the scene. When people ask who did the carving, Mila replies, "Four children and their mother."

Mila hands out a bag of goodies (packed by Nicolas and Mark) to every trick-or-treater. Candy apples baked by the kitchen staff with help from the kids. Popcorn and chocolate. And a toothbrush—after all, this is the fish bowl. If you make a mistake, you make headlines. And candy with no toothbrush equals irate letters to the newspaper. While Brian goes out with Nicolas and Mark (and a dozen camera-toting members of the media) to trick or treat in the neighbourhood, Caroline and Ben help their mother. Serge Vaillancourt, the household manager, hustles over to the governor general's house because he's had a tip-off from a ten-year-old dressed as Madonna that the witch at Rideau Hall is better than the one at 24 Sussex. He comes back later reassured that the Mulroney witch is decidedly superior. Mila greets the kids and their parents. She poses for photos, chats to the shy ones, tells those dressed up as hippies, "Hey, that's my era."

Half an hour after the festivities begin, she decides the house doesn't look spooky enough and rushes inside calling to Caroline, "Where are the white candles?" A few minutes later, a huge candelabra glows in the foyer. Then she stands outside for two and a half hours. It's damp and windy. She has a cold. But you get the idea she's having so much fun with the kids and the make-believe that she doesn't even notice the time or the temperature.

Other parliamentary spouses say you have to live a public life if you are really to understand its restrictions. Privacy is the first casualty. If you yell at your kids, people will accuse you of bad temper or worse. If you go into the liquor store, people will remark upon it and draw conclusions. Even the contents of your grocery cart are scrutinized. If you wear the same dress too many times, you will be labelled frumpy. If you change outfits too often, you are extravagant. If you take a walk on the street with your spouse, people think nothing of walking between the two of you to talk to the MP. Even Christmas, birthdays, and holidays are open season for phone calls and interruptions.

One of the reasons Mila is so good at her job is that she doesn't worry about what people think about her. She knows that you cannot please everyone. When she's on the road with her husband, she dresses to impress and wears something different every day. She bawls her children out, usually in Serbo-Croatian, whenever they deserve it—although not in front of other people. She'll suddenly take a little hand in hers and say, "Let's you and I have a chat in the other room." She doesn't change who she is for her critics.

Still, the scrutiny in the spotlight is wearing. She's been accused of being a shopaholic, of telling the Mounties to salute her, and of having an affair with actor Christopher Plummer. One of the Mounties assigned to her (who cannot be identified because Mounties are forbidden to discuss their work) says the saluting story is nonsense. He says Mila has a warm, friendly relationship with the RCMP officers.

When a group of Mounties planned a surprise fortieth birthday party for one officer, they invited Mila. It was a forty-five-minute drive for her, and they expected that she would probably be busy. But she went. They hid her in the crowd, and when the guest of honour arrived and started shaking hands with each person there, he was speechless when she appeared. She gave him a British-style rain hat. The standing joke afterwards was that the hat was too big for him that night but by the next day his head had swelled so much the hat was too tight.

The same Mountie feels that the other stories about her are exaggerations or outright fabrications. He says when they're away, she does go into shops a lot. But much of this is window shopping, in his opinion. As for the affair with Christopher Plummer, he says, ''I can't imagine how she could have an affair. Whenever she leaves 24 Sussex, we go with her.''

Christopher Plummer is happy to set the record straight. He explains that they met at the White House in April 1988, when they were both guests of the Reagans. The following night, at a dinner given by the Gotliebs at the Canadian ambassador's residence, he sat next to her. ''Her impact is immediate,'' says Plummer. ''She's an attractive, forthcoming woman. During our dinner conversation, she was very funny and I enjoyed her sense of humour.''

Soon after, Mila asked him to be the host of the Sixty-five Roses Gala she was putting on for the Cystic Fibrosis Foundation. He accepted. ''I felt very guilty afterwards, because although a lot of people had given their services free, I was paid. I decided I would like to contribute something for a charity that Mila could sponsor. I had written and arranged a one-man show. I told her I'd go up to Ottawa and do it for whatever charity she wanted and give my services free. I was paying back something I felt I owed her.''

Mila accepted his offer and used the proceeds to benefit World Literacy of Canada. It was at that event that they became better friends. He says he likes her because ''she comes on strong and natural, but she is vulnerable. There's a lovely vulnerable streak that lies behind that assured demeanour she has. She's extremely feminine, much more than one would think. It's the sweetness inside that comes out that I like most about her. And her wonderful, warm, naughty sense of humour and that underlying shyness is very endearing.''

Dozens of photos were taken of them together at the literacy benefit. One of the photos was taken while they were standing on the stage together saying thank you to the audience. However, it was cropped in such a way as to make it look as if they were having an intimate tête-à-tête. The tabloids captioned the photo ''The Lady and the Star'' and splashed it on their front pages.

Plummer thought it was funny. ''I hope she wasn't damaged or hurt by it. I think she's sophisticated enough to take all that with a grain of salt. We never talked about it, but I'm sure we would have shared a laugh over it. Gossip like that is one of the things we're used to in our dear profession.''

Mila's father has a theory about gossip. Gossip has an important social value as long as it is not malicious. ''That applies the same way to everyone. People have a need to talk about you. If you walk by my house and I don't know who you are, I wonder about you. Someone says, 'I know about her.' Then everything I know about you is what that person said, and maybe it's not true. Brian and Mila are exposed to that every day.'' He feels it is natural that people will want to know about the Mulroneys. And it is also natural that people will embellish what they do know.

He says it is the degree of gossip that matters. ''If I say I saw you dancing with a charming man at the hotel, that is nothing. If I say I saw you going into his room, that's different. A gossip generally needs more and more detail but rarely has it. So the gossip adds to the story until like a balloon, the story falls flat. But by then a lot of damage is done.''

Mila also feels that gossip serves a purpose. ''There are people whose own lives aren't going very well. They read the gossip and get solace from it. Who's going to read a story that says 'The Mulroneys are happy, their kids are nice'? Stories that are petty get more attention. People seem to need to read that sort of news. This is a worldwide thing. I haven't met anyone in public life who hasn't had untrue things written about them.''

Many of those who read the gossip don't realize how difficult life can be when you are recognized, pointed out, stared at, and discussed everywhere you go. But Mila sometimes seems oblivious to this problem. Shirley Corn remembers the night Mila travelled to Montreal to visit Shirley's first grandchild. After the visit Shirley said, ''So tell me the truth, what do you really want to do for the evening?'' Mila said she wanted to go and see the movie *Three Men and a Baby.* The line-up for the film was around the block. Shirley said, ''I'm going to the front of the line and I'm going to tell them who you are.'' Mila said, ''Don't you dare do that.'' So they stood in line. ''You could see everyone whispering to each other, 'There's Mila Mulroney, sure it is—look at her, it's Myla.'

''We finally got to the front of the line and can you believe it, the usher came out and said, 'That's it. Sold out.' So we went to another theatre. Finally we got in. We were sitting up with the gods at the back of the balcony and again, everyone in the place was staring at her and whispering, 'Nah, it can't be. Yeah, it is Mila.' But she doesn't notice it. I kept saying, 'Aren't you aware of this? Everyone in this place is looking this way.' Finally Mila said, 'Look, Shirley, if you want to make me feel important, go get me some popcorn and a Coke.' ''

Another of Shirley's stories is about the time Mila went to Montreal to visit the store Shirley had just opened, a boutique that sold accessories. ''Mila bought things to show me her encouragement for the success of my store. While I was making up the bill, she asked if she could go behind the counter. While she's there, a woman comes into the store and asks, 'Are these earrings on the counter the same as the ones in the window?' Mila says, 'They are.' Then she asks how much they are. Mila replies, 'Forty dollars.' The woman says, 'That's very expensive.' Mila says, 'They're well made.' The woman looks up, sees that the clerk she's been talking to is Mila Mulroney, and runs out of my store.'' Shirley turned to Mila and said, ''I can't believe it. I figured once you became the wife of the prime minister, I'd make a fortune. Instead, you chased the customer right out of my store.''

When the prime minister and his entire entourage (office and support staff, security, speech writers, and advisers) leave Ottawa to attend meetings or events across the country, it's like taking a stage show on the road. Mila almost always travels with Brian. ''It's one of my priorities,'' she says. ''If I go along, it's seen as an event. If I don't, it's seen as a business trip.'' But she still does it her way, often side-stepping protocol. She fills her itinerary with visits to schools, hospitals, and cystic fibrosis chapters. The trips vary from one or two days to week-long swings through a region of the country. On international trips, she sometimes takes her house-keeper to help with arrangements at the hotel (serving tea to visitors, pressing clothing for an event). And wherever she travels, executive assistant Bonnie Brownlee goes with her.

During a December 1991 swing through the western provinces that was seen as a pre-election tour, she had a schedule packed with community and hospital events. One morning she toured the Jewish Community Centre in Calgary. One of the presentations was to be of a children's judo class. But when Mila and her group arrived at the door of the gymnasium, chaos reigned. The children were running around freely, noisy and overexcited. The beleaguered teacher couldn't make them pay attention. After he'd made a few weak attempts to bring order to the class, Mila stepped in. She clapped her hands, and using what she referred to later as her ''mother voice'' said sternly, ''Okay you guys, get into line.'' She didn't have to ask twice. To the great relief of the teacher, the class began. Mila watched for a few minutes and the tour moved on.

Later, at the Cross Cancer Institute in Edmonton, she sat down at a play table with a group of children who were there for cancer therapy. She hoisted one little girl onto her lap and started to help her with a Christmas card she wanted to make. Before too long, she had a group of children involved in the project, and was conducting an animated discussion about Ninja Turtles.

The little girl on her knee, Charmaine, was clearly enjoying herself and snuggled into Mila's arms. When it was time to leave the play room, Mila stroked her face, told her to be a good girl, and spoke briefly to her mother on the way out. She moved down the hall to where an official reception was being held in her honour. Another little girl in a party dress who'd lost all her blond hair to chemotherapy walked shyly up to Mila and presented her with a bouquet.

Mila was chatting with doctors and board members when suddenly Charmaine pushed her way through the crowd. She'd left the play room, found her way to the reception area, squeezed through the legs of several hundred on-lookers and security agents, crossed the roped-off VIP area alone, and stopped in front of Mila. She extended her arms to her new friend. Mila picked her up. There was a hush in the crowd while Mila whispered to her. Then the crowd heard Charmaine's mother wondering where her little girl was and asking how she'd managed to get such a long way from the play room. There was a ripple of laughter. Mila and Charmaine said goodbye again. The entourage moved on.

At the Faculté Saint-Jean in the University of Alberta, she conducted an impromptu discussion with students from Quebec, Alberta, the Northwest Territories, and the Caribbean. They told her they were confused about the attitudes of Canadians toward francophones. She said, ''I am too. My father chose this country. We need to keep it together. We need to keep our eyes open.''

One of her trump cards is her ability to speak several languages. Not just English and French and Serbo-Croatian, but enough Russian, Hungarian, Italian, and German to get by. In the Jewish Community Centre in Calgary, an elderly Russian woman worked her way through the crowd gathered around Mila and called out a greeting in Russian. Mila whirled around, looking for the voice that had used her old country name, Milica. When she spotted the old lady, who was about half her own height, she bent down and they had a conversation. Later, the woman told a friend, ''What do you know—she speaks my language!''

She comes back from her outings with dozens of requests that range from immigration problems to sponsorships. If they concern government policy, executive assistant Bonnie Brownlee replies on government stationery. Bonnie usually finds the information the person needs or is able to redirect the request to the appropriate office. If the request regards sponsorships or fund raising, Mila responds herself on personal stationery, paid for by the Conservative party. Although she has no official position in the government or the civil service, she needs to separate the work she does on Brian's behalf as leader of the Conservative party and the work she does as wife of the prime minister.

It's a curious situation. She puts in long hours, performs ceremonial duties, represents Canada abroad, entertains scores of dignitaries from all over the world. And yet she has no official status.

Mila has a natural gift for public occasions. She can remember each name in a receiving line. Later, when a name from the receiving line is mentioned, she will turn to that person and smile. Her body language is effective. She nods her head while people talk to her. She uses her hands when she talks, flashing her long fingers in expressive gestures. Whether at a private party or a government function, she gives whoever she is talking to her undivided attention. At a reception for one hundred people, she knows she has to get around to each person, but she doesn't look over the shoulder of the person she's talking to, plotting her next move. She listens, asks questions, and charms everyone she meets. Some of her detractors accuse her of being phony. She shrugs. ''People can tell if you're bored, uninterested, or sincerely interested in them.''

She's outspoken and fearless about asking questions. At a women's health centre in Vancouver, she tells the gathering that ''women's issues below the belt are the toughest for fund raising, because no one talks about them. You can raise money for dying children, cancer, even breast cancer. But not for PMS, hormone replacement therapy, ovarian cancer, dysfunctional uterine bleeding, menopause. People don't like to talk about that.''

She's something of a cheerleader, relentlessly positive, energetic, enthusiastic. When she asks questions, she doesn't worry about sounding foolish. Nor is she shy about offering her own advice. As an expert fund raiser she will comment on local initiatives, pointing to potential hazards, daring people to try something outrageous that may raise an extra ten percent for the cause. Her friend Molly Fripp from Montreal vouches for her as an imaginative fund raiser.

Mila met Molly in 1972 while she was working in Michael Meighen's campaign office. Many years later, when Mila was living at 24 Sussex Drive and Molly Fripp was headmistress of Miss Edgar's and Miss Cramp's School, Molly called to ask for help with a school fund-raising campaign. She travelled to Ottawa to ask her former colleague if she'd lend her name to the campaign. She didn't expect a favourable response, because Mila had spent such a short time at the school and had obviously not been made to feel that she fitted in. But she also knew about the loyalty to friends and colleagues Mila had shown in the past.

''Mila knows a lot about fund raising. She asked a lot of very intelligent questions about the project, and in the end decided to agree to our request. As our final fund raiser, we held an auction, and I asked Mila to offer a luncheon as one of the items to bid on. She felt she couldn't offer to have the luncheon at 24 Sussex but did agree to host two mothers and two daughters at the parliamentary dining room. The winners were ecstatic. But imagine their surprise when they arrived in Ottawa to find that Mila had brought her daughter Caroline to the lunch, that after lunch they went to meet the prime minister in his office, and then continued on to 24 Sussex where Mila served them tea.''

For Molly Fripp, that's a minor example of the warmth and interest in others that draws people to Mila. ''It's not politics, it's part of her make-up. No one should underestimate Mila Mulroney.''

The glare of the spotlight sometimes extends beyond the immediate Mulroney family. When Mila's brother, John, was married in Montreal in 1989, the newspapers reported that Canadian taxpayers were paying for the wedding, based on the fact that three members of the household staff accompanied Mila to Montreal. According to the papers, they were being paid to be there. The personal assistant to the prime minister, Robby McRobb, explains: ''The reception was booked in an old church hall, which was filthy. Mila wanted to clean it, and a few of us went down to Montreal to help her.

I'm paid a salary. I don't get overtime. What I decide to do with my own time is my business. I chose to go to Montreal to help her. I was a volunteer.''

Other members of the family have been personally harassed by journalists. When the deindexing of the old age pension created a stir, several reporters went to Irene Mulroney's apartment in Montreal to find out how the mother of the prime minister was managing on a pension. She was frightened, thinking that the people at the door were trying to get into her home. Her daughter Olive felt it was an unfortunate consequence her mother had to pay for having a son who is the prime minister.

Similarly, when Mila's father had to testify at a trial in Montreal, the trial became national news only because he was the father-in-law of the prime minister. The trial concerned the death of an elderly man who had been having dinner with a group of people, including Dr. and Mrs. Pivnicki, at a private club in Montreal. The man left the table and went to the locker room, where he apparently urinated into the gym bag of one of the members. The member pushed him and he fell to the floor. He died later in the hospital.

Dr. Pivnicki was asked to testify about the condition he found the man in when he was called to the locker room to provide medical aid. One reporter criticized his testimony. When Dr. Pivnicki left the courthouse, powerful television lights were shining on him. Because of the inoperable brain tumour that has affected his eyesight, the glare of the television lights was too much for him; he stumbled and almost fell. The whole experience was very stressful with the added publicity. Mila says, "This could be just an emotional daughter speaking, but I think the incident made my father's condition deteriorate."

She feels she and Brian are fair game. "It's part of being here. You know that in this kind of life you're a target. But my father, my daughter, Brian's mother? Come on."

"Ever since they moved into 24 Sussex, I'm referred to as one of Brian's 'cronies' instead of his friend," Bernard Roy says. "You have to be crazy to run as a politician. Who wants to be kicked in the ass all the time and described as a cheat and a thief and a profiteer? My concern is that politics will become attractive only to people who have little to offer. That's a sad testimony about where we are in this country. A lot of people with a lot to offer won't run because they don't want to expose themselves and their families to constant unfair scrutiny."

But there are some advantages to offset the annoyances. Brian tells a story about his father-in-law that illustrates this. In May 1987, Mita Pivnicki wanted to return to Yugoslavia to attend the reunion of his medical school class. At the time, his best friend from those days was gravely ill in hospital. Dr. Pivnicki tried to locate him before travelling to Yugoslavia, but hadn't had any success doing so. He complained to Mila that he couldn't find his old friend. Mila mentioned it to Brian. Brian called the Canadian ambassador to Yugoslavia and asked him if he could help to locate the man.

The ambassador called back a few days later; he knew the name of the hospital and the hours for visiting. He suggested that Dr. Pivnicki telephone him upon his arrival in Yugoslavia and offered to send a car to fetch him at his hotel and take him to the hospital. Dr. Pivnicki was delighted, but at the same time, he was worried about his old friend. He knew that hospitals in Yugoslavia could be uncomfortable and ill equipped.

When he arrived in Belgrade, he called the embassy and a car was dispatched. When he walked into his friend's hospital room, he was astounded. The sun was streaming through one large window and there was a magnificent view of the city from another. The bed was made up with French linen sheets, and there were fresh flowers on the table and Belgian chocolates on the sideboard. "Well," said Mita, "things aren't so bad after all, my friend."

The old man struggled to sit up and in a cracked voice said, "Mita, the strangest thing has happened. Just two days ago, I was in a ward with twenty-nine men. The windows were so high up, you couldn't see the sun. The ward had bad smells and not enough food for the patients. Then, Mita, they came to me and said I was to be moved. And they brought me here. I couldn't believe my eyes when I saw this room. I asked them, 'Why would you put a sick old man like me in a room like this?' " He leaned a little closer to his friend and began to smile incredulously. "Mita, do you know what they told me? They told me that your little Milica grew up and married the prime minister of Canada."

Another advantage to the fish bowl is that it has a retreat. It's called Harrington Lake, and the whole family loves the peace and the togetherness they experience there. As well as spending the entire summer there, they go for weekends once a month and spend

Thanksgiving, Christmas, and Easter there if they aren't away. The grounds are spacious. There is a private lake for swimming and fishing in the summer and skating and pick-up hockey in the winter. Although Brian usually has a briefcase full of work to do, they enjoy long walks, and for him it's a place to read and to relax.

The house is beautiful. The official country residence for prime ministers since 1957, it has ten bedrooms and six bathrooms. Mila has decorated it with the bright colours she loves—yellow carpets in the living room, peach walls in the sunroom. There's a lot of pine furniture belonging to Brian and Mila that speaks of older, less complicated times. A huge fieldstone fireplace fills a third of the wall on the southwest end of the house. Two large windows offer a view of the lake and the manicured lawns and the surrounding acres of trees. Another fireplace graces the dining room opposite the living room.

It's very rare that they entertain anyone other than friends and family at Harrington Lake. It's where Mila likes to cook, or at least to fine-tune the meals. It's there that she has plenty of time to spend with the children. She teaches them to prepare the family's favourite foods. She shares Yugoslavian traditions with them.

At Harrington Lake, the breakfast is often served up by Brian. Mila says, "He's one of those—how shall I say—expressive cooks who calls out, 'Pass me this, hand me that,' and gets the whole family involved in his bacon and eggs creation."

When they're in Canada, the Mulroneys spend Christmas at Harrington Lake. Their tree is always decorated with the same eclectic collection of ornaments.

There's a little wreath they bought the first year they were married, a bunch of wild-coloured plastic candies the kids and Mila found in Florida one year, and an old angel for the top of the tree. "She's not a fancy angel, but she has a pretty face," says Mila. "Mrs. Mulroney gave her to us when she stopped putting up a big tree."

Christmas dinner, which is served to as many as thirty of the Pivnicki-Mulroney clan, is always suckling pig, turkey, a Yugoslavian dish called roesti, four or five salads, and Mila's favourite, Snow Eggs. "I never know what those things are called. Maybe they're known as floating islands. Anyway, they're all meringuey and delicious."

But the best part about living in the fish bowl, and even the children agree, is that they are living history. Taking part in the events of the decade or even the century. Listening. Learning. They know these are the days to remember.

Chapter Eleven

I fight with my husband. I yell at my kids. I have days when I get down. But publicly no one wants to see that.

Mila Mulroney

On the other side of the double doors, fifteen hundred people sit at dinner tables. An upbeat, fast-paced, electioneering-style video plays on several giant screens surrounding the $500-a-plate Tory faithful.

Outside the double doors, Brian, Mila, and an aide wait. When the video is over, they'll walk up the broad aisle of the ballroom in the glare of television lights to fanfare and applause. The prime minister will deliver a forty-minute speech. Then he'll take questions from the crowd. Dinner will begin.

"Three minutes, Mr. Prime Minister." Brian has had flu for two weeks and can't seem to shake it. The hotel feels too hot. He's unsettled. As he looks over his speech, the papers slip from his hands. The aide scrambles to pick them up. There is less than two minutes to go and fifty pages to assemble.

Mila doesn't move. She suppresses a grin and says to the aide, "Make sure it's in the right order." Then she moves to Brian's side. She runs her fingers through his hair, pinches his cheeks, removes a bit of lint from his navy blue jacket. She strokes the back of her hand along his face.

"Do you think I could hear this speech one more time? At three o'clock this morning, it sounded good. It sounded good on the plane too. I'm sure you could run it by me one more time," she says, and fakes a yawn.

She does it all the time. She watches him, coaches him, softens him, coaxes him. When he's angry, she makes wisecracks to cool him off. When he's nervous, she teases him. If she doesn't like a speech, she argues with him to change it. She knows when to push and when to back off.

Walking through the hotel lobby on the way to the ballroom that night, they pass a group of singers. Brian's eyes light up. She nudges his side and whispers, "Not even a hum!"

She calls him her buddy. He calls her a teenager. And she quips back, "That's why I married you, hon. You're so much older than me, I'll be forever young."

After his speech and the question period and hand-shaking and dinner, they walk back to their hotel suite together, arms around each other, playfully snuggling in the hallway while half a dozen aides and Mounties follow at a discreet distance. She tells him how terrific his speech was. He asks her how the crowd reacted. They share information, trade compliments, reinforce their bond. They're perfecting the partnership.

Brian and Mila have a very strong relationship. He needs her. He reaches out to her before a speech as if she gives him energy and confidence. He wants her with him wherever he is. Those who travelled with them during the leadership race in 1983 and during the national election in 1984 joke that the most common phrase of the two campaigns was, ''Where's Mila?''

When Brian was twenty-one years old, the woman he was in love with ditched him. He was crushed. Afterwards, he had a long, somewhat celebrated bachelorhood. Then he met Mila and was absolutely smitten by her. The only competition she's ever had has been his love of office, his determination to be the prime minister and to leave his mark on history. But even his affair with history has been shared with Mila.

After he'd won the leadership of the Conservative party, Brian said, ''I want to thank one person so very much: Mila, who has made such a contribution to my life and to the campaign.'' A year later he reflected on that win and said, ''I would never have won the leadership without her. No question about that at all. I mean that in crass, vote-counting terms. There were votes that came to me because of her. There's no doubt in my mind whatsoever about that.''

Gilbert Lavoie, editor-in-chief of *Le Droit*, was Mulroney's longest-serving press secretary. He has observed the couple in a variety of situations across Canada and all over the world. He says, ''They are equal partners. She'll push him to change a speech, even when he's being impatient—and he can be quite intimidating when he's impatient. But she'd never push him to change a policy. She's outspoken and determined and she doesn't hesitate to express her opinion. But her opinions have more to do with the office, the working of his environment, the way they handle him than government policy.''

He remembers a time when Brian was taping year-end television interviews with the networks. He looked uncomfortable sitting with a coffee table between him and the interviewer. His staff suggested that Brian sit behind a desk, and he seemed much more comfortable that way. But after one interview, Mila saw the tape and insisted that he looked much too formal. By the time the next interview began, the chairs and the coffee table were back in place.

"She's trying to protect him from himself and the others all the time," says Lavoie. "She cares about situations where he could be vulnerable. She keeps a close eye on him and his working environment."

They're warmly affectionate with each other. They hold hands across the aisle of the Challenger jet. She leans on his shoulder when she sits next to him. They make jokes about each other the way good friends do. When she's with him he's a better listener and more relaxed. Mila gives him a fundamental sense of confidence.

And he does the same for her. He's constantly praising her, encouraging her, telling her she's terrific. He plays spouse for her events as well as she plays spouse for his. Even though Mila was already a self-possessed young woman when he met her, their friends say that he has developed her confidence. They all agree that the blend of the two is perfect.

One Sunday, when Mila had to leave the house for the afternoon to co-host a telethon at an Ottawa television station and Brian was working on a speech for that evening, she decided in late morning they should have a big family brunch. She gathered the children together in the kitchen. They were joined by several members of the kitchen staff.

She pulled produce out of the fridge and created a menu as she went along. "German potato salad," she announced. Mark washed the potatoes and plunked them into a pot of water. (They have instant boiling water.) She cut up onions and threw a liberal dash of salt onto them while mixing them up with her hands. "The salt cuts the acid taste and makes them so good you can't sit next to anyone for days," she explained. She called out more courses for her menu. "Ben, make some fresh-squeezed orange juice." He suggested he make milk shakes as well. Mila moaned about the amount of fat in a milk shake. Caroline took his side and a few seconds later the blender was on. Meanwhile, Nicolas was cutting up oranges for the juice with a butcher knife. When one of the adults said, "Here, Nico, let me do that, you could cut yourself," he held up both hands and looked astonished. "No I won't. See?"

Someone chopped cabbage for coleslaw. Caroline peeled carrots and made a dish of crudités. Mila showed her how to make it attractive with lettuce. Mark made tuna salad. Esther, a staff member, rolled up cold cuts and arranged them on a plate. Her colleague, Barry, fried bacon, sausages, and eggs. Someone toasted English muffins. Mila prepared tomatoes, still instructing and teaching her brood. "Look, if you do it like this, the bread will stay warm. Nicolas, don't use that knife. Ben, add some milk to the ice cream. That milk shake is going to be too sweet. Caroline, get the pretty jug from the top shelf. The one that matches this platter. The orange juice can go in that."

Suddenly the table is laden with a feast for eight. The table setting, the food arrangements, the accessories are all colour-coordinated. It has taken thirty-five minutes. Mila yells to Nico, "Go call Daddy. Tell him brunch is ready."

Why did she do it? She had other commitments. The staff could have prepared the lunch. The kids could have eaten whenever they wanted to. "I did it because I knew Brian needed that," she said. "I could tell. I'm going to be away all afternoon. If I make a meal, I'm nurturing him. He likes that. I know when he needs me. This is my way of taking care of him. Nico is asleep on my chaise longue upstairs. The other kids are coming with me. Brian has work to do. Everyone is okay. I can go now."

She's changed in the eight years they've lived in Ottawa. She's gone from being shy about reading *Peter and the Wolf* to being executive producer of the Sixty-five Roses Gala, which was shown on nationwide television. In Brian's first term, she felt the warmth of Mila-mania. Near the end of the term, in May 1988, she felt the violence of an angry crowd. While walking to an event in Moncton, New Brunswick, she was accidentally hit by a striker's placard. The stick struck a broad belt buckle she was wearing and caused a bruise about the size of a fist on her stomach. Mila knew the blow wasn't directed at her, but she also knew that the security that had become an inevitable part of her life would now be even tighter.

From 1984 to 1988, she was the ingenue. After that, although she was still years younger than the spouses of most other world leaders, she was one of the old-timers at international summits. During the first term, she was still looking after a baby. By the end of the second, she was pushing her first-born, Caroline, out of the nest to university.

Mila is a perfectionist. She's demanding. She wouldn't ask anyone to do something that she wouldn't do herself, but she wants everyone who works with her to give as much as she does. If that is 110 percent, then that's what she expects. If she doesn't get it, she asks why. Is there sickness in the family? Is there too much stress? How can she help? She's a peacemaker. But in the long run, if people don't perform, they don't work with Mila.

She feels that a request coming from the Prime Minister's Office should be dealt with immediately, which sometimes makes people think she's unreasonably demanding. When she reads briefing notes, she quickly points out the mistakes. She edits her own speeches. She doesn't need to be told anything twice.

She has a temper. She doesn't display it often, but if she thinks people are using her, she'll get angry pretty quickly. Incompetence, sloppiness, and lying also make her furious. And she's like a lioness in protecting her children.

She believes in her instincts and often tackles a problem with more directness than one would expect. For instance, when the brother of her friend Nancy Southam committed suicide in June 1991, Mila called immediately, but as Nancy recalls, ''She didn't give me the

257

usual 'I'm sorries.' She acknowledged how awful I must be feeling and she gave me lots of advice for coping and healing. My brother has two little children, and here was Mila on the telephone telling me to be sure to show his picture to the children every day. What she told me helped—enormously. I think it wouldn't occur to most people to offer that kind of support.''

Every one of Mila's friends has a story about her availability in a crisis. She will drive through the night to help a friend through a difficult time. She's seen a lot of her friends go through divorce and says, ''I don't believe in it. Divorce causes a lot of pain and it doesn't work, anyway.'' Today, the special bond she has with the ballet group is tighter than ever before as they feel they must protect her from an increasingly prying press. Their get-togethers in Montreal are rare now because of Mila's frenetic schedule, but they do meet at least three times a year. Once at Harrington Lake for Mila's birthday on July 13, again at Cathy Campeau's for an annual girls-only dinner party, and they always go to Harrington Lake for a sleepover the night of the Academy Awards, a practice that was started as a way of keeping in touch when Mila moved to Ottawa.

Although Mila is supportive, she interprets the word ''support'' more broadly than most people. Her confidence that she knows what's best for others can become oppressive for the recipients of her benevolence. In 1985, when her parents went to Greece, she went to their home in Montreal and with the help of friends, reorganized the house, had it painted, ordered new carpets, and changed the telephone number to an unlisted one so that she could assure their privacy. She did it with such love and care, how could anyone not appreciate it? How did Boba react? ''I got used to it,'' she says flatly. Then she softens and says, ''Look, Mila is very good to us. She's a loving daughter. I'm European. I like my things scattered around me. Now everything is in place. How could I not be grateful?''

Appearances are important to Mila. She's never untidy. She'll get up at five in the morning to wash her hair if she has to. Her nails are never chipped. She used to bite her nails before she was married, but not any more. They may be touched up with tape or glued on, but they are always beautifully manicured. Her saucy bangs and her beautiful clothes are her signature. She isn't the sort of woman who pops a button on a skirt or rips a stocking on the way into a party.

Her hair is two-thirds grey (just as her father's was at her age), so she colours it every three weeks. She has her hair cut every three months and her bangs trimmed about once a month. She says she'll fight aging with diet, exercise, and attention to her appearance, but admits, ''I don't think it's fair to children when mothers try to be forever young. They deserve to get some evolution.''

The schedule she keeps usually includes coming home from an evening event at 1 a.m. and rising at 7 a.m. She credits her diet, an aerobics class, and fast walking with keeping her energy high and her five-foot-nine-and-a-half-inch, 130-pound figure slim and fit. When she first arrived in Ottawa she said formal exercise would bore her too much, that she'd stay fit with tennis. But nowadays, a leisurely game of tennis is almost out of the question, so she has resorted to a faster and more easily scheduled form of fitness.

She walks from 24 Sussex to Dows Lake, about ten kilometres away, in less than fifty-five minutes. One of the RCMP officers has to follow her, and she's talked a lot of them into joining her. So many people have been cajoled into walking with her that she says she'll get T-shirts made with ''Bodies by Mila'' written across the front.

She walks so fast that some of her fellow exercisers have to run to keep up with her. On one occasion, when they were in Montreal, she picked a walking route up the mountain. On the way back, when they were close to Sherbrooke Street in the downtown area, she heard a jackhammer and asked a Mountie, ''What's that?'' He replied, ''You've walked so fast and so far, I think we're in Beirut.''

Her friend Helen Vari has experienced the Bodies by Mila walking routine. ''We were at Harrington Lake. She said, 'Why don't you come out walking with me? You're overweight and this is a great way to burn up some calories.' She moves like a sixteen-year-old. I couldn't keep up with her. It was raining outside. A miserable day. But she wouldn't quit. She takes her diet and her body very seriously.''

She takes care to eat properly, although she admits to having a huge appetite and a weakness for German potato salad, barbecues, and pina coladas. On the road, when everyone else tends to gain weight because of the uneven eating hours and the easy availability of junk food, she puts herself on a strict regime of salads, fruit, and count-less pots of camomile tea. When she's travelling with Brian, she maps out a route with the RCMP and does her power walking. If she's in Ottawa, she attends an aerobics class every weekday morning.

Mila can recharge her batteries with a thirty-minute escape from the crowds. She still takes her psychiatrist father's advice about stress. "In this life you get to the end of your rope a lot. The night Brian won the leadership, my father cautioned, 'Don't stifle your emotions. Have a good cry, a good scream. You'll be okay.' When I blow, the room clears. I'll cry, yell, let it all hang out. Then I'm okay. Sometimes I need a little more time to decompress, time to step back from it all and say, 'Wait a minute.' If I've had enough, I'll go into a room for half an hour by myself and turn on the television. A long, hot bath works for me, and writing in my journal is good for me too. I like to take twenty-four hours off when I can. But usually my fed-up is a five-minute fed-up. I like being busy and being tested. It makes you sharper."

Although her family and friends describe her in ways that often make her sound like a saint, she is unquestionably human and down-to-earth. "I fight with my husband. I yell at my kids. I have days when I get down. But publicly no one wants to see that. They don't want to see me whining about being tired or sick or rushed or worried."

Her friend Shirley Corn likes it that her friend doesn't put on airs. "One time I was invited to 24 Sussex for a luncheon. As our car pulled up to the front door, I stepped out, looked to heaven, and thought, 'Hey, Ma, I hope you're watching.' With that, I stepped on the back of my dress and ripped the hem out of it. I was mortified when I walked into her house. But when Mila heard what I'd done, she asked the maid to get her a needle and some thread. She said, 'Get into the bathroom.' She sewed my hem, smacking me on the hip and saying, 'Stand straight.' ''

She loves music and enjoys everything from rock to classics to gospel. She's also an opera fan. When she travelled to Montreal to see *Tosca*, she was invited to meet the star of the production during the intermission. Mila, who is a great mimic, switches on a New England accent and describes the star, Diana Soviero, as a woman who regaled her with stories about growing up in the poor part of Boston and buying theatre tickets for the last row of the balcony when her family could hardly afford to buy groceries. That sort of conversation affects Mila. She cherishes the stories people share with her.

On a rare day to herself, her ideal is to ''sleep until I wake up, read the papers over lots of coffee slowly. I wouldn't get dressed or do my hair or wear any make-up, and I'd spend the rest of the day with a biography or a novel by Jeffrey Archer or John Le Carré.''

Because of her lifestyle, Mila has often been dismissed by feminists. She talks about the values of motherhood. She took her husband's name (she actually refers to herself as Mila Pivnicki Mulroney). She hasn't been outspoken about the women's movement, therefore it is assumed that she isn't a feminist. ''She is a feminist,'' says justice minister Kim Campbell, who has become a close friend of Mila's since she moved to Ottawa after the 1988 election. ''She's very much her own woman. She's a very sane woman. She's been described as 'just a wife and mother' and that may be true, but under extraordinary circumstances. She's also a public figure. She's a very sophisticated, urbane person. It matters to her to be respected."

Anyone who knows Mila insists that she's an equality-seeker. But becoming involved in a controversial cause can be a perilous trip for a public person. She feels her approach is the right one for her.

Mila's detractors also criticize her for spending too much money. When people accuse her of being a shopaholic, she replies, "Maybe I am." Even Brian jokes about it, saying that when he comes to town, the shops stay open longer if Mila is with him. He also tells a joke about his credit card being stolen. He didn't report it, because whoever had it was spending less than Mila.

She doesn't deny her spending habits. But she feels the amount of money she spends isn't anybody's business. "Brian's investment income [from the Iron Ore days] supplements his present salary and enables us to do some of the things we enjoy," she says.

Mila usually buys fourteen new outfits a year: four spring day ensembles, four winter day ensembles, two cocktail dresses for each season, and two long dresses for the year. She has a price ceiling that she won't exceed, which is in the Escada price range. She also buys three or four sweaters a season. A lot are Linda Lang's hand-knitted designs. She uses a seamstress to redesign certain pieces of clothing that she likes when they need updating. She owns about sixty pairs of shoes and boots, many of them silk shoes that have been dyed to match an evening gown. She's had some of them since she was married.

She wears one outfit during the day even if there's one function at a skating arena and another at a hospital. She changes for the evening event. If she has time between events to come home, she'll change into jeans and a sweater or a comfortable black jersey cat suit. She has one of those long lean figures that looks good in almost anything.

She wears fur and doesn't apologize for it. "I don't wear anything that's endangered. I don't believe in leg-hold traps or testing make-up on animals. But there are too many beavers in our lakes and too many seals in the ocean. And there are 100,000 people in the fur business in Canada. I think in many ways, we're going too far [with animal rights]. An artificial heart needs to be tested on an animal. It's a tragedy that a heart has to be tested in a laboratory in France because it's unsafe to do it here. I don't believe in cutting down a 500-year-old tree. But I don't believe in putting spikes in it and risking killing people in protest. There should be some kind of balance."

Most of her jewellery has been a gift from Brian. The expensive pieces, such as the Bulgari steel, topaz, and gold necklace costing $2,400 that received so much press because it was ordered through her decorator Giovanni Mowinckel, are scarce but spectacular. "Each piece has a special meaning. A necklace I love to wear was a gift when Brian became leader of the party. He gave me pearls when he became prime minister. One Christmas when we lived on Belvedere Road, he had the flu and I ran up and down the stairs for him for fifteen days. He gave me a gold watch that Christmas morning. I got ruby earrings for an anniversary that we celebrated in New York. I don't have a lot. But I have nice pieces that I wear a lot. I also have a lot of costume jewellery.''

American fashion critic, the infamous Mr. Blackwell, well known for his annual ''Worst-Dressed List,'' thinks her fashion sense rates an A-plus. When he was asked by the *Windsor Star* to rank Canadian women for their fashion know-how, Blackwell said he loved Mila Mulroney's sense of style. ''She's simply fabulous,'' he says. ''She looks wonderful from the tip of her bangs down to her toes. Her daytime clothes are simple and show clarity. Her clothes are bright enough to be elegant, positive and fun but subdued enough to make sure she doesn't overpower Prime Minister Mulroney. She opts for elegant evening gowns with conservative necklines and just enough emphasis to show her figure. Her style and expressive face are worthy of knowing.''

Despite the ups and downs of the life she leads, and despite the polls and the critics, Mila is an extraordinarily positive individual. She wants others to share in her happiness and her good fortune. When she's out shopping, she'll see something that she thinks one of her friends would love and she buys it. She buys more than two hundred Christmas gifts a year for family, friends, PMO and household staff, and government leaders and starts her shopping in June.

Mila never forgets a birthday, and thinks the day should be like a national holiday for the celebrant. She goes to extraordinary lengths to make sure the family is together—calling the Montreal crowd and Ivana from Toronto together at Harrington Lake for the celebration. Mark says the best part of a birthday party for him is blowing out the candles. "Because the whole family is there. They're all around me."

Her parties always have a theme. For Nicolas's sixth birthday, the theme was Ninja Turtles, and there had to be Ninja Turtle balloons and Ninja Turtle napkins. There's also a build-up that goes on for two or three days that makes the kids wild with excitement. Whom do you want to invite? Each child starts out with dozens of names, and with Mila's help they pare it down to about twenty, not including relatives. What shall the menu be? French fries, nachos, pizza? Then there are decorations to make and a seven-layer Yugoslavian cake called dobos torta (drum cake). One year when Mila reached into the fridge she was devastated to find that some scoundrel had taken a piece of the cake before the birthday.

Even when the party is in Montreal the whole family attends. When her brother's son Dimitri turned one, they all drove down for the party at John and Manuela's apartment. While Mounties sat in parked cars on the street outside (they arrived the day before and checked out the building, says Manuela), the Mulroneys and the Pivnickis celebrated with birthday cake inside. Manuela says, "Even if they have to be away, Mila would never forget my birthday. She called me from Paris last year. She'd sent me a beautiful sweater, exactly the one I'd commented about when we were in a store together."

Olive Elliott says her sister-in-law is like no one else when it comes to celebrating birthdays. "The thing that strikes me is her ability to remember a little something you mentioned during the year. Then she finds it for you for your birthday." Olive's hobby is miniatures. She makes wonderful doll's houses and spends a lot of time and effort on them. One year, while Mila was travelling in British Columbia, she found a miniature chair that she knew would be perfect for the settler's doll's house Olive was working on. "I was thrilled," says Olive.

Mila sometimes sends joke presents to her friends, but on one celebrated occasion, her package went astray. The joke started when Joan Burney, wife of the Canadian ambassador to the United States, and Mila were in an elevator in New York during the International Summit for Children in 1990. A woman got onto the elevator wearing a very tight green brocade bustier. Joan and Mila looked at each other, trying not to giggle. When the elevator finally arrived at their floor, they got off and burst out laughing.

A few months later, a box from External Affairs in Ottawa arrived at the Burney residence. The label read: "To: Joan Burney. From: Mila Mulroney. For: Barbara Bush." Joan immediately repacked the box and added a note explaining that Mila had sent it to her to be forwarded to Mrs. Bush.

A few weeks later, Bonnie Brownlee asked Joan, "Didn't you receive the parcel Mila sent to you?" Joan said she hadn't. Bonnie explained that it had been a joke, that Mila had found a size eight bustier in green brocade and sent it to Joan to make her laugh.

Joan immediately put a trace on the package but couldn't find it. It was another few weeks before the penny dropped. "The bustier hadn't disappeared," Joan realized. "I'd given it to Barbara Bush." Joan called Bonnie to tell her about the mix-up, adding that she hoped there hadn't been a smart-aleck note in the box to add insult to injury.

Mila called Barbara Bush and explained the mystery of the disappearing dress box. Then Barbara fessed up herself. She'd given the bustier to her daughter. The next time Barbara Bush saw Joan, the First Lady quipped, "You're no size eight."

Although she's been married since 1973, the Pivnicki family home on Marlowe Avenue in Notre-Dame-de-Grace is still part of her life. The house is filled with photos of Mila, John, and Ivana as children, as young adults, and with their own families. The fridge door is reserved for photos of the grandchildren. Mila drops in to visit her mother and father every time she's in Montreal. But her time is scarce, the visit usually short. It bothers her, because the relationship she has with her family is still very important to her. Nevertheless, her brother, sister, parents, and friends say she manages to find ways to keep the unit strong.

Still, Ivana says, it's difficult to feel close to her in public, when they are being watched by everyone else, including a couple of RCMP officers. "How can you open up in a restaurant, share your secrets and problems with your big sister, when everyone in the place is coming by to see her?" asks Ivana. "People point and stare at her and the waiters are filling up her water glass every two minutes and asking her how the meal is. I can't relax with that. But at Harrington Lake, we can have each other to ourselves."

At the lake, Mila will often offer advice to Ivana. "She may even tell me I'm not open-minded enough to take it,'' says Ivana. ''Mila has a different view of how my life should be going. I understand how she thinks, she understands how I think, we don't necessarily agree with each other. But that's okay. Some sisters won't even try to understand how the other one thinks. Not us. I think she's a hoot. I sometimes think she's too stuffy and she's more conservative than I am. Sometimes we want to kill each other, but that doesn't get in the way of the relationship we have with each other. She's my sister. I love her.''

In spring 1991, the family was shocked by the sudden collapse of Dimitrije Pivnicki. He'd had a benign brain tumour for a decade, but suddenly the tumour began to grow. It squeezed against life-sustaining areas of his brain, and the surgeon in the Montreal Neurological Institute told a devastated Boba that there was nothing more he could do, Mita was dying.

Boba called her children and asked them to come home. John, who lives only a few blocks away, was there in minutes. Mila drove from Ottawa and stayed at her father's bedside day and night for three weeks (she took a room at the Ritz-Carlton Hotel, where she got what rest she could). Over and over she called to her semi-conscious father, willing him to live, demanding that he continue to breathe, yelling, ''Do it for Mila, Tata. Don't give up.''

Ivana was not there when Mila arrived, so Mila called her at her home in Toronto, where she works at a public relations company, and told her to get to Montreal on the double. For Ivana, the call couldn't have come at a worse time. She was sick with strep throat, had a fever of

104, and, she admits, was flat broke. But of course, she rushed to Montreal, more or less in the clothes she stood up in.

Ivana arrived at her father's bedside in old sneakers without laces. Mila took one look at the sneakers and said, "What is this?" Ivana defended her style of dress, but promised herself that the next morning, she'd go to The Bay and buy a new pair of running shoes. Being a strong-willed individual, she removed the laces of the new sneakers. Mila thought she was inappropriately dressed, and said so.

"Here we were at my father's sickbed and she was focusing on my sneakers," says Ivana. "I thought that was ridiculous. When we left the hospital that night, I wanted to go out with my friends to bitch and brood about the confrontation. But not Mila. She insisted we talk it out. She demanded that I come back to her hotel. My mother even drove me there. We talked it out all right. We did it with screaming and shouting and crying. After three hours, the issue was resolved, the problem was over. But we didn't like each other very much that night."

Mila says Ivana misunderstood. "It wasn't the sneakers that were the issue for me. It was the way we were presenting ourselves to our father. He likes to see us well groomed. I thought it was psychologically important for him that we were."

Mila is one of those people who insists upon clearing the air, and will not allow problems to fester overnight. Ivana credits their upbringing for the family's interest in resolving problems, and she credits Mila's tenacity for refusing to let it go even on a night when family emotions were running high.

Surgery performed to relieve pressure on Dr. Pivnicki's brain (the surgeon removed bone from his skull so that the tumour would have some place to move) produced the results the family had prayed for. Although his breathing, hearing, and eyesight were damaged, the crisis was over.

Mila says it was the worst thing that has ever happened to her. "I felt totally at a loss. I had to leave him to other people—doctors and nurses. I had to be in the cheering section. I wanted to be able to go in there and fix it myself." All she could do was to organize the family and, says Dr. Feindel, senior consultant at the hospital at the time, "she organized the intensive care unit as well. By the time Dr. Pivnicki was well enough to go home, Mila could have been hired as staff."

During that time, Mark Mulroney celebrated his twelfth birthday, a date that is still referred to as "when Tata was sick," and John's wife, Manuela Soares, went into premature labour and gave birth to Dimitri, the baby whose birthdate is forever linked to the "crisis with Tata."

The commitment is so powerful in the family that at times it even takes precedence over Mila's official duties. One night in 1991, Mila was in Montreal to attend a PC party rally. As usual, she dropped into the family house to check on her father's health and give Boba a quick hug.

"Since my father got sick, my mother doesn't like to be alone," Mila explains. "She decided to take in a boarder. On this particular day when I arrived, she was lying on the couch. She has a pinched nerve in her neck and it was bothering her. I've never seen my mother lie on the couch, not ever. She's always overworked, always doing too much, but she always keeps going. Now she was lying on the couch, with one of those neck pillows under her head. My father was there and the boarder arrived home. My mother looked at me and said, 'Mila, can you help me with the dinner?' Of course I did. We went into the kitchen, cooked a little dinner, set the table for my father, made sure the boarder ate, and I rushed out to meet Brian at the function where he was waiting for me.

"It was as if it was nineteen years ago and I was still living at home. I may not know where all the food is kept, and things have changed in the house, but I have all the responsibility I had before I left and I take that very seriously. If they need help, they need help, that's all."

In return, Boba still helps Mila, just as she did in Montreal. For instance, on election night in 1988, Brian and Mila were in Baie-Comeau. The kids were at home in Ottawa. Mila suddenly felt concerned about them and wanted them with her. She called her mother in Montreal and asked her to go to Ottawa to arrange for the children to fly to Baie-Comeau. Boba didn't hesitate. She drove to Ottawa, supervised the packing for the four children, and accompanied them to the airport. There was a thoroughly competent and caring staff to handle the job, but Mila wanted relatives to do it. And Boba feels that's one of the roles she can play well for her daughter.

Nine years after arriving in Ottawa as a politician's wife, Mila says, "This life has to change you. I've become a little cynical, which I wasn't before. I was probably more trusting than I am now. I was innocent when we started, I'm not now. But I'm richer for the experience. I have a much wider range of interests in public speaking, for instance, and in history—areas I hadn't examined before, things that weren't part of my thought processes. I know much more about the country. I feel really lucky to have visited so many places in the country, to have met so many people. But the job makes you become stingy with your time. I'm more protective of my family and my private life than I ever was before.''

Perhaps for the first time, she recognizes her limitations. ''I used to think I could do everything. In the early days of public life, I felt I would probably have to make some choices, but really, I felt I could master anything. I don't know any more. But I do know that there are things I'll get up early for, such as preparing for an event with the children, attending an early-morning speech Brian is giving, or working on a presentation I have to make, and there are other things that will simply have to wait or maybe not get done at all. It pleases me that I've reached a peace, an understanding about what I can and cannot do.''

Her mother says she hopes Mila will return to school one day to finish her degree. But, she adds, ''I know she will always be an active part of Brian's life. Whatever he does, she'll be part of it.'' She says her daughter is full of surprises. ''No one can pin her down. She'll have an idea. She'll talk to Brian and her children. A decision will be born. And she'll act on it. That's Mila.''

Her close friends from the ballet group are equally confident about an exciting future for her. Madeleine Roy predicts, ''She'll head a worldwide organization.''

Shirley Ann Mass says, "She'll volunteer in a very high-profile way." Andrée Beaulieu sums it up. "She'll do whatever she wants—beautifully."

And Milica Pivnicki—what does she think? "I want time for my children. I want to take a trip as a tourist. I'd like to ride a bicycle through the French countryside. I won't close any doors. I haven't been out there for a while, so I have to see what's there. I've picked up a few new skills in this job. I'd like to upgrade a few others, maybe go back to school. I'd like to do something I'm comfortable in. Something I'll really enjoy, at a pace I like. I'm a great believer in never looking back. I adapt quickly.

"I'm going to love my life. I'm going to love growing old."